Afro-American Women of the South and the Advancement of the Race, 1895-1925

Afro-American Women of the South and the Advancement of the Race, 1895–1925

Cynthia Neverdon-Morton

The University of Tennessee Press

KNOXVILLE

Library of Congress Cataloging in Publication Data

Neverdon-Morton, Cynthia, 1944–
    Afro-American women of the South and the advancement
of the race, 1895–1925 / Cynthia Neverdon-Morton.—1st ed.
        p. cm.
    Bibliography: p.
    Includes index.
    ISBN 0-87049-583-6 (cloth: alk. paper)
    1. Afro-American women—Southern States—History. 2. Social
service—Southern States—History. 3. Southern States—Race
relations. I. Title.
E185.86.N48 1989
305.4'8896073'07—dc19   88-17481 CIP

In loving memory of my mother,
Hattie Oliver Neverdon

To James R. Neverdon, my father,
who continues to sustain me

Contents

Illustrations

Tables

Acknowledgments

While writing my dissertation, I became aware of the need for a comprehensive, analytical narrative of the experiences of black women in the South from 1895 to 1925. This book was written in response to that need. A 1981 National Endowment for the Humanities Fellowship for College Teachers afforded me the opportunity to spend a year collecting data and clarifying the research focus. During the years the book was being written and refined, I included aspects of my research findings in conference papers, journal articles, and essays in anthologies. Comments from colleagues on those writings reinforced my belief that this book could make a significant contribution to Afro-American women's historiography.

Once a research project is completed, there are always those to whom special thanks must be given; my list is long. No matter what words I use, none would truly express my sincere thanks to my editor, Cynthia Maude-Gembler. Because her enthusiasm and support never waned, the process of preparing a manuscript for publication never became too difficult or too tedious. I thank the following persons for their technical assistance or their continuous encouragement: Mavis Bryant; Sheridan Umphrey Ford; Ruth Petty; Elizabeth Sifton; Samuel Wilson; Lee Alexander; Robin Neverdon; Lonnie Morton; Bettye Gardner; Larry L. Martin; Chester Gregory; Ibrahim Kargbo; and all members of my family, immediate and extended.

But the white women of England and the United States have only one burden to bear, after all, the burden of sex. What would they do I wonder if they were double-crossed, so to speak, as the colored women of this country are: if they had two heavy loads to carry through an unfriendly world, the burden of race as well as that of sex?

—Mary Church Terrell,
"Being a Colored Woman in the United States"

CHAPTER 1

Introduction

In October 1895, two white women representing the John F. Slater Fund, a philanthropic organization interested in the problems of Afro-Americans, began a trip through Alabama, Georgia, North Carolina, South Carolina, and Virginia, investigating the condition of southern black women. To insure that various socioeconomic classes were represented in the study, Elizabeth C. Hobson and Charlotte E. Hopkins visited private homes as well as twenty-four schools and other public institutions for Afro-Americans. In Tuskegee, Alabama, Margaret Murray (Mrs. Booker T.) Washington called together thirty married women living within a seven-mile radius to meet with the Slater Fund representatives. The women were aged thirty to seventy years, and each had five or more children. Their husbands were all laborers, and few owned their own land or houses. As Hobson and Hopkins reported later, all the women had made a supreme effort to educate their children; all schools that were not state-supported required tuition, and students who could not afford it worked to meet their expenses.

At the end of their trip, the Slater Fund investigators asserted that, first, efforts to assist black women in the South must begin at the bottom of the socioeconomic scale; and second, schools had to be located near potential pupils. Hobson and Hopkins recommended that the Slater Fund (1) help finance the hiring of teachers for local schools; (2) support the introduction of lessons in serving and cooking, since the Slater Fund had an industrial focus; (3) support first-aid lessons, because large numbers of girls had expressed a desire to become nurses; and (4) give some women additional training at Hampton Institute, Tuskegee Institute, or Spelman Seminary. Some specific needs of black women in rural areas were identified in addition: improved roads to facilitate communication among women, night schools for those who had to work during the day, and club meetings and entertainment in the evenings.[1] Later, when husbands objected to such activities by their wives, Adella Hunt Logan, an instructor at Tuskegee Institute, argued that the needs of rural women could be met if men had a "deeper and truer respect for their women."[2]

In the earliest years of the period under consideration, then, we find articulated the dominant issues and concerns which were to guide the efforts of black club women through 1925. As Mary Church Terrell, an early black leader, put it, Afro-American women "had two heavy loads to carry through an unfriendly world, the burden of race as well as that of sex."[3] The tensions and interactions between these two sources of discrimination, and black women's varied responses to them, form the subjects of this book.

Regardless of their social class, black women often suffered humiliation or physical harm simply because of their race. In 1906–1910, the *Afro-American Ledger*, a Baltimore newspaper, reported numerous incidents in which black women were accosted sexually by white men in Maryland and other states. Black female prisoners were whipped in Georgia until 1903, when the practice was finally abolished because some overzealous guards were found to be whipping white women as well. Some black women accused of crimes never received a trial; throughout the South, lynching of women was reported as late as 1925.

A 1916 incident involved Jennie Dee (Mrs. R.R.) Moton, wife of the newly appointed head of Tuskegee Institute. Although she had traveled by train to Tuskegee in a private car which afforded her some comfort, Mrs. Moton was denied similar accommodations while traveling to Hampton, Virginia, in May 1916. She was asked to leave the Pullman sleeping car and find a seat, with other Afro-Americans, in the day coach. As a rule, the day coaches were overcrowded, dirty, and filled with smoke. Due to Mrs. Moton's husband's position, the incident received wide coverage in black newspapers. Various well-known Afro-Americans sent letters of sympathy and support to President Moton,[4] who was faced with a dilemma: he could accuse the South and make enemies of whites, or he could support the South and make enemies of Afro-Americans. Like many black men before him, Moton was unable to defend his wife and other black women against white men's verbal and physical attacks without severe repercussions. Black women in this era had to bear in mind both their own humiliations and the painful powerlessness of black men under racial oppression.

At the same time, black men generally accepted the male view that the place for women was in the home with children. The men seemed to ignore the fact that conditions in the South generally did not allow the black man to provide adequate financial support for his family so that the women could remain at home. Many black women were forced to work in order to supplement the family's income. Far too many worked as domestics, while their own homes and children suffered neglect. At times black women saw black male beliefs about the role of women as impeding not only the progress of women, but also the advancement of racial objectives.

Selena Sloan Butler, an educator, civil rights advocate, and 1888 graduate of Spelman Seminary, offered a spirited comment on the traditional male view:

> It is argued by most people that women's specific and only mission is that of maternity and obeying the injunction of the wise man, "Train up a child in the way it should go." Since so much is expected of her, is it not right that she should be given opportunity for development in the highest and broadest sense, that her physical, mental and moral nature may be prepared to fill the highest and noblest calling allotted her?[5]

In speeches to groups of men, Mary Church Terrell urged greater cooperation among black men and women, stressing the need for men to treat women with courtesy and respect. She also believed, however, that women were the leaders of the struggle for racial betterment. She spoke for many black women when she stated in 1910 at a Charity Organization Society meeting in New York City, "If anyone should ask me what special phase of the colored American's development makes me most hopeful of his ultimate triumph over present obstacles, I should answer unhesitatingly, it is the magnificent work the women are doing to regenerate and elevate the race."[6]

Black women began to challenge male views concerning feminine roles in American society. One writer proclaimed in the organ of the National Association of Colored Women, "The awakening of women is the great social phenomenon of our times. Woman no longer is represented. She has begun to think, to plan and she is able to care for herself. We, the Negro women, have our eyes open too. We know that we must stand and fight for an upward movement for the human family. Our tasks are laid at our doors, by grace and blood these tasks shall be unflinchingly performed."[7] Activists believed that when a community of women began to think, action would follow. As the black woman assumed new responsibilities, she would have to become knowledgeable about her surroundings, about national events, and about the image she projected.

The educated black female was thought to have special responsibilities to the race. In a stirring 1897 article, Selena Sloan Butler wrote:

> We must learn to patronize the professional and business men of our own race before we will claim the patronage from other races. If we do not, who will? If these men expect their support to come from other races, they may as well

fold their hands up on their bosoms, close their eyes and stop breathing; in other words, we might as well close up our school houses and stop educating young men and young women to fill those different vocations. If you are prepared in this and other institutions to be the best teachers, capable of filling the highest position in your sphere, whom will you teach? What race will supply your classroom with pupils? . . .

It is amusing as well as provoking to hear intelligent men and women, speaking on the Negro, begin with the savage period of his life, forgetting or not knowing or ignoring the fact that he once occupied a stage of civilization to which other races bowed before he lapsed into barbarism. How shall we remedy this weakness? Study the past and current history of your race and with pride tell it to your pupils in the classroom or to your children as you sit around the fireside. If you do not do this, who will?

Hang upon the walls of your homes pictures of the men and women of your own race who have given a chapter that deserves to be recorded in the history of the civilized world. . . . We should appreciate everything that represents the achievement of our people, whether modern or ancient. Then, fill your libraries with books that are the product of the Negro brain. Do these things, and I prophesy that almost every child of the succeeding generation will speak with as much pride of his race and the Negro blood in his veins as does the Anglo-Saxon of his race and the blue blood which comes to his veins.[8]

Although black women saw little change in racial attitudes, they persisted. Amelia Perry Pride, a graduate of Hampton Institute who was a community worker in Virginia, wrote, "As to my undertaking too much, I would rather wear out working among all classes of my race than to rust out seeing so much to be done. . . . I have only to speak to the women in Lynchburg and they follow me in whatever I undertake."[9]

To be sure, black women were not monolithic in their thoughts and actions. Margaret Murray Washington of Tuskegee stated, "We cannot find the average colored woman any more than we can find the average women in other races."[10] Regional as well as individual differences influenced the ways black women viewed themselves. Some had advantages — urban versus rural location, family structure, education, and personal income were four such variables — which shaped their social status and self-perceptions. Differences in class and interests separated groups of Afro-Americans. In many cases, when highly educated black women sought opportunities to enrich their lives through the formation of Greek letter sororities and elitist social clubs, the effect was to widen divisions among members of the race. But it was a mistake for such women to believe that they could live isolated from the masses of Afro-Americans and from problems seen as affecting only the lower classes. Racist attitudes touched all Afro-Americans. To their credit, may who belonged to select groups were also active in other organizations which sponsored community programs. Women like Amelia Pride of Lynchburg were able to elicit the support of other women because they no longer focused on the social status of the individual woman or her husband. As they worked to improve conditions in the home, school, and community, the women were concerned with positive results for all. As Mrs. I.C. Norcum of the Virginia State Federation of Colored Women's Clubs put it in 1911:

> Woman thinks not of what she can get but more of what she can give. . . . No longer does a woman, who wants to help those who need her, air the best garments in her wardrobe on these errands of mercy. Her approach is not heralded by the swish of a silk skirt as it was during the old days when women went slumming, but womanhood and developed soul shine through her every action. Community uplift . . . instead of enervating the one we have helped and making him a dependent beggar, we lift him up.[11]

Differences between urban and rural women were obvious. Nevertheless, Adella Hunt Logan of Tuskegee Institute believed that "the needs of country folk are about the same as those of town and city residents. Means of social uplift do not differ greatly. . . . In home, in church, in school and social service, the country woman is in her handicapped way doing what she can. Probably not all she can, but she is a potent helper."[12] In keeping themselves morally "straight and strong," rural women were seen as aiding the general improvement of Afro-Americans in rural areas.

Because many black female social activists encountered similar problems in their communities, they shared crucial areas of interest—especially the home, the family, health care, education, and social justice. At the 1899 Hampton Negro Conference, Lucy C. Laney argued that educated colored women had the responsibility to help Afro-Americans develop more hygienic habits for their homes and persons, to assist those who were imprisoned, and to help eradicate the burden of prejudice. She stated, "Women are by nature fitted for teaching very young children. . . . In the kindergarten and primary school is the salvation of the race." Still, only women of character and culture could "do the lifting, for she who would mold character must herself possess it."[13] Moreover, educated black women, Laney felt, must be public lecturers willing to give advice and set directions for others. They were to develop neighborhood classes in cooking and sewing; at church, teach in Sabbath schools, conduct Bible classes, and lead young people's meetings and women's societies; and, even more importantly, "come forward and inspire our men and boys to make a successful onslaught upon sin, shame, and crime"[14]

Southern women focused on many needs of Afro-Americans: the plight of working women, limited economic opportunities, inferior housing, severe health problems, the political strait jacket of Jim Crowism, care for the aged, programs for the very young. But the key to solving all these problems, leaders of black women were convinced, was education of the masses of black citizens. Education was seen as the first step toward racial equality, and racial equality was the essential precondition for development of the individual Afro-American's full potential. Thus individual growth and group improvement were viewed as inextricably intertwined. In order to structure longlasting, meaningful programs in areas of concern, the women encouraged group reliance. At the same time, they recognized and taught the value of self-reliance. In focusing on the development of skills, the women hoped that their efforts would have a multiplier effect in the black community. Once the individual matured and prospered, her knowledge, energy, finances, and time could be utilized to further the goals of the entire race.

To promote mass education, black women formed clubs, founded institutions, became teachers, and created innovative informal educational programs of many types. No matter what type of social service activity was planned, some educational aspect was included. Throughout the period under consideration, the kind and quality of education appropriate for Afro-Americans in the South were subjects of continued debate. Black women participated in the debates, but they also developed educational institutions, designed curricula, helped formulate educational policies, and taught in the classroom. But much teaching took place outside formal educational settings. The women used whatever forum was available, whether discussing such issues as proper dress, suffrage, or the treatment of black South Africans, or providing practical experiences in gardening, home nursing, sewing, or child care. The home was considered the major focal point of informal education, and every willing family member was included in some aspect of the educational process.

As it became clearer that all black women—rich and poor, urban and rural— would have to work together to achieve the dual goals of racial and individual betterment, class differences among the women diminished in importance. They not only established local clubs, but in time formed or joined state, national, and international organizations, to share experiences, pool resources, and wield greater influence to achieve common ends. The National Association of Colored Women served as the coordinating body for many social service programs. Key black women leaders were involved at all levels of social activism.

Despite the gulfs that often separated them from white women, at times the Afro-Americans were able to join forces with whites to achieve limited ends. At other times, as in the woman suffrage movement, black women's efforts to enlist the support of white women met with bitter disappointment, and the Afro-Americans chose to struggle on alone. At the same time, black women knew that they would need the involvement of black men if many of their group goals were to be realized. Issues of suffrage, housing, adequate schools, positive self-image, and employment directly affected all Afro-Americans during the years 1895–1925.

The racial aspirations, missionary zeal, and educational commitment shown by the leaders of black women's groups in those years took shape within the broader intellectual climate of Afro-American society as a whole. Southern industrial, liberal arts, and women's colleges for Afro-Americans were important centers of black intellectual ferment, part of a wider flowering of Afro-American thought and culture during this era. Hampton Institute, Tuskegee Institute, Fisk University, Atlanta University, Spelman College, and Morgan State College were magnets that drew southern students, male and female, who hungered for knowledge and opportunity. The colleges instilled in these students a lasting sense of responsibility to utilize the education they had been so fortunate to receive, not simply for personal advancement but to enhance the future possibilities of all Afro-Americans. Most of the colleges thus became centers of outreach programs bringing education and social services to the masses.

These institutions also maintained close networks of graduates, exercising broad influence on southern black society as a whole. At several of the colleges, annual conferences brought together graduates and others for continuing education and thoughtful, often provocative consideration of issues crucial to black Americans. The conferences held at Tuskegee Institute, Hampton Institute, and Atlanta University stressed the interdependence of all Afro-Americans and the importance of education for the masses; if people acquired certain habits or skills early enough in life, social problems might be greatly reduced or eliminated. Although the Hampton and Tuskegee Conferences focused on industrial education while the Atlanta Conferences advocated college training for blacks, all evolved methodologies for assessing the strengths and weaknesses of the black community. Tuskegee and Hampton Institutes, drawing on those methodologies, implemented community action programs.

The conferences encouraged women to develop programs for the masses, and taught methods of implementing the programs in a given community. But the black women who led the southern club movement did not depend solely on the conferences for direction. The programs they established attest to their own discerning eyes, innovative minds, and organizational skills.

Black women who were able to attend colleges and professional schools were prepared for service to those who did not possess their educational, financial, or moral backgrounds. The educated black female was instructed actively to seek out the areas of greatest need and go there. The challenge to extend their service beyond the United States to all who formed part of the African diaspora motivated some young women to live in Africa or the Caribbean. Others, however, saw that residents of the rural South were as deprived as those in the least technologically advanced nations. Even with families and jobs, countless black women found time to render service to those less fortunate than they. Instead of seeking payment for their services, the women often gave freely of their income to further the causes they supported. The Christian tenets to which they subscribed, and the educational institutions they attended, taught that to give of themselves and of their funds was part of their responsibility.

Because the number of black female graduates was restricted, while the need for services was so great, it was essential that more women, with or without formal training, who possessed a commitment to racial advancement, become involved in community concerns. In the year between the Hampton Conferences of 1899 and 1900, more than ten women's clubs were formed in the South; thereafter, the club movement expanded rapidly.

The regions in which the colleges were located became focal points for social service networks, largely composed of black women. Here we shall examine the activities of women in and around Hampton, Virginia; Tuskegee, Alabama; Nashville, Tennessee; Atlanta, Georgia; and Baltimore, Maryland.

Leaders of black women's clubs cooperated in the creation of such organizations as the National Association for the Advancement of Colored People (NAACP) and the National Urban League. While black men have received extensive attention for their leadership in these national organizations, it was often black women who implemented the programs for which these groups became widely known. This less glamorous but equally crucial work by women has gone largely unnoticed by historians. Moreover, the period 1895–1925 in black history has focused on the viewpoints and personalities of two key figures, W.E.B. Du Bois and Booker T. Washington. Unfortunately, this emphasis has tended to highlight the conflicts among Afro-Americans, obscuring the positive advances made by the race as a whole.

In the United States generally, 1895–1925 was an era of social change, during which many self-help and social service programs were initiated throughout the country. The Progressive Movement, and particularly Theodore Roosevelt and the Muckrakers, helped to bring about needed reform and a restructuring of white society. Afro-Americans, however, were generally excluded from the Progressive Party and from the effort to change the American social order. Consequently, Afro-Americans had to create their own social service organizations to aid the victims of an oppressive society. Especially in the South, these organizations were headed by black females. By examining the activities and philosophies of black women and their leadership groups, historians may gain a more complex and comprehensive understanding of key issues and particularly of the positive programs and changes initiated by Afro-Americans during this period.

The significant social, economic, and political gains made by Afro-Americans could not have been achieved without the diligent labor of countless black women who were dedicated to advancing the interests of all Afro-Americans. Although they shouldered the double burden of race and sex in a racist and sexist nation, they never lost their hope and their initiative. This study pays tribute both to the leaders whose names are well known, and to those who until now have been hidden behind the "great women" of history.

CHAPTER 2

The Colleges

Issues in Afro-American Higher Education

Between 1895 and 1925, black intellectuals debated the aims and content that should dominate in higher education for Afro-Americans. As early as 1901, James Weldon Johnson, principal of Central Colored Grammar School in Jacksonville, Florida, raised the key question: "Is the Negro to remain in this country a separate and distinct race, or is he to become one of the elements in the future composite American?"[1] If Afro-Americans were going to remain separate, then they should receive a different type of education, in accord with characteristics quite different from those of white people. If, on the other hand, Afro-Americans were to become integrated in the future American race, Johnson thought that they should receive the same type of education as whites.[2] The question was crucial, because the race's collective goals were intimately linked with the type of education seen as best for most Afro-Americans.

The issue was far from resolved by 1925. Therefore, during 1895–1925, black educators and other intellectuals continued to outline their views about the basic knowledge and skills which all Afro-Americans should have, and about the type of curriculum that would best help Afro-Americans achieve their ultimate goals.

Hampton Institute originated the concept of a higher education for Afro-Americans focused on trades. The concept was further elaborated by Booker T. Washington, a Hampton graduate who became head of Tuskegee Institute, in his famous address at the 1895 Atlanta Exposition. Washington proposed that Afro-Americans be educated and work along industrial lines rather than trying to move quickly toward social equality in the South. Whites supported this approach because Washington's philosophy would not drastically change the existing southern social and economic systems. Many Afro-Americans accepted the industrial focus because, despite its limitations, it would permit them to upgrade the quality of their lives.

Charles H. Turner, professor of biology at Clark University in Atlanta, suggested eight basic skills and qualities needed to raise "vagrant Blacks" and poor whites to a new level of life: "Manners of a gentleman, cultured homes, business honesty, thrift, Christian morality, marketable skills, leadership qualities, and love for justice—contempt for lawlessness."[3] In his opinion, industrial education had not been entirely successful. He therefore suggested that all classes of Afro-Americans and whites receive the highest possible degree of education, to instill in them his eight virtues. Turner was not alone in calling for a moralistic education; many black intellectuals saw good character and morals as key elements in individual success and in the eventual solution of problems faced by their people.

As the debate continued, black intellectuals became convinced that Afro-Americans should know about their own culture and history. Roscoe Conkling Bruce, who served for fifteen years as assistant superintendent in charge of colored schools in the District of Columbia, in 1905 championed an enriched curriculum for black colleges in the South. To meet the needs of students, the curriculum, he felt, had to be flexible. He recommended including courses in the aspects of natural science which related to trade and industry, courses in history and social science emphasizing the traditions and progress of Afro-Americans in Africa and North America, and courses on current sociological problems of Afro-Americans.[4]

After 1905, there was no black intellectual who did not discuss the need for Afro-Americans to learn about themselves. W.E.B. Du Bois, as the champion of Pan-Africanism, offered a scheme for education which would give all Afro-American students the basic tools for life. Their first four years were to be devoted to reading, writing, and understanding basic mathematics; there was to be no vocational training in the primary schools. Until age fourteen, students were to concentrate on the "three Rs" and related subjects. If the student was not suited for academic training, then vocational education could be introduced. Every Afro-American, however, was to learn to speak French, and many were to be fluent in Spanish and Portuguese. These languages were emphasized because most people of Negro descent outside the United States spoke French or Spanish. For Pan-Africanism to succeed, the ability to speak the three languages was a must.[5]

Archibald Grimké, the black activist who founded the Washington, D.C., chapter of the National Association for the Advancement of Colored People, developed a center at Howard University to collect research materials about Afro-Americans.[6] In 1915, Carter G. Woodson founded the Association for the Study of Negro Life and History.

In 1924, E. Franklin Frazier urged a new type of education which would make Afro-Americans the primary object of study. For Frazier, the major flaw of traditional education for Afro-Americans was the attempt to mold conduct and character; he believed that these qualities resulted from habit. His new approach demanded that Afro-Americans become aware of themselves, first of all. With this enhanced awareness, they could determine how to resolve existing issues. The new education was to be based on sound scholarship and careful selection of students.[7]

By 1925, even though new curriculum directions were being sought, black institutions of higher education were attempting to offer the same basic courses as most white schools did: English, the sciences, history, geography, philosophy, and modern languages. According to Dwight O.W. Holmes, in 1916 more than 97 percent of the 92,593 students enrolled in black institutions were performing at college level. This was a marked increase from earlier reports.[8] Because graduates would become teachers, colleges placed special emphasis on Afro-American history and racial issues in addition to the standard academic programs.

Howard, Fisk, and Atlanta Universities became known for their professional programs, while Hampton and Tuskegee Institutes continued to concentrate on industrial training and related areas. In all the colleges, however, the increased emphasis on Afro-American culture and history encouraged the development of social service courses and programs to deal with the problems of the masses.

Afro-Americans often saw education as a means of escaping poverty, enhancing their ability to secure employment, and redressing social inequalities and injustices. Throughout the period when black educational institutions were developing, whites debated not only the kind of education Afro-Americans should receive, but also whether they should be educated at all. The Afro-Americans who provided most of the impetus for the establishment of educational institutions saw as key issues adequate funding for the schools, establishment of curricula to meet the needs of Afro-Americans, qualifications of teachers and administrators, better physical facilities, and black control of schools for Afro-Americans.

Many Afro-American educators, intellectuals, and leaders demanded that only black scholars, formally trained, should be hired to teach at black institutions. They felt that Afro-American teachers would identify more readily with the students and understand the problems that arose because of the students' race; teachers could serve as examples to the students, inspiring them to achieve similar positions; and white institutions would not hire Afro-Americans, even if they were highly qualified. Supporting these three basic beliefs were two additional suppositions: Afro-Americans observing black teachers at work in black institutions would feel a heightened sense of racial pride; and if the institution were successful, whites would have to acknowledge that Afro-Americans were capable teachers.[9]

Nathan B. Young maintained that every black college should have at least one Afro-American on the board of trustees, as well as one or more on the faculty. He felt that all whites, whether competent or not, should eventually be fired and replaced by competent Afro-Americans.[10] In contrast, Professor D.J. Jordan of Morris-Brown and Clark did not want all the whites removed, because he felt that by discriminating themselves, Afro-Americans would forfeit the right to protest acts of discrimination by whites. He did say, however, that some whites were at black schools because they could get better pay for less work. He described some white faculty and administrators as often "haughty, unsocial and unsympathetic."[11]

Nevertheless, whites felt that they had definite roles to play at black institutions. They stressed their ability to convince philanthropists to give funds to support the institutions, arguing that since Afro-Americans did not contribute significantly to endowment funds, they should not expect to control the schools. Between 1895 and 1925, most black institutions continued to employ a large number of whites on the faculties. In 1912, 461 teachers were working at twenty-two black universities — 74 white men, 127 white women, 160 black men, and 100 black women, or a total of 210 whites and 260 Afro-Americans. Fewer black women were hired than black men or white women.[12]

Those blacks who were hired as teachers often served as administrators while also fulfilling their teaching obligations. By 1912, it was becoming more difficult to secure efficient white administrators for black institutions. While two-thirds of the presidents of the black colleges were white, they were, in many cases, assisted in the management of the institutions by Afro-Americans. The more stable academic institutions had white presidents: Atlanta, Claflin, Clark, Fisk, Howard, Leland, New Orleans, Rust, Shaw, Southern, Tougaloo, Virginia Union, and Walden.[13] Many of these institutions did not have black presidents until after 1925. This refusal to allow Afro-Americans to head their own institutions was due to a combination of tradition, prejudice, and the belief that funding by whites would be available only if whites held key positions at the college.

By 1925 it was obvious that the industrial schools had not transformed the masses of Afro-Americans into an industrial people. Since black communities formed a separate section of a biracial society, black professionals had to provide services needed by Afro-Americans. With the great influx of Afro-Americans into urban settings, teachers, doctors, preachers, and businessmen were desperately needed; rural Afro-Americans too needed professional services. As Dr. Alain Locke declared at Hampton's fifty-eighth commencement, "the education of the Negro is not a conflict between two theories of education, or two kinds of education, but is a mutually supplementary program of the collegiate professional and collegiate economic, technical and vocational with the important field of teacher training and social service training harmoniously balanced and divided between them."[14]

By 1925, it was also clear that one type of education would not exist to the exclusion of the other. The industrial-academic controversy was largely being resolved by choice. High schools in the South most often offered dual programs of study. Black students and parents chose those programs and schools which seemed best suited to their needs. The level of scholarship and attendance at the black schools demonstrated that they would survive if funds remained available.

As Afro-Americans debated such issues, whites as well as Afro-Americans attempted to clarify the issue of education for women. Both white and black laypersons and educators in 1895–1925 offered arguments against the education of females. Buell E. Gallegher, president of Talladega College in Alabama from 1933 to 1943, in *American Caste and the Negro College,* provided a summary of the views held by laypersons and educators:

> (1) biologically determined differences in temperament and (2) inherited inferiority in mental ability make the education of women beyond the elementary stages a dubious affair. But if they must be educated, then let the curriculum be designed especially for the needs of women as indicated in (3) the preponderance of intuition rather than reason in feminine psychological processes; in (4) the social demands that women restrict themselves to the arts of graceful consumption rather than invading the masculine areas of production and distribution, and (5) the actual fact that three-fourths of the women do become homemakers, so that education should fit them for continuance in their place. And if women, with their defense complexes aroused, object that they do not want to be given this special education designed to fit them for a peculiar place in society, then (6) it must be admitted that the whole idea of educating the two sexes in the same manner implies an effort to assimilate the two sexes, making them physiologically as well as psychologically alike, which is patently absurd and therefore explodes the whole affair.[15]

Despite arguments during the Progressive era, against educating females, more and more white women were gaining formal education beyond the secondary level. In 1890, 2,500 white females graduated from colleges; 8,500 graduated in 1910. Many became teachers and social reformers.

The first black female college graduate, Mary Jane Patterson, completed her studies at Oberlin College in 1862. Between 1895 and 1925, most of the black college graduates were women. However, black men generally determined the kind of education needed and the specific courses to be offered at a particular institution. The postsecondary education of black women emphasized missionary responsibilities and moral values, as we have seen, while extracurricular activities shaped their personal philosophies and their responses to racial goals.

This chapter examines the education available for black women at two key types of institutions: the "industrial" education epitomized by Hampton and Tuskegee Institutes; and the "liberal arts" or "academic" education offered by Fisk University in Nashville, Atlanta University and Spelman Seminary (later Spelman College) in Atlanta, and Morgan State College in Baltimore. Spelman also represents the attempt to provide education specifically for women, while the other institutions were coeducational. All of the institutions incorporated some aspect of domestic science in the program offerings for women, thereby indicating that education was an extension of the home and was gender based. We shall further examine professional training programs—for teachers at several of these colleges, for nurses at Hampton and at Meharry Medical College in Nashville, and for social workers at the Atlanta School of Social Work.

Hampton Institute, Virginia

Organization and Curriculum. Originally known as Hampton Normal and Agricultural Institute, Hampton Institute served as the earliest model for black colleges with an industrial focus. Hampton's founder and first principal, Gen. Samuel Chapman Armstrong, agreed with Robert C. Ogden, "guiding spirit" of the Southern Education Board, that "good organization and business methods should prevail at Hampton."[16] Armstrong, who believed that for success one had "to look within self rather than without self,"[17] vowed that Hampton would not become dependent upon government support or private philanthropy. The South, he felt, was the place for Afro-Americans to improve themselves. In 1909, Booker T. Washington, an early Hampton student who became the first principal of Tuskegee Institute, recalled that Armstrong recognized the difference between "working and being worked" and had emphasized the former in formulating Hampton's objectives: "His idea was to bring hand and head together."[18]

The school was established in 1866, on the eastern shore of Hampton Creek, below the town of Hampton, Virginia, in facilities that had once served as Camp Hampton, a United States Army base hospital. In 1867 the land and buildings were purchased by the American Missionary Association of New York for $19,000. On 1 April 1868, the institute opened with fifteen students and two teachers. It was charged "to train teachers for the public schools and make industrial leaders for the race."[19] The term "industrial leaders" meant "better farmers." In 1870, the Virginia State Assembly made Hampton a quasi-public institution; thus the school became eligible for federal land-grant funds.

At the outset, requirements for admission to Hampton attempted to guarantee that students would enter service careers. All students were required to remain at the school for the three-year course and to become teachers upon graduation. Hampton sought to educate all who were willing to learn. From the beginning, the school was coeducational; families were accepted and small houses erected to accommodate them. At first, anyone could be admitted who was between the ages of fourteen and twenty-five, was of good character and health, and could read and write intelligently and do arithmetic up to long division. In 1895, knowledge of fractions and decimals was also required, and the minimum age for admission was raised to sixteen.

Beginning in 1900, a concerted effort was made to upgrade the basic academic proficiency of students. Before admission to the three-year agricultural course, all students were required to complete a three-year academic course at Hampton or equivalent training at other schools. During the academic year 1901–1902, academic subjects were integrated with the industrial courses. Arithmetic problems were introduced into the shop and model farm curricula. History was taught in relation to daily problems, and geography was related to agriculture. The geography of Africa was introduced into the middle year in order to further racial awareness. In 1904, the academic course was extended by one year. The academic year was eight months, with one school week equivalent to four days. On the fifth school day, all students worked, some for wages.

During the school year 1905–1906, the course of study was increased to four years and the social studies component was strengthened with racial data from the U.S. Census. As of 1913, academic subjects were also incorporated into the trade and agricultural courses. Diplomas were granted only to those with a skilled vocation who had completed the four-year course.

Students were expected to become self-supporting in agriculture, trades, teaching, or business.

In time, to limit its total number of students, Hampton again revised entrance requirements. Beginning in 1919, students were required to take entrance examinations in arithmetic, English, geography, and physiology. The exams were supplemented with standard group intelligence tests designed to identify gifted students and eliminate those whose skills were extremely limited. In time, only students capable of performing at the college level were admitted.

The year 1920 marked the midpoint in Hampton's transition to the college level. The institution became a private foundation, with only 5.7 percent of its $458,911 working budget coming from government funds that year. Hampton's status as a land-grant college was given to Virginia Normal and Industrial Institute at Petersburg, Virginia.[20] In 1920, Hampton had 2,300 students, including those at Whittier Training School, the summer school, the ministers' conference, and the farmers' conference. The 73-acre main campus, plus two farms, Whipple and Shellbanks, comprised 913 acres. The first college courses were introduced in five schools: Normal, Business, Home Economics, Trades, and Agriculture.

Since the majority of students still came from the rural South, administrators did not amend the entrance requirements further until 1922. In that year, students were required to have completed the eighth grade before being considered for admission. Even then, in order to insure that all students developed the basic skills, the curriculum continued to include subject matter that should have been taught in the public schools. Under Hollis Burke Frissell, who served as principal from 1893 to 1917, Hampton began to shift from a primary focus on agriculture and industrial training to a four-year college program awarding the Bachelor of Science degree. Under James Edgar Gregg, principal in 1918–29, the transition was completed.

Even in 1922, however, each student was required to take some course work in agriculture. While Hampton still accepted the motto "training for life," changing conditions in the South necessitated curriculum changes. Hampton's basic divisions in the 1922–23 school year were the Academy, the standard secondary school to prepare students for work at Hampton; the college-level Normal School for teacher training; the Business School, which awarded a diploma; and the three-year basic or four-year college course in agriculture. The first class to graduate from the four-year course in agriculture and trades received their diplomas in 1918. In 1922, the B.S. degree was granted to students who successfully completed the four-year teacher training course; and on 1 September 1923, the B.S. degree was awarded to

1

Fig. 1. The expansion of Hampton Normal and Agriculture Institute's physical plant was evident in an 1890 aerial view of the campus. Note the Business Office, left forefront; Gymnasium, behind; and the Wigwam, Indian boys' dormitory, far right. *Courtesy of Hampton University Archives.*

Fig 2. Although segregated in the dormitories and dining halls, Native American and black female students at Hampton Institute were taught in the same classrooms. *Courtesy of Hampton University Archives.*

Fig. 3. In 1916, Sarah J. Walter, a member of Hampton Institute's Normal Department, supervised Lucy Hunter's practice teaching. *Courtesy of Hampton University Archives.*

2

3

4

5

6

Fig. 4. Skills learned in a 1900 cooking class at Hampton Institute were utilized when preparing meals for the Abby May Home. *Courtesy of Hampton University Archives.*

Fig. 5. Hampton students in the dressmaking classes acquired skills which enabled them to earn money while attending school. *Courtesy of Hampton University Archives.*

Fig. 6. Among Alice Bacon's major accomplishments during her tenure at Hampton Institute was the founding of Hampton Training School for Nurses and Dixie Hospital. *Courtesy of Hampton University Archives.*

Fig. 7. A training room for nursing students at Tuskegee Institute was similar to those at most nursing schools. The curriculum and teaching tools were continually updated in order to ensure that students received the best training possible. *Courtesy of Hampton University Archives.*

four graduates in agriculture education. Hampton officially changed its name to Hampton Institute on 20 May 1930; by 1932 it was fully accredited and empowered to award the master's degree.

Despite this progress, some Afro-Americans raised questions about the quality of instruction received by students at Hampton and about their ability to become leaders of racial advancement. John Hope, president of Morehouse College, saw Hampton as a school preparing Afro-Americans to be teachers in the classroom, on the farm, and in the community. In 1917, he stated that preparation at Hampton ought to qualify students to become leaders, in excellent positions. He identified two views concerning the quality of academic preparation needed for effective leadership. He wondered whether the type of teaching and discipline at Hampton sufficiently developed student initiative. The students there, in his opinion, "received and executed orders admirably" owing to the military training there, but thought it was unclear how much independence they had developed. Future teachers needed enough independent work to enable them to be self-reliant once they assumed their positions. Dr. Hope suggested that a study be made of the influence of the library on the students' scholarship. The Hampton student, he asserted, was well-read "considering that when he finishes Hampton he has received only an academic education perhaps not equivalent to preparation for entrance to college; but I ask this question, does the Hampton student develop much power out of his reading?"[21] Such were the questions raised by advocates of liberal arts education for black students.

Women at Hampton. From its earliest days, Hampton was committed to the education of women. By 1900, the institute had to refuse admission to two-thirds of its applicants because of limited facilities, but it continued to admit large numbers of women. Hampton administrators endorsed the idea that women's influence was a key factor in the progress of Afro-Americans. The institution could assist in this progress by training women who possessed "broader intelligence, higher ideas of morality, and proper methods of homemaking."[22] Women were admitted to the day program as boarders, and to the night school. In 1905, courses in the day and night programs were correlated, to facilitate smoother transitions from one to the other.

Many parents of the female students at Hampton expected the institution to serve "in loco parentis." During 1895, the first-year students were expected to live in companies of ten for three months at a time in Abby May Home. Every aspect of the students' lives was monitored as they received instruction in domestic science. Their instruction began with the upkeep of their own rooms. Each room was shared by two girls and was inspected on Sunday mornings, with the more advanced students serving as captains during the inspection. Teachers served as primary supervisors for the girls' behavior and academic performance.

Rules governed the personal appearance of the female students too. There were clothing requirements for classes and after-school hours. Every girl was instructed to bring a gossamer (light raincoat) and rubbers or the money to purchase them. Those in the Work Department had to wear plain easy-fitting wash dresses and aprons. The girls were also expected to wear Warner waists, garments similar to modern camisoles. All day school girls had to purchase gymnastics suits. After 1909, to encourage the development of personal taste, the girls were not required to be in uniform, although the Work Department continued to have dress requirements until 1925.

The physical education program was designed to round out the student's personal and academic development at Hampton Institute. A required medical examination before entering the school helped to identify possible medical problems; dietary concerns were ascertained, and physical and orthopedic records were maintained. A required physical education course of two periods a week was individually designed to include instruction in personal hygiene and, during the fall and spring, outdoor activities. The girls' athletic association sponsored inter-class tournaments as part of the recreational program. Little time was provided for unsupervised activities during the school's early years.

When Hampton admitted Native Americans in 1878, women were among them. In 1882 the Wiona Lodge for Native American female students was built. By 1900, 132 Native Americans were enrolled, including 57 females and 78 males from numerous tribes. The Native Americans were segregated from the black students in separate dormitories and, until 1912, dining halls. Male and female Native Americans were also kept separate except for such special activities as the Society of Christian Endeavor and the Minnehaha Glee Club. Black and Native American students were taught together in the same classes, except for lace work classes given only to Native American women. By 1912, Native Americans and blacks were eating in the same dining hall, but at separate tables.

In spite of efforts to segregate the students, David Owl, a Native American who came to Hampton in September 1909, felt that they developed an ability to work with others; "while the races were in a measure separate, the more basic school activities united us into one big student body." Some Native American female students married black students and "developed into congenially integrated families of culture." Mr. Owl did not know of any Native American male students who had married black female students.[23]

The gradual intermingling of the races brought negative responses from some private citizens and governmental officials. Congressman Carter of Oklahoma stated that Native Americans and Afro-Americans should not be educated at the same schools. In 1912, the U.S. House of Representatives failed to pass the appropriation bill for Hampton Institute, despite a letter from eighty Native American students at Hampton to U.S. Sen. Charles Curtis requesting that the funds be continued because they chose not to attend other educational institutions. The funds were not continued, but Native American students attended Hampton until 1923.

Like the Afro-American women, female Native American Hampton graduates became productive members of their communities. Many returned to tribal reservations to work with Native Americans. The greatest number became teachers, while others married and raised families. Susan LaFlesche, of the class of 1886, became the first Native American female to earn a medical degree. She interned at Women's Hospital in Philadelphia and then became government physician at the Omaha Indian School at Omaha, Nebraska.

Teacher Training. Most women who entered Hampton Institute at the upper level planned to become teachers. Only in 1918 did the first class without teacher training graduate. Because of professional and state demands, continual efforts were made to strengthen Hampton's teacher training program. Whittier Public School, located on the campus, by 1900 had four hundred students; this school served as a laboratory for the teacher trainees. The course of study and teaching methods for the school were under the direction of the Normal Department, which also supervised the teaching. In 1900, the program was a two-year course consisting of general and specific courses. Students were required to take arithmetic, literature, history, geography, nature study, manual training, form and color, domestic science, and physical training. Some of the more specialized courses included psychology, education, and Negro and Indian Society.

The academic courses were revised in 1905, and the program was lengthened to four years. Most of the subjects from the advanced normal course of 1898 were incorporated into the academic course. By 1910, seniors were required to practice teach at Whittier Public School for a period of six months, five days a week. Attempts were made to establish an advanced course for the preparation of teachers for the higher grades. The program enrolled ten students but was discontinued in 1912. The subjects of the advanced course, however, were incorporated as the academic course was revised in 1913. The Academy became a four-year secondary unit. The Normal Course continued to prepare teachers only for the elementary levels.

By 1912, the reputation of Hampton Institute was described as "tarnished" because poorly prepared graduates of the Normal Department had been placed in positions in secondary schools. A significant number of black teachers had been rejected by the State of Virginia because they did not meet state certification requirements. Some teachers were given emergency certificates, but others had to undertake additional training, and Hampton responded by upgrading specialized courses and provided the required training. With more women on campus, additional dormitory space was needed, and the position of Lady Principal was suggested.

In 1922, Virginia passed the West Bill, which required all public school students to take physical education. Institutions with normal programs had to train their students to teach such courses in order for them to receive certification. To satisfy the requirement, Hampton developed a thirty-six-hour lecture course in school hygiene and a one-quarter course three hours a week in methods of teaching school children physical education. The courses were offered at Whittier Training School.

In 1922, Whittier Training School had five-hundred pupils in eight grades who attended for a nine-month school year. A ninth grade was added that same year. Girls in the school were required to take industrial activities for nine years. Up to the fourth year, boys and girls had the same industrial program. Beginning with Grade 5, the girls were instructed in domestic arts and were expected to work in the community. A trained nurse instructed the girls in the care of the sick. Parents were expected to be aware of the school's curriculum and to assist in its development. An active Whittier Parents' Association was formed and met monthly to support the school. An internal evaluation of Whittier Training School and the Normal Course in 1923 produced recommendations for enhancement: more men in the program, more courses in human geography, courses in the history of Afro-Americans and in ecology, practicum experiences in rural and county schools, and new methodologies to fit the needs of school districts and pupils.

Domestic Science. From its inception, the Domestic Science Program at Hampton Institute was designed for female students. Stress was placed on practical application of the skills which were taught. As early as 1900, cooking classes prepared meals for the Abby May Home everyday. The girls were taught to do the marketing for the meals as well. By December 1902, dietetics was included in the course offerings, and the diets of selected teachers were used as the basis for planning meals.

Beginning in 1902, the girls served as waitresses in the teachers' dining room. Because off-campus employment opportunities were limited, serving as waitresses allowed the girls to earn money and gain additional training. Other skills taught in the Domestic Science Program also made it possible for the students to earn money while attending school. Basketry and hand-weaving of cloth were introduced into the curriculum in 1900; the products were sold locally and at fairs. The girls also were paid for doing fine-laundering for the teachers and the institute.

Home Training proved the most profitable course for the students. When the Domestic Science Building was erected in 1898, household arts were fully integrated into the curriculum. The four-year program required women to take courses in cooking, sewing, and handicraft arts. Every four months each female student was assigned a duty in general maintenance or cooking at the institute. Each task was paid by the hour, and the efficiency with which the task was performed determined the rate of pay.

The practical experiences enabled a number of students to secure summer positions as domestics. During World War I, northern whites requested cooks, laundresses, waitresses, and housekeepers, prompting discussion of the advisability of allowing the young women to work in the North. The North was seen as a region which could and would easily corrupt the morals of the students or develop in them unrealistic expectations regarding the quality of life for Afro-Americans. If the southern way of life was to be maintained, the infiltration of northern ideas and ideals could not be tolerated. For many, then, the question of whether black female students should work in the North during the summer months required much deliberation by the white administrators and faculty members. A major deciding factor was the availability of jobs in the North and the opportunity for the female students — many of whom were responsible for paying all or part of their educational expenses — to earn better wages than they could if they remained in the South. Thus, despite objections, between seventy-five and one hundred girls were sent to the North during summer 1917 to work for white families.

While Domestic Science students were paid for some services, volunteer work in the college's neighborhood also formed an integral part of the curriculum. Having been instructed in the principles of scientific farming, girls planted beautiful gardens and yards in the Hampton community. The students were taken to farms to critique planting methods and to broaden their knowledge of dairy work and poultry raising. They made some of the simple furnishings for the Domestic Science Building and were also responsible for minor repairs, painting, and papering of the building. The volunteer activities were structured to teach the students skills they personally would need and to instill in them the habit of sharing their knowledge with others.

The primary objective of the Domestic Science Program, however, was to train teachers of industrial and domestic science. During the first two years of the program, the students took academic and methods courses. They observed at Whittier Training School and did practice teaching there, and some thought was given to extending the practice teaching to other local schools. By 1922 the program had become known as the Home Economics School, but it still featured many of the same courses.

Extensions of the Domestic Science Program were developed as early as 1908. The Matrons Course for "young women who wish to prepare for the work of school matron, including inspection of rooms, care of girls in dormitories, and the planning of their work"[24] was either a one-year or a two-year program. The two-year program granted a diploma and was developed in order to provide a "broader preparation for the work of supervising the social and domestic life of a boarding school."[25] In 1912, because of the popularity of the program, an advanced Matron's Course was added in the Home Economics School; and in 1914, the course was extended to four years. In the senior year, students spent the majority of their class time in special training for the efficient operation of kitchens, dormitories, and hospitals. After 1918, at the request of supervisors and principals, institutional management for matrons of boarding schools was also offered during summer sessions.

Hampton Training School for Nurses. Throughout its history, Hampton responded to requests for special courses and programs. A request for nurses training by Hampton student Susie Hicks led to the founding of the Hampton Training School for Nurses. By necessity, lay nursing had been practiced by many black women before 1895. As a rule, hospitals that accepted black patients were few in number, and many of those permitted only white physicians and nurses to practice in their facilities. Training schools for black medical personnel tended to be linked with the rare health care centers operated by and for Afro-Americans.

The nursing programs of Meharry Medical College and Hampton Institute were representative of the stablest and most effective training available for black females. Although both nursing programs were affiliated with black educational institutions, Meharry's was founded by a black male physician, while Hampton's was founded by a white female. The two programs became well known in the South because of their curricula, their graduates' skill and professionalism, and their impact on health care in the black communities in Nashville and Hampton. In spite of internal conflicts among the chief administrators and opposition from the white communities, both nursing programs were still in existence after 1925.

The Hampton nursing program began on September 16, 1890, when Dr. Addison, a black physician in Hampton, held a meeting at his home to solicit the support of Afro-Americans for a hospital and nurses training school to serve black citizens. This group deliberately maintained only an unofficial advisory role, however, and Alice Bacon, a white woman who was former editor of the *Southern Workman,* Hampton Institute's newsletter, is credited with founding the school in 1891. She became the principal organizer and sought support from local whites.[26] Thus, Dixie Hospital was established near King's Chapel Hospital, to serve as the practicum center for black nursing students and to provide medical care for local people. Although some teachers and board members from Hampton Institute also served the training school and hospital, the two institutions remained financially and administratively independent.

The school and hospital were incorporated on 4 March 1892. That May the incorporators leased 3.4 acres of land at ten dollars a year for five years from the Normal School Trustees of Hampton.[27] In Bacon's home on 6 June 1892, the incorporators delineated the rules of governance and defined operational procedures for the school and hospital. Bacon was elected secretary-treasurer; in reality, she personally assumed the task of developing and promoting the hospital and school.

Bacon's role in the administration of the training school and hospital underwent examination in 1896. Miss S.B. Swanton, the white superintendent of the training school and hospital, was overseer of the fiscal and administrative plans of the hospital. She was also responsible for assigning students to hospital duty and district work. One of her principal tasks was to monitor the educational progress of the students. If the fledgling institutions were to survive, Bacon, as the chief fiscal officer, and Swanton had to be in basic agreement regarding plans and approaches. When a dispute developed between Bacon and Swanton over educational approaches, the board formalized administrative procedures for the key personnel. The rules were adopted on 1 June 1896 and remained in force until 1906. Bacon maintained her sovereignty; in protest, Swanton resigned.[28] Dr. Francis Weidner from Hampton Institute replaced Swanton.

At the same time that the board formalized administrative procedures, it also formalized admission, curriculum, and student conduct regulations. Applicants had to be between the ages of twenty-one and thirty-five and possess a "good common school education and be thoroughly sound, mentally, morally and physically."[29] The students had to provide a certificate from a responsible person attesting to their moral character and a certificate from a physician verifying their physical condition. All entering students were placed on probation for three months. At the end of the first month, candidates for admission who appeared to be making satisfactory progress were permitted to wear the school cap and begin the regular program. Those who passed the mental and physical fitness exams at the end of the third month were enrolled as student nurses.[30]

Upon official entrance into the nursing program, each student signed an agreement to remain at the school for the entire two years. Any student who was released or dismissed before the culmination of the program was not eligible to receive fifty dollars awarded upon graduation. Only the school's executive committee had the power to authorize the dismissal or release of a student, and any student accused of misconduct or inefficiency was entitled to a hearing. The rules for student nurses were explicit and stringent, regulating rest periods, clothing, vacation periods, and general conduct.[31]

Because, Bacon was "convinced that colored women cannot long retain a hold upon the profession of nursing without training at least equal to that enjoyed by white women," academic requirements were also defined.[32] Methods of instruction included lectures, demonstrations, and recitations from textbooks. The primary instructors were the superintendent, the head nurse, and members of the medical faculty. Daily lectures were given by physicians from the Hampton Soldiers' Home. The course included surgical, medical, and obstetrical nursing; physiology; anatomy; and the ethics of nursing. There were no set schedules for exams: "the final test of a nurse's scholarship . . . must lie in her ability to put the instructions received into daily practice in the hospital or at outside cases."[33]

At the end of the fiscal year, on 31 May 1897, sixteen females had graduated and five were to graduate during the summer. It was decided in that year to admit one male, a graduate of Hampton Institute, for the two-year course. His program included lectures deemed most appropriate for him, and his hospital assignment was in the male wards.[34] The young man, Alex Sinclair, graduated in 1903.

The school continually updated its curriculum so that students could secure excellent positions after graduation; as a result, the program was increased to three years in 1902. During the first year, students received basic instruction and practice work in the hospital. The second year included lectures by physicians, practice work, and four hours a week of textbook instruction. Exams and practice in and outside the hospital were required in the third year.[35] Practicum experiences became an integral part of the curriculum and were weighted heavily in grading. The practicum experiences were not only vital academically, but also allowed students to earn money for their school expenses and personal needs.

During the probationary period, room and board were provided for all students. Upon arrival, each applicant deposited money with the treasurer to cover her return trip home if it became necessary or was requested. After probation, the students received a monthly allowance to cover expenses. After 1903, those who worked with regular ward patients were paid $7.50 per week, and those who attended to contagious cases received $15.00 per week.

Even though some whites objected, the hospital accepted any patient, Afro-American or white. Because some white patients refused to address the black nurses as "Miss," the administrators required that all patients use the title "nurse" when addressing the students. The mixed-patient policy and regulations like these did not deter whites from seeking admission to the hospital; in 1912 it became necessary for the hospital to move to larger quarters with sixty-five beds, off Hampton's campus. From 1891 to 1923, the hospital provided care for more than fourteen thousand patients.[36]

Community Work. At Hampton Institute, the central philosophy was that academic knowledge was to be used for community improvement. At first, students took this to mean that they were to work after graduation to improve the places where they would live. However, in 1895, Elizabeth Hyde, Lady Principal, stated in her annual report, "I feel that we must do more for Hampton and the vicinity. The school has done a good deal already, but it has been in an indirect way and the policy has always been that of withdrawing the school from its bad surroundings."[37] By 1910, on Sundays groups of young men and women were being sent into the areas surrounding Hampton to work directly with the residents on a number of projects.

"Training in Community Work" was a course "designed to give the knowledge and training needed in dealing with the perplexing and almost insoluble problems confronting the young men and the young women of the colored and Indian races." According to Hampton's catalog, the course would prepare the students to relate their special work to the needs of the communities in which they are to live, and will train them for effective influence in the home, in the school, in the church, and in other activities for social betterment.[38] In 1915, as a step toward implementing the objectives of the course, the neighborhood near Hampton was divided into four districts, with one or more teachers and their student helpers sponsoring club meetings for the residents in each one. Later we shall explore in some detail the programs established in the Hampton area as a result of the initial outreach efforts of Hampton Institute. Here we simply emphasize the philosophy and experience that women students at Hampton were exposed to on a daily basis. The orientation toward community service, evident in Hampton's academic programs, its teacher training, its affiliated nurse training, and its extracurricular activities, had a profound impact on the thinking and future undertakings of its graduates.

Hampton Institute graduated its first class in June 1871. Hampton carefully kept in touch with former students, whether graduates or not, thereafter. Each was sent a Christmas letter, along with an inquiry sheet asking for current positions and activities. Synopses of the inquiry sheets and excerpts from them were often published in the school's reports and in its bulletin, the *Southern Workman*. The first synopsis reported, "Almost all the girls and young men we sent out last spring, after three years at Hampton, are teaching successfully and doing well in every respect in their first setting out in the world for themselves."[39]

After graduation, many of those who had attended Hampton continued to attend the institute's summer sessions and special workshops in order to extend their skills. A large percentage clearly considered themselves persons who had been given special opportunities and thus charged with special responsibilities. The annual inquiry sheet of 1922 asked, "What are you doing in addition to your regular employment to help your community?" Answers from two thousand graduates and ten thousand former students indicated that may were innovators and leaders in their communities. Many of the graduates naturally became champions of the Hampton industrial concept. At the same time, they institutionalized the idea of self-help for Afro-Americans.

Approximately 90 percent of the early graduates of Hampton became successful teachers who were involved in many aspects of life in their communities. Some male and female graduates established schools using Hampton as the model. Among these were Calhoun Colored School, Calhoun, Alabama; People's Village School, Mt. Meigs, Alabama; St. Paul Normal and Industrial School, Lawrenceville, Virginia; Kittrell College, Kittrell, North Carolina; Maryland Industrial and Agricultural Institute, Laurel, Maryland; and, of course, Tuskegee Institute, Tuskegee, Alabama.

Tuskegee Institute, Alabama

Philosophy and Early Years. Booker T. Washington, the first principal of Tuskegee Institute, was a former slave who had been educated at Hampton. Out of his experience there, he developed his philosophy of Afro-American education. He felt that prior to the Civil War, every plantation had been an industrial school. Afro-Americans had been trained as carpenters, blacksmiths, wheelwrights, brickmasons, engineers, cooks, launderers, serving women, and housekeepers. Under slavery, however, no intellectual training had been included with the training of the body.

Before opening Tuskegee Institute, Washington spent one month in the Tuskegee area meeting the people. He found many living in the same places and in the same manner they had before emancipation. In the plantation districts, large families lived together in one room. He believed that many of the residents accepted the idea that "education was rather a desire for escaping work."[40] Washington saw industrial education as a means of fostering a strong economy, the habits of thrift, a love of work, ownership of property, and a desire for bank accounts. Without industrial development, he saw no wealth and no leisure for Afro-Americans; without leisure there would be no "opportunity for thoughtful reflection and the higher cultivation of the arts." Washington further stated, "No race can be lifted until its mind is awakened and strengthened."[41] Industrial training, therefore, had to be coupled with intellectual and moral training. According to Washington, the industrial schools should seek to "fit students for occupations which would be open to them in their home communities."[42] He recognized that whites would readily support Afro-Americans who received an industrial education.

One of the earliest rules at Tuskegee was that no student could attend unless he or she studied a trade as well as the "basics" of education. Parents of some students complained that they did not want their children to work in many of the trades for which they were being trained at Tuskegee. Washington replied, "I do not wish to be understood as meaning that the education of the Negro should be confined to that kind, industrial, alone, because we need men and women well educated in other directions; but for the masses industrial education is the supreme need."[43] He recalled, "During the first ten years of its existence, a large part of the time and energy of the Tuskegee school was spent in convincing the students, their parents, and the white and colored population of the North and South, of the value of industrial education, and in planning its methods."[44] By 1900 Washington felt that the battle had been won.

As at Hampton, at Tuskegee the primary axiom was "learning by doing." Tuskegee was established in 1881 as an experimental farm to aid the black farmers of Alabama. Washington was concerned that while 85 percent of the black population before the Civil War had lived in the country districts, after the war relatively few were being trained as farmers.[45] He therefore advocated agricultural and industrial education as a means of providing more and better farmers. He also felt that the schools should teach students how to utilize effectively all the materials available in nature. In 1899, Congress granted 25,000 acres of land to Tuskegee. Of this, 5,000 acres were later sold to supplement the endowment fund. The young male students cultivated 800 acres of the land owned by Tuskegee. As part of their training, students also erected fifty-six of the sixty buildings on campus. Washington stressed self-help and advocated that Afro-Americans build upon their strengths. "I sometimes fear that as a race of people we have so formed the habit of considering our disadvantages that we overlook our advantages."[46]

While stressing self-help, Washington did not hesitate to seek financial and moral support from whites. On 16 October 1901, he dined with President Theodore Roosevelt at the White House and as a result received national publicity. Though responses to the visit were mixed, the visit helped establish Washington in the eyes of the nation as a leader of Afro-Americans and brought additional funds to the institute.

By 1912, Tuskegee Institute was situated on 2,345 acres and had buildings valued at $1,339,248. The endowment fund totaled $1,401,826, not including 19,910 acres of unsold government land valued at $3,000.[47]

Tuskegee did not undergo as many curriculum changes as Hampton did. After Washington's death in 1915, Major Robert Russa Moton faithfully executed the plans and activities formulated for the institution by Washington. Born in 1864 on a plantation in Virginia, Moton, like Washington, had attended Hampton. After graduating in 1890, Moton became a teacher at Hampton and was placed in charge of six companies of black and Native American students, thereby acquiring the rank of major. Journalist William H. Crogman stated that Moton belonged to "the conservative element of the race."[48] The programs and courses during Moton's administration reflected his conservatism and did not introduce many new educational directions. The enrollment and financial worth of the institute, however, continued to grow. For the 1920–1921 academic year, enrollment was 2,240; Tuskegee had a budget of $411,827 and income of $457,300. In 1925, John D. Rockefeller, Jr., turned over to the Hampton-Tuskegee Fund securities worth one million dollars. The securities were "to aid the sound work achieved by the two institutes in helping to solve the race problem."[49]

Women at Tuskegee. Even though Booker T. Washington readily accepted funds and curriculum suggestions from whites, he had a strict rule that only Afro-Americans could be fulltime resident members of the staff at Tuskegee. Women were always employed in large numbers at Tuskegee, teaching in many of the disciplines. Well-known black women served in various capacities; among them were Hallie Q. Brown, Adella Hunt Logan, and Mrs. (Josephine) B.K. Bruce, widow of a former U.S. senator. In 1896, thirty-eight females were members of the faculty and staff. Through 1925, women continued to be active members of the staff, assisting in structuring the program offerings, recreational activities, and community projects for the female students.

Margaret Murray Washington, third wife of Booker T. Washington, became a guiding force in the development of activist programs among female students, faculty, and staff, and among citizens far beyond the campus. An 1889 graduate of Fisk University, Mrs. Washington had become lady principal of Tuskegee in 1890. She married Washington two years later and lived to serve Tuskegee for thirty-five years, until her death in 1925.

Booker T. Washington was firmly committed to education for women. He believed that an education at Tuskegee could insure the moral and spiritual development of women and at the same time give them industrial skills to complement their analytical skills and enable them to secure jobs in the North or South. Washington did not oppose a literary or academic education for women but felt that those subjects should be included in the industrial program.

Women students at Tuskegee generally were enrolled in one of three programs: domestic science, teaching or nursing. Regardless of the program, academic as well as behavioral regulations were enforced: "It is the policy of the Institute to give special attention to the training of girls in all matters pertaining to dress, health, etiquette, physical culture and general housekeeping."[50] Girls were supervised by the lady principal and the female teachers. Special rules for female students' conduct were presented to them on their first day in attendance. Each week the young ladies were required to attend special talks relating to sex education, care of the female body, and other topics relating specifically to women. The students could not leave the grounds of Tuskegee without being accompanied by a teacher. Nor were they permitted to participate in political meetings or conventions.

A typical Sunday morning in such a student's life in 1912 suggests the limited personal time afforded women at Tuskegee. The rigorous schedule was considered an important element of education for life discipline. A bell would alert the students to rise, and ten minutes later another bell would announce breakfast. All students had to be presentable when they entered the dining hall and were expected to bring their personal napkins. Table etiquette was monitored. Immediately after the meal the students returned to their rooms, which were cleaned and then inspected by a corps of teachers and/or workers. The students' clothing was also checked.

The proper clothing for the girls after classes was determined by the parents, with the advice of the matron. The school uniforms, sold at Tuskegee, consisted of a dress and hat for spring and another for winter. The girls provided overshoes and gossamers (light raincoats) for wet weather. Gym outfits, also sold by the institute, were required. The clothing regulations remained in force until 1925.

On Sunday a call to prayer was issued after room inspection. Students, carrying their personal Bibles, marched to hear a sermon and a choir performance. Sunday school followed the morning service. After dinner and a quiet rest, at three o'clock a bell summoned the students to a prayer meeting and band concert. The religious and moral lessons continued, as students listened to an address by Booker T. Washington or another well-known person at the evening chapel meeting. Washington believed that the activities of the day provided lessons "in punctuality, in decency of appearance, in table manners, in keeping clean surroundings, in placing a value upon time, even the day of rest."[51]

The daily schedule prevented women students from making significant personal decisions and from exercising free thought and movement. Even so, some felt that it was necessary to maintain strict supervision because the school was situated in a hostile environment. Movement by the students was restricted in part because many whites still resented the intrusion of Afro-Americans who were striving to elevate themselves. Even though the school reached out to Afro-Americans in the vicinity of Tuskegee, social and racial distinctions were observed. It would be many years before the existence of Tuskegee was not considered a threat to the traditional southern social structure. The curriculum was designed to equip students for occupations considered "safe" by many whites and Afro-Americans.

Domestic Science. Just as important as the girls' deportment and personal habits was their academic performance. Dorothy Hall, the Girls' Industrial Building, was dedicated on 22 April 1901. The erection of the building marked the formal beginning of industries for girls at Tuskegee. The courses and the amount of time needed to complete them were plain sewing, two years; dressmaking, three years; millinery, eight months; cooking, four years; laundering, one year; mattress making, two years; and basketry, four years. Postgraduate courses in sewing, millinery, and cooking were offered. Although it was still considered a field more suitable for males, in 1899 girls were permitted to enroll in tailoring. It was noted that the girls demonstrated the same aptitude for the field as did boys; girls in the tailoring division made all the overalls, common pantaloons, vests, and coats used by the students and industrial instructors.

Products from other courses were utilized by faculty members and students. In 1903, students in plain sewing began to furnish the underwear and work shirts for the young men. Between 1910 and 1914, over 2,500 articles were made each year in the plain sewing division. The dressmakers and milliners made dresses and trimmed hats for most of the students and teachers; the millinery division made and trimmed approximately five hundred hats a year. The upholstering division made all of the mattresses and brooms used by the school, and the girls in the laundry department were responsible for all of the laundry work of Tuskegee.

The students' schedules alternated between one day in academic classes and the next in a trade class. Industrial classes were designed to make the students proficient teachers in the trades, so that they could perform services for the community. All female students at Tuskegee were required to take courses in cooking and domestic science. Sewing, millinery, laundering, and homecrafts were among the required courses. The Domestic Science Department, as it was known by 1923, regarded housekeeping, the preparation of foods, and the remodeling and remaking of old clothes as sciences, and stressed efficient, cost-conscious, timely skills.

Subject matter in the trade courses was correlated with course content in the academic subjects. No modern foreign languages, Latin, or Greek was taught. Mathematics, English, geography, and history were the basic academic disciplines offered. In English, students were exposed to two years of rhetoric and English classics. Problems in plane and concrete geometry were based on the trades. Where possible, economics, American history, ancient and medieval history, physics, and chemistry were also related to trades or other practical concerns.

The Normal Department. The Normal Department also had as its base the industrial core courses. During the students' last two years, they were required to teach in classrooms, under supervision. Instruction was given in lesson planning and presentation. The students were also exposed to supervised teaching in model schools in the community. The Children's House on Tuskegee's campus served as the public school for the institute and the principal practice teaching site, preparing students to enter the "A Preparatory Class" at Tuskegee. Funds for the model school came from the county government, from Tuskegee general funds, and from student tuition. The Normal Department designed the school's curriculum to complement the goals of the institute. Specialized courses in business, social work, and community work were not included until after 1915.

Nurses' Training. One program for females which received national attention because of acute shortages was nurses' training. Nurses' training, which began at Tuskegee in 1892, in 1899 became affiliated with the school hospital. The course of study lasted three years. For two years, the trainees performed tasks and received instruction at the hospital; the third year they received lectures and bedside instruction, with one or two days a week designated for hospital instruction.

Admission requirements included letters of recommendation, good moral character, and good physical condition. Applicants could be fourteen years of age and older. Those who chose to attend the night school, at less cost, had to be sixteen years of age or older. By 1910, all students had to have completed the requirements of the academic department before being admitted to the three-year nursing program.

In an effort to improve the quality of nursing instruction and to provide better medical care for residents of the surrounding area, several changes were made in the nursing program after 1908. As an addendum to the home-household course, the head nurse at the hospital instructed all female students at Tuskegee in the care and training of children. With the dedication of the John A. Andrew Memorial Hospital in 1913, both health care and instruction were vastly improved. Community outreach was further strengthened when the Tuskegee Health Center, established in November 1921, employed a public health nurse who divided her time between the Health Center and a movable school which traveled to the rural communities around Tuskegee. The Health Center, staffed partly with student nurses, presented health lectures in the community and organized Mothers' and Girls' Health Clubs. Involvement in the various health care units of Tuskegee augmented the student nurses' classroom instruction, with the result that they were hired to work as nurses throughout the United States and in foreign nations. Some returned to Tuskegee after 1923 to take postgraduate courses in surgery and nursing.

Graduates. Tuskegee Institute's graduates and former students rendered many services to their communities and to the nation. From the time of the first graduate, Virginia Adams Driver Thomas, who became a housekeeper in Prattville, Alabama, to the end of 1925, former students primarily chose human service occupations. Tuskegee maintained contact with its former students and assisted them whenever possible. For example, graduates in agricultural fields were sold farm instruments and land tracts at low rates. Committees of teachers from Tuskegee were sent to evaluate the progress of institutions begun by former students. The committees examined the physical plants, teaching methods, financial status, extension services, and other aspects of operations, to ensure that Tuskegee's own concepts and methodologies were implemented and maintained. By 1916, graduates had established seventeen schools located from Louisiana to Virginia.

Atlanta University

Organization and Early Years. The group of intellectuals and educators who favored a liberal arts education for Afro-Americans gained increasing attention for their concerns toward the end of the period 1895–1925. Liberal arts institutions, however, were established as early as many of the industrial ones. A cluster of such schools grew up in Atlanta, Georgia. One which became known for its academic excellence was Atlanta University. Granted a charter by the Georgia Legislature in 1867, Edmund Asa Ware founded Atlanta University "for the liberal and Christian education of youth."[52] The school opened in October 1869, with eighty-nine students — sixty-two men and twenty-seven women. College courses were introduced in 1872, and the first college class graduated four women in 1876. The institution was controlled by an independent board of trustees and received no financial support from the City of Atlanta, the State of Georgia, the national government, or benevolent societies.

By February 1895, 216 students were enrolled in the College, Normal, College-Preparatory, and Sub-Normal Departments. The faculty and staff consisted of fifteen persons. Situated on sixty-five acres, the university had no endowment; insufficient funds forced the school to reassess its priorities throughout its early years. In 1894, the grammar school was closed, and Atlanta University supported three general courses of study: high school, normal, and college. In 1895, the university was able to provide annual scholarships of forty dollars for some students but could not continue to employ the teachers of cooking and nursing (note the areas of instruction in which personnel were eliminated). The institution was not able to eradicate its debts until 17 October 1921. At that time, payment from the Drew Legacy finally enabled the institution to operate free of debt.

The criteria for admission became more selective after 1898, and the curriculum was broadened. In November 1898, the purpose of the institution was defined for the first time: "The higher education of carefully selected Negro young men and women in both academic and industrial lines, is emphasized by this Institution as necessary for the elementary and industrial training of the masses."[53]

In spite of the addition of the word "industrial" to its statement of purpose, Atlanta University's primary objective continued to be providing a liberal education. Like most black institutions dedicated to providing a liberal arts education, Atlanta included a number of industrial courses in its basic curriculum. Offering industrial courses was in line with a national educational trend and also encouraged white philanthropists to give funds to liberal arts institutions.

George Towns and W.E.B. Du Bois. George A. Towns, one of the two black faculty members at Atlanta University in 1895, became a leading spokesperson for a liberal arts education for Afro-Americans. He stated, "Negro masses should be reached indirectly through the highly and liberally educated Negro teachers."[54] Towns criticized the rise of many industrial schools patterned after Tuskegee. In 1899, as a student at Harvard University, he devoted an English paper to the question, "Is the Idea of the Tuskegee and Calhoun Schools the Solution of the Negro Problem?" The purpose of the two schools, he wrote, was "to reach the masses directly and give them a common-school education, industrial and agricultural training, with the hope that the masses may improve their conditions and become a commercial importance by accumulating property and thus to solve the Negro problem."[55] He concluded that this idea was not the solution, since it would not remove all the barriers to the incorporation of Afro-Americans into the American system. Further, he argued, the type of education advocated by Tuskegee and Calhoun would not bring Afro-Americans up to white American standards, nor would it supply candidates for the higher economic classes.

Dr. W.E.B. Du Bois shared many of Towns' views. In 1896 he was invited by Booker T. Washington to teach at Tuskegee. Washington hoped to quell some of Du Bois' criticisms of industrial education by making Du Bois a member of Tuskegee's faculty. Instead, Du Bois accepted a one-year position as professor of history and economics at Atlanta University, at a salary of $1,000.[56] Atlanta was a logical choice for Du Bois; later, in *Souls of Black Folk* (1903), he criticized industrial schools and strongly advocated the cultural emphasis of Atlanta University. His major criticism of industrial education was its compromise with white racism. As his stay at Atlanta University lengthened and as his leadership role at the Atlanta Conferences developed, Du Bois became more and more vocal in his opinions. The comments of Towns and Du Bois brought open criticism from the Atlanta University trustees and from private citizens but did not decrease the number of applicants to Atlanta University.

Community Work. In an effort to help students earn tuition, gain experience, and assist rural Afro-Americans at the same time, Atlanta University extended its summer vacation period so that "the students may go to the dark corners to do missionary work in country schools, and earn money to come back and continue their studies."[57] They were expected to teach a variety of subjects, including religious studies. When Georgia's public school system, in February 1896, changed its term to five months a year, the action decreased opportunities for students to teach during the summer. Atlanta University administrators sent a note to county school commissioners requesting that school sessions include the summer months of June, July, August, and September, when Atlanta University was not in session.

Because the demand for teachers was greater than the supply, Atlanta University students were given qualifying certificates which were readily accepted by the school districts.

Women who graduated from Atlanta University generally regarded their school years as highly productive, motivating ones. Comments from graduates of the Normal Department indicated that many had been imbued with a missionary zeal which prompted them to seek the less glamorous jobs. Adella Hunt Logan, an Atlanta graduate, had been approached by Ware, former president of Atlanta University, to teach at Atlanta but had chosen to teach at Tuskegee instead. In a letter to Atlanta's President Bumstead, she wrote, "[Ware] did not see why I should prefer so crude a field to the work so well organized and pleasant as that of Atlanta University."[58] Apparently many felt, as she did, that the "crude" work was more valuable. In 1922, over fifty thousand black children in rural southern schools were being taught by Atlanta University graduates.

Spelman Seminary, Atlanta

Early Years. Believing that black females were ultimately to provide the major support system for the race, black and white intellectuals and educators founded schools to meet what they considered to be the special needs of black women. Among those schools were Haines Normal and Industrial School in Georgia, founded by Lucy C. Laney, a member of Atlanta University's first graduating class; Hartshorn Memorial College in Virginia; the National Training School for Women and Girls in Washington, D.C., founded by Nannie H. Burroughs; St. Augustine's School in Florida; and Palmer Memorial Institute in North Carolina, founded by Charlotte Hawkins Brown. In time, Spelman Seminary in Atlanta would be recognized as the most prestigious all-female institution for black women to attend.

Like some other educational institutions for Afro-Americans in the South, Spelman owes its origin to white northerners who traveled south to help others. Sophie B. Packard and Harriet Giles chose Atlanta as the site for an industrial school for women because "its healthful climate, railroad connections, and spirit of enterprise, have made it largely the political, commercial and educational center of the state."[59] The city was also thought to be in need of moral elevation. Packard was a representative of the Woman's American Baptist Mission Society, and the Baptist Congress gave financial support for the venture.

The institute opened on 11 April 1881, in the basement of Friendship

Baptist Church, where a black clergyman, Father Frank Quarles, was pastor. Starting with eleven students and one hundred dollars, the two white women offered instruction in domestic arts, housekeeping, and homemaking. The institute's aim was to build character within a Christian framework; the founders felt that "Christianity and morality are the foundation of our own teaching, for if these are neglected, all else is vain." The school's motto indicated its religious orientation: "Our Whole School for Christ."[60]

Interest in the educational endeavor grew, and several black ministers organized the Baptist Educational Society to raise funds for a separate school building. Assistance also came from outside the black community. Mrs. John D. Rockefeller had become interested in the project in 1880, when she had heard Packard lecture. In 1882, the first Rockefeller gift was sent to further the venture. The school was able to relocate in 1883, but its independent status was threatened by the Home Mission Society, which wanted the institute to merge with Atlanta Baptist Seminary for men, Morehouse College. Another financial gift from the Rockefeller Foundation enabled the founders to argue successfully for their school's continued existence as a separate entity. Gratified by the level of financial support from the Rockefeller Foundation, the founders officially named the new school Spelman Seminary, in honor of the mother of Mrs. Laura Spelman Rockefeller.

In 1893, Spelman had four units: high school, domestic arts school, nurse training program, and normal department. However, because of the impending nationwide economic slump, enrollment began to decline. In 1895, the board of trustees agreed that academic standards would be maintained in spite of the need for additional students. In 1895, 550 students registered, the majority in the English preparatory program. The school was proud to announce in its 1895 statistical table that it had been responsible for one thousand religious conversions since the founding of the school.[61]

Nevertheless, enrollment continued to decline until the 1897–98 academic year. Giles, Spelman's president, attributed the decline to three factors. Market prices of cotton had fallen and since the majority of boarders came from the rural districts of the South, parents apparently were no longer able to pay the required fees. An epidemic of yellow fever and smallpox in Atlanta prior to the opening of the term had also contributed to the decline. Finally, Spelman's requirements may have been too stringent for many.

In the annual report released in March 1898, the president wrote:

> It may be that our insistence on greater accuracy and proficiency before promotion and graduation, in which we were sustained by your vote two years ago, had discouraged those who wish speed in education at the expense of thoroughness,

but we are confident that a high standard of scholarship will eventually make a name for Spelman that will surely attract the best young women, and will promote the progress of the Negro race more effectually than a lax and flattering management.[62]

The year 1900 brought a return to financial prosperity for the country, along with increased enrollment at Spelman. The most significant increase was in the higher classes. Of 598 students enrolled, 285 were boarders and 313 were day scholars. Students came from eighteen states, South America, and Africa.[63] The enrollment increased to 631 students in 1903; as a result, some day students and those interested in the Dressmaking Department were refused admittance because of lack of seats. The high price of cotton in 1904 again boosted enrollment.

Many students worked during summer 1903 to help pay their fees. In spite of their college experience, the majority of the young women worked in menial positions: domestic service, 62; needlework, 33; teaching, 31; laundry work, 17; clerical, 16; farming and gardening, 15; music, 7; and miscellaneous, 19.[64] Their goals for the future evidently merited hard labor in the present.

Spelman administrators were interested in attracting not only qualified students but also better prepared and more committed faculty members. Even though some black females were hired as instructors and staff members, more whites were employed. Dr. Sophie Jones in 1885 became the first black woman to join the faculty; she taught nursing and supervised the school's infirmary. Lugenia Hope taught millinery in the 1907 term, when there were also two other black instructors. Some Spelman graduates were hired to teach selected courses or assist in the departments. As of 1909, five graduates were faculty members. Margaret Nabrit Curry, of the college class of 1924, was the first Afro-American to be appointed to the Spelman College faculty.

Faculty members' duties were varied. They were expected to supervise student extracurricular activities and serve as role models. All faculty members were encouraged to seek additional training and attend seminars so that they might bring new techniques and knowledge to the school. It was understood that the seminary could not hope to maintain its academic standards if it did not have a well-informed, dedicated faculty.

Student Life. Approximately 33 percent of the original Spelman enrollees were between the ages of twenty-five and fifty.[65] By 1907, 41 percent of the students were under sixteen, 52 percent were between sixteen and twenty-

8

Fig. 8. As at other educational institutions of the period, Spelman Seminary's 1897–98 faculty was predominantly white. Because of its all-female student body, all administrators and faculty members were women. *Courtesy of Spelman College Archives.*

Fig. 9. In 1908, nine dressmaking majors graduated from Spelman Seminary; the instructor is the white woman. At most institutions in 1895–1925, the number of graduates from all programs was generally small. *Courtesy of Spelman College Archives.*

Fig. 10. Nora Gordon (*center*) was a member of the 1895 missionary training class at Spelman Seminary. *Courtesy of Spelman College Archives.*

9

10

11

12

13

Fig. 11. Upon graduation from Spelman Seminary, Congolese students Lena Clark (*second left*) and Maggie Rattray (*seated*) returned to the Congo as missionaries. Nora Gordon (*far left*) was the first Spelman graduate to serve as a missionary to the Congo. Emma Yongeblood (*second from left*) continued her education at Meharry's School of Nursing. *Courtesy of Spelman College Archives.*

Fig. 12. After marriage to a minister of the American Baptist Missionary Union, Lena Clark Whitman (*right*) returned to the Congo. As part of her duties she taught reading. *Courtesy of Spelman College Archives.*

Fig. 13. Lugenia Burns Hope and her husband John (*rear center*) pose with an early graduating class of the Atlanta School of Social Work. *Courtesy of Atlanta University Center Woodruff Library.*

five years of age, and 7 percent were over twenty-five. One-half of the students were residents of Atlanta.[66] As the average student age decreased, the supervisory responsibilities of teachers increased. The boarding students were divided into nine "family life" groups, each headed by a teacher who assumed the authority of a mother "ruling" her family. The teacher was responsible for assigning her students daily tasks, instructing them in manners, neatness, orderliness, and healthy ways of living, and fostering their moral development.[67] Students were expected to account to their head teacher for their time outside of classes. Nonresidents of Atlanta were not accepted as day scholars and had to be boarders unless their parents or guardians submitted written requests. Nonresidents had to return to their homes when the term ended.

Strict discipline, dress, and conduct codes were enforced to ensure the attainment of Spelman's primary objective: to develop Christian women. Through the establishment of such codes, administrators became the judges of what was proper or suitable for the students. Although the administrators' intentions may have been benign, they nevertheless isolated students from social events and realities. A case in point occurred in 1910.

In that year Dr. W.E.B. Du Bois began a campaign to acquaint students at black colleges with the newly-formed NAACP. The colleges were generally eager to receive him, but Lucy Hale Tapley, president of Spelman, refused to permit Du Bois to visit Spelman's campus. She stated that she was aware of and concerned about the plight of Afro-Americans but did not wish the girls at Spelman to know about problems she felt they were too young to handle.[68] Given the wide age range of the students and their probable experience away from the campus, Tapley's behavior appears over protective.

Throughout Tapley's tenure in 1910–27 and afterwards, Spelman maintained its rigid control over every aspect of the students' lives. After 1914, students were permitted free periods between 3 and 5 p.m., and after dinner until the evening meetings. The free time could be used for playground activities, tennis, reading in the library, or meditation. However, the student's whereabouts still had to be known. In 1925 the school did make recreational programs through the Alkahest Lyceum Bureau of Atlanta accessible to students. By that time, the school term was nine months, with no vacation period during the year.

Industrial Training. If little attention seems to have been given to activities outside classes, it was because the academic progress of the students was of prime importance. Spelman's focus was clearly enunciated in its charter, which supported the intention of the founders to stress academics as well as industries. In 1896 each student was required to take courses in the Industrial Department. It was considered especially important that students enrolled in the academic areas take courses with an industrial focus, so that "as [they] enter lives of useful services . . . they would have higher ideas of true living."[69]

All students were required to perform domestic duties for the college and thereby put into practice theories learned in class. The one-hour daily housework duties were rotated, so that each student was exposed to all tasks. Students were responsible for the preparation of nearly all of the meals and were paid for their services. The advanced students took courses in theory and were responsible for preparing the teachers' meals. Laundry work, basketry, gardening, sewing, printing, and fine needlework formed part of the industrial offerings. The Home Economics Department, offering many of these courses, was formally organized in 1918.

Teacher Training. Many of Spelman's departments were organized according to traditional patterns. The Teacher's Professional Department combined theory and practice. Like other black schools, Spelman established a training school for practice teaching. Spelman began to upgrade its requirements for admission to the normal program much sooner than did other schools, however. As early as 1908, applicants had to be high school graduates who were willing to complete the entire three-year course. Spelman's insistence upon high standards in its departments brought recognition from many parts of the United States. In 1925, the American Child Health Association of New York City chose Spelman to offer a health education course to public school teachers. Spelman had incorporated the course in its department in 1923. In 1926, the course was included in the Extension Teaching Program, which had been introduced in 1925. Public school teachers (twenty-one in the initial year) were able to register for courses leading to a degree.

Nurse Training. The excellence of Spelman's Nursing Program also won recognition. One of the earliest nursing schools for Afro-Americans, the full program developed in 1886. Two course options were available: professional and nonprofessional. The three-year professional course included service in the Mac Vicar Hospital, opened in 1900, and class work. The nonprofessional course taught skills designed to enable the students to care for the sick in their homes. Because of the program's excellent rating, private donors gave funds to both the hospital — begun by Spelman because of insufficient facilities for Afro-Americans at Grady Hospital in Atlanta — and to the nursing program. The program's rating also enabled its graduates to secure jobs in Georgia and other states. In 1919 Ludie Andrews and Charity Collins passed the state board examination in Georgia and were licensed as registered nurses; they were the first Spelman graduates to pass the exam. The trustees closed the program in 1928.

Missionary Training. Probably the most distinctive department at Spelman, and one which also boasted of its graduates' success, was the Missionary Training Department. It began in 1892 with the purpose of training "Missionary teachers, family missionaries, church and Sunday school workers . . . for the United States or foreign lands."[70] Missionary work was considered so important that students who had worked in the mission field received one hundred dollars for a minimum of five months service to help defray their school expenses. Religious training and skills needed to convert others were the major concerns of the department. Because it was expected that many of the students would eventually fulfill their missions in Africa, several African languages were taught as part of the program.

When the program ended in 1906, twenty-seven persons had graduated. Some chose to work in the South, while others accepted African missions. In 1889, Nora Gordon, an 1888 graduate of the Higher Normal and Scientific Course, became the first Spelman student to travel to Africa. Although she had already accepted a teaching position in the Atlanta public school system, she decided instead to travel to Palabala in the Congo to serve as a helper in the local mission. Officially, she was a missionary of the board appointed by the Women's Baptist Foreign Missionary Society of the West. In 1891 she worked in Lukungu, Congo, with another Spelman graduate, Clara A. Howard. Gordon returned to the United States in 1893 and married Rev. S.C. Gordon of Jamaica in 1895. They returned to the Congo to work at Stanley Pool.

Evidently Nora Gordon had internalized both the teachings of Spelman and the condescending, ethnocentric attitudes of those who see themselves as having something "special" to offer others. In "Some Characteristics of the Heathen," an article published in the *Spelman Messenger,* Gordon described Africans in some of the same terms whites used to describe Afro-Americans in the United States. She noted that the Congo native was "proud, ignorant, superstitious, and degraded"; he "viewed foreigners as not better than he" and had a "dislike for Belgians." Her solution was the traditional approach: "The Congo Missionary's work is two-fold. We must civilize as well as christianize, the people."[71] Unfortunately, the approach used by

Gordon and others would precipitate new problems which are still with us today.

Having accepted the tenets of Christianity and believing that complete adherence to them was the way to achieve a better life, many black females were eager to proselytize. In the United States, since the days of slavery, the black church had facilitated the improvement of both individual and race. Thus, for many Afro-Americans the practice of Christian principles was a natural and necessary response to the harshness of everyday life. At the same time, the Christianity taught by the missionaries promoted restrained behavior which could not permit radical reaction to the economic and social systems of the United States and the colonized African nations. As a result, missionaries gave more attention to modifying behavior and "saving souls" than to combatting systems of government oppressing peoples of color.

Nora Gordon returned to the United States in 1900, bringing with her Emma Yongeblood, a Congolese. Yongeblood enrolled at Spelman, graduated, and then completed the nurse training program at Meharry Medical College in Nashville. After her graduation from Meharry, Yongeblood secured a job in a hospital in Tennessee. In 1901, at the age of thrity-four, Gordon died at Spelman.

Other Congolese students were either brought to Spelman by alumnae or sent by white missionaries. Three of these were Flora Zeto, Margaret Rattray, and Lena Clark. All returned to the Congo to convert the natives and establish schools and missions. Excerpts from articles written by Lena Clark for the *Spelman Messenger* reveal the influence education at Spelman had upon her and her decision to become a missionary. Clark had been adopted by Dr. Joseph Clark, a missionary from Scotland to the Congo, and had been converted before her arrival in the United States. She wrote, "I sailed from the New World" on 27 April 1891. "Now, after a pleasant stay in this Christian school, I am going back to help my dying friends in Africa." She viewed missionary work as "benevolence reaching out in every direction to lift up the unfortunate." She believed missionary work and training were assets as one interacted with members of one's family and community and when one started a family of one's own. Christian training, she believed, enabled a woman to instill values in her children. She indicated that she hoped Spelman's daughters would be "going out to save Africa's sons and daughters."[72]

Whether for duty in Africa or at home, Spelman's administrators and faculty worked assiduously to develop missionary zeal in the students. Many of the campus clubs incorporated missionary activities as part of their programs. One club, the Congo Mission Circle, specifically prepared its members for work in Africa. The circle was an organization logical for Spelman, since the Baptist Home Mission concentrated its efforts in the Congo. Nora Gordon and her husband were active members of the circle during the early months of 1895. The Reverend Mr. Gordon delivered lectures to the members in an effort to correct common stereotypes of the Congo. Members of the circle also engaged in missionary work in Atlanta; they distributed religious tracts and papers and encouraged residents to attend Sunday school.

The campus YWCA also carried out missionary activities in Atlanta. The chapter was organized in spring 1884, and every Spelman student and teacher became a member. Three of the most active YWCA committees concentrated on missionary work, young converts, and temperance. The temperance committee formed a separate society in 1891. Members were to proselytize and convince people to take the temperance pledge. One member, Trudie Howser, persuaded 103 Spelman students to sign the pledge. Given the ban on alcoholic beverages and the school's teachings, the signers probably required little persuasion. Other campus clubs also reflected the Christian and missionary orientation of Spelman. They included the Christian Endeavor Union, the Volunteer Mission Board, and the Social Purity Society.

Spelman Alumnae. The moral lessons and training imparted by Spelman's administrators and teachers influenced many black women during the period 1895–1925. By 1924 Spelman reportedly had taught 15,000 students during its forty-four-year history. Of that number, 959 had received diplomas and degrees. Spelman became a four-year college on 1 June 1924. Up to that time, students receiving college degrees had completed part of their requirements at Morehouse College. Many of Spelman's graduates continued their studies, taking professional courses at schools such as Meharry Medical College, Hampton's Library School, and the Atlanta School of Social Work.

In March 1925, Spelman was able to identify 851 living graduates. Of that number, 90 percent were teachers.[73] Many of the graduates, loyal to their alma mater, actively participated in the Spelman Alumnae Association, founded in 1892. Many of the graduates clearly believed in the kind and quality of education offered at Spelman. A Granddaughters Club, organized in 1910, was still functioning in 1925. A statement by Millie A. Harris, a 1902 academy graduate, suggests the sort of work done by Spelman alumnae and the esteem in which they held the institution:

I am now teaching at Hightower, Ga., but will soon finish my term and return home. I have been trying to be a loyal daughter even while away at work. I have taught three terms since I left school. During my last summer's term, I organized a B.Y.P.U. [Baptist Young People's Union], which is now in a flourishing condition. The Sunday-school is now in a much better condition than I found it. Five of my scholars pledged me regarding temperance matters. I cannot think of anything I need but a pledge.[74]

Atlanta School of Social Work

Without the official banner of a discipline, Afro-Americans had been practicing social work since the antebellum period. But as a structured body of knowledge concerning social action developed, Afro-Americans saw the utility of formal training for members of their race. The Atlanta School of Social Work became the first independent institution to offer such training.

Walter R. Chivers, professor at Morehouse College, believed that it was through the efforts of Lugenia Burns (Mrs. John) Hope that the Atlanta School of Social Work was founded. As organizer of Atlanta's remarkable Neighborhood Union and a fulltime staff member of the Atlanta Anti-Tuberculosis Association, Hope had broad expertise and a firm commitment to racial betterment. She served on the board of the School of Social Work and taught the community organization course, which included such topics as publicity, finance, committee organization, social programs, recreation, and community movements.

With fourteen students and Gary W. Moore as director, the school opened on October 4, 1920. Moore, a teacher of sociology at Morehouse, had come to Atlanta in 1912 as a fellow of the National Urban League. His assignment had been to teach economics and sociology, to develop a Department of Social Science at Morehouse, and to foster practical work in Atlanta itself. Moore also hoped to persuade the Neighborhood Union to affiliate with the National Urban League. As we shall see, he did not succeed in this latter objective.

A committee of Afro-Americans and whites, headed by Dr. John Hope, president of Morehouse College, was responsible for managing the school. In 1922 E. Franklin Frazier became director. Frazier, who had completed a research fellowship at the New York School of Social Work, remained at the school until 1927.

The Atlanta School of Social Work was incorporated in 1924 and offered a one-year course. The list of petitioners for incorporation showed the cooperation of colleges, agencies, and foundations, whites and Afro-Americans. Individual contributions kept the school alive during its early years; funds were also given by the Rosenwald Foundation and the Laura Spelman Rockefeller Memorial Foundation. Through 1925, the institution continuously sought adequate, stable financial support. Volunteer services proved most beneficial to the new school, as directors of social agencies and members of the medical profession freely gave their time and knowledge. The faculty consisted of a teacher in casework and fieldwork, a number of executives of Atlanta social agencies, and E. Franklin Frazier.

Courses were originally designed after patterns suggested by the National Urban League. The approach focused on casework and human behavior, and stressed benefits to individuals rather than to community units. The school's curriculum reflected social change and attempted to keep abreast of national trends, but Afro-American concerns remained central. By 1924, courses were offered in casework, human behavior, social investigation, physiology, home nursing, community organization, play leadership, social problems, and fieldwork. Students spent three days in coursework and two days in the field. In order to be near social services agencies utilized for practicum experiences, the school in time moved to 239 Auburn, the top floor of the Herndon Building. Expanding its services, the school provided extension courses for forty-six public school teachers, conducted a short course for ministers' wives at Gammon Seminary, and presented two lectures a week to the senior normal students at Atlanta University.

After he became director, Frazier introduced into the curriculum courses which stressed sociology and research. In part because of his innovative approaches to social work, the school was accredited on 29 December 1928 by the American Association of Schools of Social Work, founded in 1919. It was the first school for Afro-Americans to meet the association's accreditation requirements.

Graduates of the Atlanta School of Social Work, most of whom were women, received certificates which qualified them for a number of positions. The graduates were employed throughout the United States as district agents and executives in "colored" departments of associated charities, as probation officers, as Urban League officers and assistants, and as welfare workers in industry, church social service departments, the YMCA and the YWCA. The graduates' activities firmly established the formal framework for social work in the black community.

Fisk University, Nashville

Organization and Early Years. From its inception, Fisk University in Nashville, Tennessee, received positive national attention for its innovative curriculum, its demand for academic excellence on the part of all students, and the quality of its graduates. Fisk included industrial courses in its liberal arts program. Founded by John Ogden, Erastus M. Cravath, and Edward P. Smith on the site of the former Union Hospital; Fisk began to accept students on 9 January 1866. The school was named for Gen. Clinton B. Fisk, assistant commissioner of the Freedmen's Bureau for Tennessee and Kentucky, who acquired the school's site and gave $30,000 to its founders. The school was incorporated as Fisk University on 22 August 1867, pledging to train young men and women of all races. Because of the affiliation of Cravath and Smith, the school was placed under the control of the American Missionary Association.

Fisk, like other institutions for Afro-Americans, encountered financial difficulties during its beginning years. In 1871, the board of trustees decided that, becuase of its inability to remain financially solvent, Fisk should close. To prevent the closing, George L. White, treasurer and instructor for vocal music, developed a plan to raise funds. He organized the Jubilee Singers, composed of four women and four men, who presented concerts throughout the United States and Europe. In seven years, in addition to gifts of books and paintings, the group raised $150,000, of which $100,000 went to erect Jubilee Hall. Individuals, foundations, and the Jubilee Singers contributed funds which kept Fisk open through 1925.

As of 1871, Fisk University consisted of a high school, normal school, model school, theology department, commercial department, and the college; most females, however, were admitted to the normal department. All female students, regardless of their major, were required to take courses in domestic science. Until the class of 1907, only men were enrolled in the Theology Department. Cora Adginora Pair-Thompson, a member of that class, distinguished herself as a missionary and teacher in Brewerville, Liberia, in West Africa.

George Haynes and the Department of Social Science. In 1910, at the request of the Committee on Urban Conditions Among Negroes, which became the National Urban League, George Edmund Haynes, a 1903 B.A. graduate of Fisk, established the Department of Social Science at Fisk University. One major task of the new Committee on Urban Conditions was to help train black young people for social service work in direct contact with the masses. In developing a model training program for black social workers, Haynes would make Fisk the training center for Nashville as well.

From 1911 to 1915, Haynes outlined program activities for the new Fisk Department of Social Science. His first task was to win approval for the social science concept from black institutions of higher learning. His plans also included the publication of "Fisk University Studies in Negro History and Negro Life" based on specific studies of localities; and the establishment of a Social Science Museum to contain African materials, relics of Negro history in the United States, charts and illustrations for teaching social and economic theory, and a collection of photographs and models of playgrounds, camps, schoolhouses, and tenements.[75] He knew that the proposed projects would cost a great deal of money, but he felt that a small beginning could be made. His recommendation to the trustees of Fisk University was that a room be designated to house the materials and that the publications initially be issued in small booklets.

After 1912, interest and support for the Department of Social Science developed to the point that Haynes hired an assistant, Ellie Alma Walls, who held a B.A degree from Fisk (1911) and an M.A. degree from Columbia University (1912). Responsible for teaching applied sociology, statistics, and methods of research, Walls also assisted in the theoretical sociology, economics, and Negro history classes and supervised fieldwork for students at Bethlehem Center in Nashville.

The first year of the training course ended 9 June 1915. Myrtle L. Alexander, who had earned her undergraduate degree at Fisk in 1914, completed the course and was awarded a certificate. Immediately upon completing her requirements, she left to begin a job in New Orleans. Her success prompted further interest in the training course. Haynes decided to develop a strong organization for students in social science and to seek affiliation with other institutions. Atlanta University and Wilberforce were selected as two educational institutions where training courses and social science departments might be patterned after those of Fisk.

George Haynes also recognized the need for Fisk to seek support from local colleges and national groups. During the 1915–16 academic year, he planned to offer a series of special lectures on social problems of interest to college classes and faculty members. Haynes appealed for speakers in four areas: "Health and Community Welfare," "Rural Education in Relation to the Improvement of Country Life," "Relation of Physical Education to Community Welfare," and "Home Economics in Relation to Community Welfare." Fisk was not able to offer honorariums to the lecturers, but five faculty members from George Peabody College, a white institution in Nashville, agreed to speak. The lectures were scheduled for fifty-five minutes a week, and attendance by students was voluntary.

Women Students at Fisk. All of the female students at Fisk were exposed to lecturers and faculty members who attempted to increase their social consciousness. However, such students' social activism was greatly limited by the attitudes and actions of administrators, faculty members, and local citizens. The women students were often regarded as needing to be shielded from harsh realities until after graduation. The restrictions tended to establish a special society for the female student which precluded her practicing the values she was being taught.

As early as 1867, a dormitory was designated for female students. The "walls were hung with mottoes and creeds which were constant reminders that she must ever be noble, loyal, and true."[76] Males and females were not permitted to visit one another in their rooms, nor were they permitted to participate in unchaperoned activities. Intimate relationships were discouraged, and restrictions aimed at protecting the morals of the females. Young women had to be in the dormitory before dark and were permitted one caller per week during the hour from 4:30 to 5:30 p.m. The rule of two to one supported the belief that there was safety in numbers. Restrictions became even harsher during the administration of white President Fayette McKenzie in 1915–26. Students could be expelled if close contact between them was suspected. Merely walking with a member of the opposite sex was considered poor conduct.

Fisk University believed that it had a special mission in educating black women. The *Fisk University News* in 1916 stated, "Fisk University recognizes the absolute necessity of the right education for young women. The highest interest of every community depends largely upon the intelligence, frugality, virtue and noble aspirations of its women."[77] In fulfilling their charge, administrators continued to regulate the social activities, academic choices, and dress of females. In spite of the strict regulations, so many females continued to apply for admission that normally Fisk had to refuse admission to hundreds of them each year.

Since it had been expected that the beginning of World War I would cause Fisk enrollment to decline, the "heavy" registration of young women was "almost surprising."[78] Some parents, however, expressed concern about the safety of their daughters when Fisk served as a United States Army receiving camp. The president of Fisk responded by declaring that the Army camp would be kept separate from the university; any female student who had any contact with the soldiers would be sent home.

With the beginning of World War I, as President Wilson called for preparedness, Fisk women began to train as Red Cross nurses. Local speakers and others involved in war activities gave motivating lectures to the students. Faculty members taught first aid and the proper making of bandages. Some young women were selected to make items for the Red Cross. The university paid for their services, and they used their earnings to help pay their school expenses. Fisk administrators saw all levels of contributions as vital, indicating the students' concern and love for their nation.

Fisk's Elitism. Even before World War I, however, some Fisk students had expressed concern over the students' relationship with the wider community. An editorial in the April 1916 issue of the *Fisk University News* stated:

> When we pass our fellow man upon the streets, speak to him, no matter what his condition of life may be. Tip your hat to the ladies. Have a word of cheer for everyone. Let the people feel that we are one of them. Let Fisk be known by the services it has rendered to the community. What's the good of an education if we can't apply it to the everyday needs of life? If some disaster should come to Fisk, these would be the first to lend a helping hand. Can't we do as much as they? Send our boys and girls into their Sunday schools, churches, clubs, etc. Let them take part in their exercises. It is unreasonable to expect people to help us all the time, especially when we never return the favor. Fisk, open your eyes and look around you! Don't stay here on this hill aloof from the people. Learn to know them and their needs. It is with them that we have to mingle after we leave here. All of these things tend to bring about a spirit of brotherhood that cannot prove anything but lasting.[79]

Unfortunately, Fisk was gaining the reputation of being an institution for the elite. A father of two boys wrote to President McKenzie in 1916 that his sons desired to attend Fisk but that his finances could not support them. He stated that many people considered Fisk an "aristocratic school and that only rich Negroes would be admitted." McKenzie, in an open letter published in the December 1916 issue of the *Fisk University News*, pointed out that Fisk was willing to accept any student who would study. He further stated, "If we have any preference here, our preference is for the poor boy who is not ashamed to work with his hands to earn his way." McKenzie's response, however, did not fully eradicate Fisk's elitist image.

It was not possible fully to eradicate the elitist image, because Fisk, as well as other black educational institutions, did foster an educational philosophy and a type of training that sharpened class distinctions within the race. Black college graduates often possessed personal habits and outlooks different from those of the masses. However, the April 1916 editorial identified the crucial concern. Different personal standards, habits, and educational experiences must not be allowed to isolate one group of Afro-Americans from another. Due to social restraints and limited economic opportunities, black graduates had to interact with Afro-Americans from many backgrounds; it was necessary that the interaction begin before the students graduated. It was also essential that students study under, and work in the community with, black professionals who had developed and maintained links with those aspiring to improve their status in life.

Student Protests Against McKenzie. Fayette McKenzie, a white man who became president of Fisk in 1915, ruled the college with an iron hand. He was charged with not consulting alumni or black leaders in making decisions for the institution, but instead cultivating and consulting white southerners. Open attacks on McKenzie began about 1920 and reached serious proportions in 1924. Students identified five major problems: regulations were too strict, chapel should not be compulsory, athletic associations and a student government should be permitted, McKenzie should relax his dictatorial policy, and Afro-Americans should be in charge of departments. There were only fourteen black faculty members.

Following student riots late in 1924, and a 1925 strike involving seventy-five percent of the student body, it was announced that McKenzie would resign at the end of the academic year.[80] During the interim, the trustees endeavored to stabilize the institution and to resolve some of the students' concerns. Of particular importance was the board's efforts to hire more black teachers. The sexual and racial composition of the faculty and officers at the end of the 1915–16 academic year[81] is shown in table 1. As at a number of black institutions, white female instructors were in the majority at Fisk and thus were in a better position to serve as role models for the female students. However, at the time, white females were not always the best role models for young black females: many of the whites saw themselves as missionaries and exhibited the negative characteristics associated with that group.

Because many female students felt that black women would best identify with their needs and goals, they continued to petition for the hiring of more black women. The board in principle approved the hiring of a black dean of women, but it was not until 1929 that Juliette Derricotte was employed in that position. On 18 February 1926, the board ended its direct rule over Fisk by announcing the new president, Thomas Elsa Jones, another white man.

Fisk Graduates. Fisk University remained an institution staffed primarily by whites who believed that "the object of education is service" and that the places to serve were Africa and the rural South.[82] Many of Fisk's female graduates accepted the belief of the faculty and administrators and chose positions in which they could fulfill the charge.

Althea Brown Edmiston serves as an excellent example of such a graduate. Edmiston earned her B.A. degree from Fisk in 1901 and in 1903 was sent by the Southern Presbyterian Church as a missionary to the Belgian Congo. In a letter published in the *Fisk University News* in December 1915, Edmiston told of her activities and accomplishments:

> In addition to my helping in the hospital and the school, I have a home of sixty-five new girls. I had to make three dresses each for them, besides other garments and aprons. I had a native man to help me sew and we made up more than four hundred garments. The girls look very well in their new clothes, all in uniform. For Sunday, they have white trimmed in blue; for school, blue trimmed in white.
>
> I also have been typewriting my Bakuba Grammar. I have 275 typewritten pages. I shall start typewriting the Dictionary very soon. The work of the Lord continues to grow. There were 1,020 present at our Sunday school yesterday. I have charge of the women's department; I have them divided into nine classes, with native teachers to help do the teaching. Mr. Edmiston keeps very busy everyday. He has charge of the experimental farm, in addition to his evangelistic work. He is away from home all day, including Sundays at times. Our dear little boy is growing nicely and speaks the native language fluently.[83]

Table 1. Fisk University Faculty and Officers, 1915–1916

	White Male	Afro-American	White Female	Afro-American	Total
Professor	3	3	2	0	8
Assistant Professor	0	1	0	0	1
Instructor	4	3	9	6	22
Music Teacher	0	0	7	0	7
Officer	3	0	7	3	13
Total	10	7	25	9	51

Source: "Fisk University Faculty, 1915–1916," George E. Haynes Papers, 1909–1922, Box 4–Folder 22, Special Collections, Fisk University Library, Nashville, Tennessee

Table 2. Fisk University Alumni, 1875-1923

	Male	Female	Total
Theological	15	1	16
Normal Department	31	387	418
Home Economics Department	0	43	43
Social Science Department	0	7	7
The College	512	303	815
Music Department	11	50	61

Source: Catalog of Fisk University, 1923-1924, pp. 93-95.

She and her family remained in the village until after 1925. As of 1929, she was residing in Selma, Alabama. Edmiston's life was a testimony to the vision and hard work that so many black women of the period considered necessary.

Other female graduates of Fisk University also chose service fields. *Fisk University News* reported in April 1919 that 42 percent of all Fisk's living graduates were teachers. Many of them had remained in the South. A summary of the alumni from 1875 to 1923 (see table 2) reveals the large number of women who had graduated and indicates that the majority of the 42 percent who were teaching in 1919 were women. Because fifty-three students graduated from two departments, the total number of graduates during the period cited was 1,307.[84] These figures do not reflect the 294 females who attended the graduate programs through 1923. It was also true that the majority of students in the Department of Social Science was always composed of women.

Meharry Medical College, Nashville

History. Meharry Medical College began in 1875 as the Medical Department of Central Tennessee College. The other departments of Central Tennessee College later failed, but on 13 October 1915, a new charter was granted to Meharry, making it a separate institution. Beginning in 1899, females were graduated as physicians; most classes, however, had only one to four female graduates. In limited numbers, females were also enrolled in allied health areas such as pharmaceutical studies. The majority of women admitted to Meharry Medical College, however, entered its nursing program at Mercy Hospital.

Dr. Robert Fulton Boyd, the first black physician to earn a living practicing medicine and surgery in Nashville, opened Mercy Hospital on private property. The hospital soon became an adjunct to Meharry Medical College. In an effort to halt the advancement of Afro-Americans in Nashville and to eliminate competition with City Hospital, opponents of Dr. Boyd sought an injunction to close Mercy Hospital soon after its completion. Their grounds were that white workmen from Mercy's construction site had been admitted as patients. The injunction was denied, because white physicians instead of Afro-Americans had attended the workmen. Meharry administrators, faculty, and students supported Dr. Boyd because Meharry students were excluded from internships and observations at City Hospital in Nashville and would have medical privileges only at Mercy.

Nurse Training. After an assessment of need, the first Meharry Nurse Training School was organized at Mercy Hospital about 1900. The two-year course included classroom and clinical experiences. By 1905, the hospital had grown to twenty-three beds and 257 students. The house nursing staff consisted of 6 females under the supervision of Corinne L. Patterson. The nurse training classes were under the direction of Dr. Josie E. Wells, a Meharry graduate. All of the students participated in the weekly clinics held at the college and had an opportunity to observe Dr. Daniel H. Williams of Chicago performing surgery during the week to ten days he spent at the hospital every year.[85]

In time, Meharry personnel began to object to administrative procedures at Mercy, and disputes with Dr. Boyd arose. To prevent division of the black medical professionals in Nashville, Dr. Boyd proposed the organization of a school hospital to be named in honor of George W. Hubbard, the first president of Meharry. J.C. Napier, a local black politician, was named president of the George W. Hubbard Hospital Association; Dr. Wells, secretary; and Dr. Hubbard, treasurer. The wives, daughters, and sisters of the Meharry faculty formed a club to assist in the fundraising campaign. Pledges were secured from private citizens, churches, and benevolent societies.

The north wing of Hubbard Hospital was completed in 1910, at which time the Nurse Training School was transferred there from Mercy Hospital. Charmian C. Hunt, a nursing graduate of the Woman's and Children's Hospital in Boston, became the first superintendent of nurses in the new hospital. The first probation class of twelve females entered the training school and began one of two programs. Those seeking nonprofessional certificates enrolled in a two-year course. Those seeking professional certificates were required to complete three years of training, of nine months each year. The granting of nonprofessional certificates was soon discontinued, so that the faculty could concentrate fully upon preparing those in the three-year course.

The Hubbard Hospital was completed in 1912, at a cost of approximately $43,000; Andrew Carnegie contributed the last $10,000. Dr. Robert Boyd died in 1912 and bequeathed to Meharry $5,000 for the hospital and $2,000 for the school. Private rooms were available for those who could afford to pay, and wards were available for the indigent. The hospital had beds for seventy-five patients and treated nearly all its outpatients free of charge.[86] The hospital soon became known for its service to the community and was praised for the excellence of its medical team.

The Nurse Training Department was carefully monitored to make sure that the best qualified females were admitted and that only those who had mastered all the necessary skills were permitted to graduate. Those seeking admission had to be at least twenty-one years old and must have completed four years of a high school or its equivalent. Maturity, good health, and good moral character were also required for admission. Candidates for admission were placed on a two-month probation and dismissed at the end of that period if their progress was not deemed satisfactory. The rigorous course of study included such subjects as anatomy, physiology, chemistry, theory and practice of nursing, urinalysis, obstetrics, and surgical nursing. The courses were taught by graduate nurses and by the Meharry faculty.

The nursing program graduated its first students from the new facility in 1913. Lula Woolfolk, Hulda Margaret Lyttle, and Rhoda Pugh, a transfer student from Wilson Infirmary, received the professional certificate. It was anticipated that the nurses would take the state examination for full certification, but the secretary of the state board and white nurses objected, and the students were not tested. It was not until 1914 that Pugh and Minnie D. Woodard-Smith, visiting nurses on the staff of the Nashville City Health Department, were permitted to sit for the Tennessee State Board examination. Permission was granted only after the Rock City Academy of Medicine and Surgery and the Nashville Negro Board of Trade intervened and met with the mayor of Nashville and other public officials. The two black nurses were called from work to report for testing at 1:00 p.m. They were examined in ten subjects, and although tested under a great deal of pressure, passed. Their success paved the way for other Afro-American nurses in Nashville.[87]

In order to ensure the success of its graduates, admission, retention, and scholastic requirements were strengthened after 1915. Students were told to bring enough money with them to pay railroad fare home in case they did not pass the probation period. Because married women were not permitted to live in the nurses' home, if a student married during the school term, she was dismissed from the school. After 1922, students had to have completed a four-year course at an accredited high school before applying for admission. Because of the requirements and the limited funds and facilities, admission quotas were kept small. From the time of the establishment of the school until 1934, the number of graduates was fewer than three hundred. Graduates were professionally employed in their field in nearly every state of the Union.

National Association of Colored Graduate Nurses. Founded in 1908, largely through the efforts of Martha Franklin, a graduate of the Women's Hospital in Philadelphia, the National Association of Colored Graduate Nurses (NACGN) attempted to interest black women in nursing as a profession. A separate organization for black nurses was seen as necessary because, even though some black nurses were members of the predominantly white American Nurses Association (ANA), that association never fully embraced its black members. The southern division of the ANA barred black nurses from membership.

Members of the NACGN from various states met annually to present papers and consider issues relevant to their field. The state chapters often sponsored activities to raise money and obtain supplies for black hospitals in their communities, directed relief work during natural disasters in their locales, and provided scholarships for women who wanted to pursue a career in nursing. During World War I, under the leadership of Adah B. Thomas, the NACGN successfully petitioned the U.S. War Department to permit black nurses to serve. NACGN remained an association for black nurses only until its merger with the American Nurses Association in 1951.

Morgan State College, Baltimore

Unlike many other black colleges, during its formative years Morgan State College in Baltimore, Maryland, did not acknowledge a special mission to educate females. Morgan did, however, develop an academic program which stressed excellence, and soon it had a substantial number of female applicants. Known originally as Centenary Biblical Institute, the university was chartered by the State of Maryland in November 1867. Its name was changed in 1890 to honor Dr. Lyttleton Frye Morgan, who had chaired the board of trustees. From 1890 to 1907, the university utilized only one main building and graduated few women.

In 1907, Dr. John Oakley Spencer, fifth president of Morgan, encouraged the Carnegie Foundation to give $50,000 to the institution for a library building and other facilities. Morgan initiated a campaign among Afro-

Americans in the community to raise $25,000 of the $50,000 it needed in order to qualify for the Carnegie Foundation grant. The trustees of Morgan were committed to raising the other $25,000. The Ladies Auxiliary, chaired by Emma E. Truxton, assisted in raising funds, and the Colored YWCA served as the collection unit. By November 1911, a total of $65,000 had been raised by Morgan and its supporters.

With the increase in capital, the college began searching for a site which would accommodate its expansion plans. As of 1912, Morgan was the "only school of advanced degree and degree-conferring powers in the State of Maryland for Colored People."[88] Because of its unique status, many sought admission to the institution. The enrollment in 1912 was three hundred. The curriculum included a college preparatory course, normal course, and collegiate program.

When Morgan decided to move from the city, an injunction was granted to stop the move. A new segregation ordinance was passed and Baltimore County responded by requesting a similiar ordinance. On 23 February 1917, Mayor James H. Preston called a meeting of two hundred persons to discuss the development of a black community with Morgan as the center. The community was to benefit the better educated and more economically secure Afro-Americans. To win support from whites, it was indicated that congestion and unsanitary conditions brought about health problems which affected whites as well. Many Afro-Americans in Baltimore were living under such adverse health conditions. A committee was appointed to study conditions and make recommendations. Dr. Spencer, president of Morgan, served as chair.[89]

The concept of a planned college community was not unique to Morgan. In order to be near their places of employment, to secure better housing, and to live near others who shared similar views and aspirations, many faculty members bought homes in planned and unplanned communities near their campuses or lived in housing provided by the institutions.

In June 1917, a tract of land at Hillen Road and Arlington Avenue in Baltimore was purchased for Morgan. Two years later, in September 1919, the Morton Estate adjacent to the college was purchased. The Citizens Investment Company in 1925 began to implement the recommendations for a planned community. The community was labeled Morgan Park, and by the beginning of the summer, six houses had been erected. Houses situated on 6,300-foot lots required a down payment of $500 in cash and weekly payments of $18. Lots measuring 50 by 125 feet were priced at $1,050 and up.[90] Advertisements in the *Afro-American Ledger* showed sample homes owned by Afro-Americans. Those Afro-Americans who had the financial resources began to purchase the lots, and a new social schism emerged among Afro-Americans in Baltimore.

This schism was also evident in the level of direct interaction Morgan had with the black community. In Hampton and Tuskegee, the colleges served as the centers of the black community, and the towns developed around them. While in Nashville, Haynes aggressively pursued links with the community so that Fisk University's Social Science Department would have a laboratory for the actualization of its social science theories. Even in Atlanta, where there was no dominant affiliation with any one college, women, particularly the members of the Neighborhood Union, did actively involve the cluster of colleges in their program activities. Morgan's physical separation from the majority of the black residents of Baltimore and its efforts to remain financially solvent did not foster the development of extension services. Because of the many active charity organizations and black women's clubs in Baltimore, the need for an educational institution to assume the leading role in coordinating community betterment was not as great as in other areas. Instead, in Baltimore, churches became the key supporters of women's social activism. Union Baptist, Bethel A.M.E., Perkins Square Baptist, and Sharpe Street Methodist were just four of the many churches that assisted the women in identifying community needs, determining plans of action, and raising funds. Often the churches also served as the sites for meetings and program activities.

Conclusion

In the years immediately following the Civil War, institutions of higher learning were established in Hampton, Tuskegee, Atlanta, Nashville, and Baltimore. Each of the insitutions admitted females and designed courses and programs which were deemed suitable for them; national and gender-specific patterns of curriculum offerings, student conduct and dress codes, and graduation requirements were evident. At the same time, because it was believed that educated black women had a special responsibility to assist in the "lifting of the race," courses and programs were developed to enable them to accomplish this task. Emphasis was placed upon household management, community organizing, health care, farming for personal use, and the care and teaching of children.

Career options in domestic science, nursing, and teaching were seen as legitimate, respectable ones for black women. As a result, many black women made great personal sacrifices to attend the institutions or to send their children. Upon graduation, the females returned to their homes or went to new communities with a clear mission. There it was often these graduates who, as social activists, led the effort to structure self-help and social service programs for their fellow Afro-Americans.

CHAPTER 3

Black Women Workers

Black Women in the Labor Force

During the period 1895–1925, most black females were not college or training school graduates. Even though there were successful black female entrepreneurs in all of the regions, the majority of black women in the labor force held menial, unskilled, low-paying jobs deemed suitable for women only. The women's absence from home for long periods while working to earn money for their families often resulted in problems within their households. Inadequate health care, lack of supervised day care for children, poor housing conditions, and inability to engage in personally enriching activities were some of the concerns shared by many working women. Because these problems impacted negatively upon the individual and the race as a whole, women—the educated and the illiterate, the professional and the unskilled—found it in their best interest to work together to resolve the problems.

In 1900, there were 1,316,872 black females in the United States, comprising 11.4 percent of the total female population. Of black women, 34.8 percent were wage earners. Of the wage earners, 76 percent worked in agriculture, primarily domestic agriculture. The next highest percentage of black female workers (66 percent) were laborers who performed unspecified jobs. Of 1,285,031 female servants and waitresses in America in 1900, 345,386 (27 percent) were black; 65 percent of all laundresses were black.[1]

Generally, black women began to work at an earlier age than white women did. While 40 percent of black females over the age of ten were working in 1900, only 16 percent of white females were. Of even greater consequence to homes and families, 26 percent of all married black women worked in 1900, compared to 3 percent of all married white women.[2]

In 1910, 70 percent of the black population lived in rural areas; black rural residents owned 15,702,579 acres of land, valued at one billion dollars.[3] Female workers of the rural South struggled to subsist, at the same time that they were engaged in a "bitter struggle against prejudice and its traditions."[4] Wives of some farmers cultivated the land, while their husbands held other jobs to supplement the meager living they could earn from the farm. Many women still worked long hours in the fields on land owned by someone else; they received inadequate pay which kept them in debt and in poverty. Girls tended to marry young, and the vicious cycle repeated itself.

In both rural and urban South, many black women continued to work as domestic servants, in a system that retained many of the characteristics of slavery. Women were required to spend long hours away from their homes, carrying out physically exhausting duties for which they received little pay. Some experienced sexual harrassment by white males in the homes. And even here, inequities existed: male domestics were paid an average of $15 per month, while women received only $8 a month. If women became cooks, they could earn as much as $12.50 per month. Generally, only men were hired as cooks in public places, where they earned as much as $25 per month.[5] Despite the poor pay, exposure to sexual abuse, and health hazards connected with such work, for southern black women, domestic servitude was often the only available employment. As a result, black women remained the principal domestic servants through 1925. As might be expected, only black women questioned the system in an open forum; they became agitators for domestic service reform. Many southern white women accepted the system as a natural feature of the southern milieu.

Dr. R.E. Jones, founder of the Woman's League and Hospital in Richmond, attempted to help resolve the problems of Richmond's employed females. All workers and clubs were consolidated under the league and met twice a month at the league's hall. Lectures were designed to improve the personal and work habits of the women. A listing of white women who desired domestic assistance was kept at the league; in the private homes of Richmond, 95 percent of the domestic help was black. Even though economic disparities existed between men and women domestic workers, the women who secured jobs through the league were afforded greater protection.

During the period 1895–1925, as the nation industrialized, employment outside the home became a viable option for women. But while more skilled and professional positions became available for women in America at large, all too often black women were not considered likely candidates for the new job openings. However, because the pay was better even for unskilled jobs in the cities, black women increasingly left rural areas for urban ones, North and South. Unfortunately, as we shall see, many of the women were ignorant of urban conditions and fell prey to unscrupulous men and women.

In 1916 and 1917, unprecedented numbers of Afro-Americans migrated to the North, where they anticipated better wages and greater personal freedom. R.R. Moton, at a 1916 conference held by the National League on Urban Conditions Among Negroes, said, "Wherever the Negro is offered larger opportunities, whether in Alabama, in Pennsylvania, or in Africa, there he will go. People regardless of race will always go where they think there are opportunities."[6] Nevertheless, he advised Afro-Americans to remain in the South and retain their property. In spite of the havoc resulting from the boll weevil attack of 1915, many farmers, according to Moton, were recovering because of the practice of rotating their crops and raising their own livestock. In his opinion, the Negro migration was also assisting in the dissolution of absentee landlordism in the South.

In another appeal to Afro-Americans to stay in the South, a former governor of Alabama declared, "The open season for shooting Negroes is over in Alabama. The reaction toward justice and fair play has begun in the South. I have never been more hopeful for the ultimate solution of the race problem. We must, however, be governed and controlled by the idea of service. That man or race who needs me is my neighbor."[7] Such sentiments from southern whites were in vogue because whites would suffer economically if they continued to lose their field hands and laborers to the industrial North.

Many black female migrants sought employment as dressmakers, seamstresses, and launderers in factories and mills, and other types of jobs in tobacco factories and in cotton, silk, and knitting mills. When black females were hired throughout the South to help manufacture cigars, cigarettes, and cheroots, this was seen as progress for the race. Although black women began to secure jobs in industry, they remained underrepresented in skilled positions. In Baltimore, for example, in 1910, out of 5,276 clerical positions, black women held only 58. Although some held responsible positions as teachers (12 percent of black women) or as dressmakers, seamstresses, and milliners (12 percent), 18 percent of employed black women in Baltimore were launderers and servants.[8]

Richmond, Virginia, and Augusta, Georgia, became known as cities where black women could find work. In 1901 in Richmond, women were able to earn as much as three dollars per week in tobacco factories. In Baltimore, the pay scale at a few factories was even higher. One extraordinary company, Wise Brothers, which manufactured shirts and overalls, had a "colored girls' department" in 1900 but discontinued it after the economic panic of 1907. In 1909, the firm resumed hiring black women, and by 1912 employed over 260. These women were paid an average of five dollars per week, while some earned as much as ten dollars per week. Because of its excellent pay and —rare indeed— fringe benefits, Wise was able to retain its workers. The company operated a restaurant so that employees could purchase food for half the cost charged in public eateries. Coffee cost one cent; pie, three cents; soup, three cents; and a plate of food, six cents.[9]

Organizing Black Women Workers

As increased numbers of women flooded the labor market and as the nation moved closer to World War I, more and more women left the rural areas and relocated where jobs were available. Many of the industrial jobs were unskilled ones. Young girls and women were employed in stores, factories, laundries, brickyards, lumberyards, and similar plants. As the number and kinds of jobs increased, it became necessary that black women be trained to operate new equipment. The new industrial opportunities were accompanied by increased responsibilities and job hazards. Black women held jobs that required them to perform such tasks as cleaning engines for railroads, carrying lumber, operating power machines in clothing factories, and operating cleaning machines in steam laundries.

Many disadvantages associated with factory work now became evident. The black women were not always fairly compensated for their new workloads. It became necessary for them to agitate for fair wages, reasonable hours, sanitary working conditions, and the required preliminary training.

Female employees of the Norfolk American Cigar Company's local stemmery, for example, became dissatisfied with the low wages and poor working conditions. The women had been earning seventy cents a day for a ten-hour day and fifty-five-hour work week. The company refused to honor a request for a wage increase to $1.25 for women floor laborers and recognition of a union. The three hundred black female employees who struck shut down the factory and presented the following statement:

> In view of the present living conditions the *Journal and Guide* is of the opinion that there are justice and reason in the demand of the women. We do not believe that under present conditions any adult laborer, man or woman, can subsist upon much less than the factory women are asking. The average woman who works in the factory of the American Cigar Company has to provide every week for house rent, food, fuel, clothing, insurance, church dues, lodge dues and incidentals. The items will run as follows:

House rent..$1.00
Fuel 75
Food...3.00
Clothing...1.00
Insurance...25
Church dues 25
Incidentals...25

At $1.25 a day the women would earn $6.87 a week, as the working time at the factory is 5-1/2 days.

Every item mentioned above is absolutely essential to the existence of a working woman. Insurance, church dues and lodge dues are just as essential as bread and meat. Were it not for these three things every working woman of the tobacco factory element that got sick would most likely die from lack of attention and be buried as a pauper.[10]

Confronted by the alarming employment statistics and harsh economic realities, black women established organizations to present a more unified front in seeking economic redress. Some of the organizations, such as the National Association of Colored Wage Earners, founded in July 1896, are still in existence. Others were organized but disbanded because of ineffective leadership, financial difficulties, or lack of support, or because goals were short-term in nature. Still others, such as the Women's Business League, were reorganized by different leaders during the period. The Women's Business League was reorganized on 22 October 1912, and again during 1923, when two hundred persons joined to promote Afro-American business enterprises.

Appeals were also made to whites for assistance. Leading black women sent a statement to the First International Congress of Working Women, held from 28 October to 5 November 1919: "We, a group of Negro Women, representing those two millions of Negro women wage-earners, respectfully ask for your active cooperation in organizing the Negro women workers of the United States into unions, that they may have a share in bringing about industrial democracy and social order in the world."[11] The appeals were not heeded, and in 1921 some of the same prominent black women met in Washington, D.C., to found what was heralded as "the first labor organization of our women in the world." Organizers were selected to develop a membership of ten thousand which would implement a national program. The objectives of the proposed labor union were:

(1) To develop and encourage efficient workers;
(2) To assist women in finding suitable work;

(3) To elevate the migrant class of workers and incorporate them permanently in service of some kind;

(4) To secure a wage that will enable women to live decently;

(5) To assemble the multitudes of grievances of employers and employees into a set of common demands and strive, mutually, to adjust them;

(6) To enlighten women as to the value of organization;

(7) To make and supply uniforms for working women; and

(8) To influence just legislation affecting women wage earners.[12]

These objectives were not realized, because the labor union never became operative. To fulfill such ambitious objectives would have required a total realignment of class, wealth, and attitudes in America.

The Impact of World War I

As of 1918, one million women were at work in American industries. Compulsory "fight or work" work laws had been enacted in Delaware, Georgia, Kentucky, Louisiana, Maryland, Massachusetts, New Jersey, New York, Rhode Island, South Dakota, and West Virginia. Concerned about the impact of the laws on black women particularly, Walter White, assistant secretary of the National Association for the Advancement of Colored People (NAACP), undertook a survey of enforcement of the compulsory work laws. The resulting "Report of Conditions Found in Investigation of 'Work or Fight' Laws in Southern States" covered Alabama, Florida, Tennessee (Memphis), Mississippi, Georgia, and Louisiana. Although authorities had stated that the national "work or fight" order did not apply to women because of family duties, the NAACP survey of southern states found that the ruling had been applied to black women. The thousands of dollars raised for Liberty Loans, the conscientious efforts to conserve food, the voluntary involvement in war industries, and family obligations were ignored as black women in certain areas were forced to "work or fight." An employment card system was enforced in Memphis and Mississippi. Black women were not permitted to live on allotments from male relatives at war. Memphis went a step further and made it mandatory to report black women who were not working.[13]

With the onset of World War I, black women compaigned actively to prohibit the United States' entry into the war. Moreover, as essential members of the labor force, black women constituted a crucial component in national defense plans. Although they were seen as a vital segment of the "Second Line of Defense," black women were not rewarded justly for their labors; national plans were still conceived in terms of past attitudes and stereotypes. Among the needs were black foremen, more training for workers, and equalization of pay between whites and Afro-Americans. Nevertheless, black women participated in the war effort because many viewed participation as an opportunity to further personal and group goals. For many black Americans, the slogan, "Making the World Safe for Democracy," represented a hope that they too would share in the American dream.

On the federal level, black women became involved in efforts to improve the working conditions of women in industry. The Women in Industry Service (WIS) was the section of the U.S. Department of Labor which after World War I became the Women's Bureau. The section was formed to oversee the role of women in ordnance efforts, but its scope broadened as the war progressed. Helen Irving, a graduate in Home Economics from Howard University, and Elizabeth Ross (Mrs. George Edmund) Haynes were appointed to serve as special aides to Mary Van Kleeck, director of WIS, and to bring a black perspective to the section. Elizabeth Haynes had assisted her husband, the Fisk University Social Science Department head, when he was director of the U.S. Department of Negro Economics in 1918. In fact, Van Kleeck had noted Mrs. Haynes' involvement in the Department of Negro Economics.

On 17–18 February 1919, an informal conference on the problems of Negro labor was held in Washington, D.C. Mary Van Kleeck, director of WIS; Helen B. Irvin, WIS's industrial agent; and Marcy C. Jackson, industrial secretary of the National Board of the Young Women's Christian Association (YWCA), spoke about the special problems of black women in industry. Although the conference issued resolutions, only one addressed the problems of black women.

In 1918, WIS initiated a study of labor conditions for women in America, involving a national investigatory tour between 1 December 1918 and 30 June 1919. Although a segment of the study focused on the black woman, Virginia was the only southern state visited by the service's representatives. Northern cities were examined more closely, because the service wished to analyze the impact of migration upon the labor force. Previous data suggested that many of the black women who had migrated to northern industrial cities had come without skills. It was inevitable that conflicts between labor and management would occur. WIS recommended methods that employers could use to improve working conditions for the women and advised the women that they needed to improve their skills so as to seek better jobs. The study attributed the success of Afro-Americans in the munitions plants partly to management-sponsored training. Elizabeth Haynes and Helen Irving investigated plants in Chicago and confirmed that where training was provided for women who had already attained a basic education, work production and quality increased.

The study's conclusions and recommendations were released to the public by WIS. The article, "Colored Women Represent Their Race in State and Nation," which appeared in the *New York City Tribune* on 23 March 1919, carefully described Irving's and Haynes' skin colors, clothing, and manners. The writer noted approvingly that Irving spoke in a "wholly detached manner. . . . She had the charm of not appearing to possess consciousness of her race. Her talk of Negro working women is as dispassionate as it would be if she were speaking instead of white women." In addition to reflecting white racial attitudes, the article covertly suggested how professional Afro-Americans should respond to crucial issues affecting other black people.

As domestic service secretary of the U.S. Employment Service from 1920 to 1922, and as its examiner in 1922, Elizabeth Haynes candidly elucidated the distinctive problems facing black women in numerous lectures and informal talks. The majority of black female workers were still in domestic and personal service, agriculture, and manufacturing and mechanical industries. In fact, some of the women had been displaced after World War I by returning soldiers and declining labor needs. Companies no longer paid the minimum wage but expanded the duties of workers. Even those who were in private service felt the impact. Domestics who had been paid ten dollars a week found their wages reduced to seven or eight, with the added responsibility of laundry. Even with over two million black women in the labor force, there was still a demand for additional welfare workers, district nurses for rural women, and missionary school teachers.[14]

Mechanisms for augmenting the professional categories of female workers and for ensuring upward job mobility were of prime importance after World War I. Women who were successful as teachers were encouraged to pursue careers as principals. Educators were also requested to consider positions as registrars or deans of women as viable career options. The National Urban League, in an effort to increase the number of social workers, offered fellowships for study at accredited colleges or universities.[15] In 1923 the league indicated that there were 150 black social workers; seventy-five were women employed at forty local organizations.

When black men returned to their homes and communities after World War I, many problems had to be faced. One key concern was how black people could maintain the progress they had made since 1914. Of equal importance were the steps necessary to ensure justice and safety for all black Americans. Racial tensions had not lessened as a result of the Great War.

On 28 May 1918, riots broke out in East St. Louis when whites attempted to prevent the movement of Afro-Americans into the city; rumors that Afro-Americans were killing whites circulated among the residents. It was reported that three thousand persons, including white women, hunted down Afro-Americans, attacking black women and men. As whites feared changes which the end of the war might bring about in the United States, overt actions against Afro-Americans increased. Lynchings and race riots were used by whites to control the black populace.

To retain the social, economic, and political advances and to further the goals of the race, black women again had to assume leadership roles in developing and implementing self-help and social service programs. One immediate goal was to facilitate the readjustment of the returning veteran. New groups developed, but some groups simply shifted focus to accommodate new needs. Generally, black Americans after World War I found it extremely difficult to move the race ahead. Local groups such as the Neighborhood Union and the Colored Empty Stocking and Fresh Air Circle, and national groups such as the National Association of Colored Women reverted to firmly established programs. Calls to national leaders for aid went unheard or unhonored.

By 1920 it was generally accepted that there were significant similarities in the problems of urban and rural black communities. Of Afro-Americans in the United States, 40 percent—four million or more—lived in urban areas. Migration had both advanced the race and increased social welfare problems. Most of the newly arrived migrants had relatives or friends who remained in the rural South. Those kinship and friendship ties entailed interaction. What was needed was greater cooperation and dialogue between urban and rural residents who were qualified and committed to seeking solutions to the social welfare problems. The ultimate goal was stated by Monroe Work, director of research and records at Tuskegee Institute:

> We are at present working largely on the theory that after all it is a good thing for the Negro to get out of the country into the city, out of the south into the north. A broader and perhaps more correct view of the situation is to look at it from the standpoint of endeavoring to secure for the Negro in every part of the nation, north and south, in the city and in the country, the same advantages of education, of health, of sanitation, of protection from mob violence and other wrongs which the Negro in the most favored communities of the nation enjoys.[16]

By 1925, black women in the South, in urban and rural communities, faced more pronounced hardships in spite of the economic advances which had been made during the last thirty years. Of black women who were part of the labor force in 1925, the majority was still in agriculture. There was a decline in the number of women in agriculture between 1910 and 1920 and an increase in women in industry. Certain statistics, however, remained constant. A higher proportion of married black women than of white married women worked, and more black women than white women under sixteen and over sixty-five worked. Marriage appeared not significantly to alter the status of black women. Birth and death rates were influenced by the necessity to work.

CHAPTER 4

Lifting the Race Through Teaching

Overview of Schools for Afro-Americans

By 1895, state educational reports and surveys by private citizens and agencies provided a profile of education for Afro-Americans in the South. Many of the needs and concerns identified were not unique to any one state or school district within a state. Throughout the South, school buildings were generally in poor condition, though kept clean by students and staff, and had extremely poor sanitation facilities. The number of children eligible to attend school was far greater than the number in attendance; even so, there were not enough schools for black children.

The shortage of schools was particularly acute at the high school level. In 1910, of the black high school students, half were in private schools financed primarily by Afro-Americans; only in the border states did a significant number of black high school students attend public schools.[1] Generally, the whites who operated public schools were reluctant to provide education that would raise Afro-Americans above their current living levels. Many more high schools were available for white students than for Afro-Americans. Black citizens were forced to pay school taxes, yet they also had to pay tuition for high school training in private schools. Those public high schools which were available for Afro-Americans generally operated on a five-month term in poorly built and equipped facilities. Many of the teachers were still underqualified.

Depending upon the school district and the school's focus, teachers were responsible for instructing students in a wide range of subjects, including English, German, Latin, history, algebra, chemistry, housekeeping, dressmaking, cooking, biology, and mechanical drawing. By 1915, each school system had fully incorporated some phase of industrial education into the curriculum for black children. In 1917, for example, the State of Maryland

adopted a uniform curriculum for Afro-Americans which included industrial education:[2]

Grades 1–8: Hygiene; Nature Study and Agriculture; Geography; Physical Education; History

Grades 4–5: Afro-American History; Reading; Language and Grammar; Spell-
ing; Arithmetic; (for girls only) Handwork

Grades 5–7: Canning; Cooking; Care of the Home; Music; Drawing; Writing;
Applied Design; (for girls only) Handwork and Sewing

At the high school level, private schools, unlike most of the public ones,
were following the college preparatory or classical course of study. Despite
the fact that most private schools had limited funds, facilities, and equipment, they continued to train most of the Afro-Americans who became
teachers in the public school systems.

Rural schools faced even more adverse conditions than urban ones. Most
were located in isolated settings, had insufficient facilities and equipment,
and received little direct supervision from local or state authorities. Even
so, the rural schools provided the only education available to the vast majority of black students in the South. Because of farming schedules, most
teachers were employed for a few months of the year to teach in ungraded
one-room school buildings. Pupils ranged in age from six to twenty-one
years.

Because of their location, poor facilities, and inability to pay competi-
tive salaries, rural schools often had to hire inexperienced teachers. Both
colleges and school districts encouraged college students who were training
to be teachers to gain experience teaching in rural schools during the summer. Thus the trainees could make money for tuition and related expenses
during their own school terms.

A 1912 appeal for funds from a black female teacher in Lowndes County,
Alabama, suggests the conditions and needs of rural southern schools:

Where I am now working there are 27,000 colored people and about 1,500
whites. In my school district there are nearly 400 children. I carry on this work
eight months in the year and receive for it $290, out of which I pay three teachers
and two extra teachers. The State provides for three months' schooling, but practically I am working without any salary. The only way I can run the school eight
months is to solicit funds from persons interested in the work of Negro education. I have been trying desperately to put up an adequate school building for
the hundreds of children clamoring to get an education. To complete it and furnish it with seats I need about $800.[3]

Even faced with these obstacles, the rural teacher was expected to teach,
organize the community, and establish School Improvement Leagues. The

leagues, composed of parents and friends, had as their primary objectives to improve the quality of life for the community and to enhance the schools. The teacher was also expected to set an example for the students by being neat, prompt, and consistent in her behavior.[4] The tasks were formidable ones, requiring more funds than were allocated by the states and more energy than it seemed humanly possible to expend.

Afro-Americans Organize for Change

Because Afro-Americans saw education as the key to improving conditions for the masses, leaders were concerned with a number of issues directly related to the educational process. One major concern was who would teach. The U.S. Census of 1890 reported over 25,000 black teachers in the United States. The great majority was composed of women; generally, unmarried educated women became teachers. This choice was widely approved, since the women would work with children and not compete for jobs viewed as "man's work." In many southern cities, however, whites staffed most public schools. Black women had to protest in order to receive teaching positions even in schools for black students. When they were able to obtain positions, their instructions were heeded by thousands of youngsters who were enabled to see a possible exit from the socioeconomic and political systems that had bound many of their parents to a life of poverty and unfulfilled hopes.

Rarely were black teachers justly compensated. According to a report from the Board of Education in Atlanta, the highest salary for any teacher in 1894 was $2,000 a year, and the lowest was $350. The average salary for white teachers was $553; for black teachers it was $369. The highest salary for a black female teacher was $1,800.[5] In Hampton, Virginia, in 1912, the forty-nine white teachers were paid a total of $23,343, an average of $476, but the twenty black teachers were paid only a total of $4,041, or an average of $202.[6] Inequities in salary, regardless of training and experience, led some teachers to resign. Teachers in rural districts were paid still lower salaries than those in urban areas.

By 1919, the South, like the nation as a whole, was becoming increasingly urban. Some 2,300,000 Afro-Americans, a fourth of the total black population in America, resided in the South's urban centers. Of that total, 770,000 were children, only 500,000 of whom were in school.[7] Urban educational institutions still had great need of financial assistance. Nor did conditions improve significantly by 1925. In that year, the elementary schools for Afro-Americans in the South were far below the standards of other schools in the United States. And Afro-Americans were still carrying the burden of providing their own secondary education.

By 1925 it was clear that whites in the South were not going to assume their public responsibility to provide equal educational opportunities for Afro-Americans. Throughout the South, Afro-Americans used petitions to draw attention to educational problems. Petitions requested new or improved educational facilities, or funds to maintain existing structures. Two representative petitions circulated in Atlanta, Georgia. Personnel, students, and friends of Atlanta University, Clark University, Morehouse College, Morris Brown College, and Spelman College were able jointly to bring about changes in the city's educational structure.

In 1919, there were 400,000 black schoolchildren in Georgia. Property owned by the county school boards was valued at $445,885. Of that amount, $69,240 (15 percent) was in black schools. There were 824 schoolhouses for whites and only 143 for Afro-Americans. Since 1890, the U.S. government had contributed $400,000 for agricultural education in Georgia, but only $100,000 had gone to Afro-Americans.[9] In 1919, a petition was sent to the Georgia legislature, requesting fairer distribution of funds for schools. The key proposal was, "The money provided for the support of such schools shall be divided between the white and colored races in proportion to the amount of taxes paid by each race."[8] The memorial received limited positive response from the state.

On 2 July 1919, the Georgia Association for the Advancement of Education Among Negroes sent another petition to Gov. Hugh M. Dorsey. It requested seven fundamental changes in the educational system: increased salaries for teachers, longer school terms, better school facilities, establishment of a normal school and district agricultural schools, increased state financial support, more equitable distribution of federal funds, and the creation of an office of assistant state supervisor of Negro schools, to be headed by an Afro-American.

Government officials began to grant some of the requests. In Atlanta, on 1 January 1920, the board of education voted to convert the white Ashby Street School, located in a predominantly black neighborhood, into a junior high school for Afro-Americans. The city's leading white ministers had supported the appeal to the board. An eighth grade was added, making the school the first high school for Afro-Americans in Atlanta. A new black high school, encompassing grades seven to ten, opened in 1924. The school had 1,700 students and 42 teachers. It was expected that the school would add eleventh and twelfth grades by 1926.[10]

Many of the requests made in 1919 would not soon be met. Georgia still had 261,115 black illiterates in 1925. From 1919 to 1925, the State Illiteracy Commission supervised services for only 35,000 black illiterates. Faced with the appalling statistics, the governor appointed a committee to survey the state's educational needs. The committee felt that one million dollars was needed to update the system. They recommended that $122,500 of that amount be appropriated to schools for Afro-Americans.

Other recommendations from the committee clearly demonstrated the lack of concern for and commitment to education for Afro-Americans. Sumter County had 4,948 illiterates out of a total of 5,138 black residents. Yet the Sumter County school district was cited as needing to economize because it had only 6,583 children of public school age; 4,961 of them were Afro-Americans. Other suggestions included cutting the salaries of black teachers who earned over $25 a month (the highest salary was $47 a month); shortening the school term for Afro-Americans from eight to six months; abolishing four schools, even though they were crowded; and releasing three special teachers. The recommendations were grossly unjust because, out of $22,027 allocated to Sumter County, the state treasury provided only $4.44 per black child, a total of $6,400.[11]

Training to Improve Teachers' Skills

By 1910, schools for Afro-Americans in Hampton, Tuskegee, Nashville, Atlanta, and Baltimore were staffed primarily by black teachers. However, in the effort to meet the demand for black teachers for black children, whites did not always enforce the educational requirements for teachers. For example, in spite of the fact that many black teachers in Nashville had graduated with normal degrees, 50 percent of such teachers in 1909 were Fisk graduates who had not received normal training. Graduates of academic courses, preparatory courses, or grammar schools were regularly hired as teachers throughout the South.[12] The State of Virginia even attempted to lower the passing grade required for Afro-Americans on the state teachers' examination. Convinced that quality was more important than quantity, educated Afro-Americans opposed the plan.

To increase the competence of teachers, Hampton Institute, Tuskegee Institute, and local school districts began to offer normal training in the summers. Expenses for some of the teachers were paid by county superintendents or the General Education Board, a philanthropic organization.

The number of applicants to the summer normal school always exceeded the number of places available.

Hampton Summer Institute. Three hundred teachers and principals attended the July 1899 Hampton Institute. In conjunction with the institute, Hampton also offered a vocational trade school featuring classes in whittling and sewing for children. Because of the popularity of Hampton's curriculum, the Peabody Fund and the State of Virginia, through the advocacy of Superintendent of Public Instruction, J.W. Southall, bore half the expenses of the institute in 1901. In 1903, the summer institute was lengthened to six weeks and stressed courses of particular value to rural teachers. All of the teachers were required to take courses in agriculture or nature study, but other course selections were elective. To supplement what the teachers learned at the institute and to serve as reference material for all teachers, Hampton published free leaflets for teachers and superintendents. The leaflets contained suggestions for classroom activities, instruction methods, and facts relating to several disciplines. If bulk quantities were desired, they could be purchased for fifty cents a dozen.[13]

Hampton discontinued the summer institutes for several years after 1905 but offered them again beginning on 15 June 1909. Because the administrators of the institute wanted to expose the teachers to as much instruction as possible, the program was varied but highly structured. In 1912 the school day began at 8 a.m. with devotional exercises and continued with six class periods of fifty minutes each. Sample course titles were: "Home Life in the Country," "Care of House," "Condition of Rural Schools," "Problem of Dressing Appropriately." [14]

Students came from throughout the United States to attend the summer institute. In 1912 Virginia had the largest number of enrollees, 187; North Carolina had the second largest, 64. The ages of students and their educational training and teaching experience varied greatly, as table 3 shows. A total of 125 students had previously attended one or more of Hampton's summer institutes.[15]

By summer 1917 the classes had become more specialized to meet the needs of specific personnel in education. From the nine states where there was a state supervisor of Negro schools, a total of fifteen leading teachers were selected for special classes. Classes in institutional management were developed for four matrons from prominent boarding schools; eleven school principals and industrial teachers together had another specially designed program. All the courses were intensive and were scheduled for four days

Table 3. Hampton Summer Institute, 1912

Numbers of Students	Years of Experience
11	None
20	3–6 months
92	1–2 years
90	3–5 years
75	6–10 years
24	11–15 years
10	16–21 years
13	22–30 years
7	30–40 years
342 Total	

Source: "Summer School," September 1912, Extension File, Archival and Museum Collection, Hampton University, Hampton, Virginia.

a week. For Virginia enrollees who were seeking certification for promotion to a higher professional classification, the requirement to obtain credit was a minimum of twenty lessons in each course.[16] Based on the positive response to the classes for principals and the apparent need for high school teachers, Hampton incorporated aspects of the summer institute in a four-year course to training high school teachers and principals in its regular program. The course was offered for the first time in 1920; the first class graduated in 1924.

The decision to offer courses not included in the summer programs of other institutions greatly increased the number of Hampton's applicants in 1920. Of 540 persons who enrolled, only 98 were men. To provide dormitory space, the Stone Building was converted into a women's dormitory for the session. Even so, lack of dormitory space necessitated rejection of 100 to 200 applicants. The new courses included (1) a two-summer course for teachers of physical education and community recreation workers; (2) a two- to three-summer course for primary school teachers and one for grammar school teachers, to enable teachers to receive the Virginia Elementary Professional Certificate; (3) high school courses for teachers seeking special certificates in history, English, mathematics, and science; and (4) a special course for North Carolina teachers of vocational agriculture, requested by North Carolina educational authorities.[17] The summer institutes proved invaluable in strengthening the skills of black teachers throughout the South.

Normal Training in Baltimore. A different type of training for black women teachers originated in Baltimore. As early as 1869, the Baltimore Normal School for the Education of Colored Teachers had been founded in the city; however, the school later relocated outside the city limits and became known as Bowie State College. In December 1900, the Baltimore City School Board authorized the formation of a training class for black teachers at the Colored High and Grammar School. This was to become the one teacher training institution that remained in the city of Baltimore.

In 1900 the board specified that the training class for black teachers could use two rooms in the school building and assigned Elizabeth Smith, the second assistant in the white Teachers Training School, as the instructor. When classes began on 4 January 1901, the course was limited to one year. In 1902 the class, still sharing space with the Colored High School, was named the Normal Department of the Colored High and Training School and offered a two-year program. It was not until 1909 that the training department became a separate unit, with its own principal and a new location. From the inception of the class, the majority of the students were female. Descriptions of policies and procedures in the early years used "she" when referring to students. In 1910 the faculty consisted of the principal, three assistants, a supervisor of practice teaching, and instructors of music, drawing, manual training, physical training, and sewing.

Applicants for admission to the school had to pass an entrance examination on the following subjects: English, including grammar, composition and literature; history and civics; arithmetic; plane geometry; physics; botany or zoology; geography; physiology; and hygiene. Graduates of colleges approved by the superintendent were eligible to enter the second year of the program without taking the entrance examination. Graduates of the Colored High School could also be admitted without taking the examination if faculty members provided recommendations which attested to the graduate's ability to work with young children. Preference was given to those Colored High School students who had earned the highest averages,[18] but nonresident students were also accepted. In all cases, the admission requirements were designed to identify the most dedicated and promising students.

The first term of ten weeks included "General Methods and Principles of Teaching," with a review of basic skills, introduction to selected methods courses, and supervised practice teaching. Students attended classes for twenty weeks during the second year, when instruction concentrated on method courses in reading, geography, language and grammar, nature study, history, literature, and arithmetic. Practice teaching in the city's elementary public schools for Afro-Americans was also mandatory. Because of the significance accorded the practicum experiences, the supervisor of practice carefully graded students according to "skills in teaching, class management and helpful cooperation with associates in the details of school routine."[19] The grade earned was important because it, along with the first-year course grade, was used to determine who was eligible to serve as a substitute teacher in the public schools. Eligible seniors were paid $1.50 for each day of service as a substitute teacher.

The practice teaching grade was also highly significant after graduation. To quality as teachers in the elementary schools, those completing the training school course had to pass a professional exam. Only those with an average of 75 percent and no grade lower than 50 percent could sit for the exam. The exam, which covered course material from the entire program, was given twice a year in February and June. A passing professional exam grade was weighted equally with the practice teaching grade, and the total score determined whether one would be placed on the "preliminary list" of teachers. If the probationary teachers did not execute their duties in a satisfactory manner after placement on the list, they could be required to complete the second year of courses again.

Through 1925, the training school maintained its quarters in six classrooms of the senior high school building. The school was renamed the Fanny Jackson Coppin Normal School in 1926 but did not move to its present location at 2500 W. North Avenue until 1 July 1952.

Education Activism in Baltimore

The concern for training of black teachers in Baltimore both reflected and encouraged keen concern for education on the part of black citizens in the community there. Active efforts had long been made in Baltimore to improve various aspects of education for black children.

As early as 1895, there were twenty-one schools for Afro-Americans in Baltimore. One was a manual training school staffed by 6 male teachers, and the other schools, including one high school, had a total of 167 female teachers and 21 male teachers. In 1895, for these twenty-one schools, the school board allocated $141,776 for current expenses; all white schools together received $1,007,797. That year the board also requested funds from the City Council to build a new elementary school building, since the black school in question had 800 pupils but only 20 teachers; the board recognized that the children were "performing their school work under many disadvantages."[20] Funds were also requested to build a "colored" grammar school in West Baltimore.

In 1885, the Colored High School, with a principal and several assistants, had become a separate unit within the High and Grammar School on Holliday Street, where the Peale Museum now stands. In 1897, a separate bulding was erected for the advanced students, but in 1901 the school was relocated at Pennsylvania Avenue and Dolphin Street.

In 1895 a Baltimore newspaper, the *Afro-American Ledger*, initiated an editorial campaign calling for the hiring of black teachers. It was perfectly satisfactory to have black teachers and separate schools, the paper argued, but if whites taught Afro-Americans, then white children should have some black teachers. In time the editorials took a stronger position, urging Afro-Americans to vote for the mayoral candidate who would no longer permit white teachers in black schools. In April 1896, the City Council agreed gradually to eliminate white teachers from black schools. Only black graduates of Maryland schools were to be certified as eligible teachers.[21]

The first Baltimore public school staffed by black teachers opened in March 1896, with George W. Biddle as principal and Louisa Smith as his assistant. By 1902, half of the schools for black children had black teachers; by 1904, three-fourths; and by 1907, all of them. In 1910, the school board appointed three black administrative supervisors to oversee the affairs of the completely segregated system.

As late as 1920, there were only 27 public schools for Afro-Americans, compared to 128 for whites. Frederick Douglass High School and Booker T. Washington Junior High School provided the only training beyond the elementary level; black women made up the majority of teachers.

Afro-Americans in Baltimore were acutely aware of the poor public schools for their children. In 1898, Baltimore's black teachers organized mothers' meetings which were held monthly at a primary school for girls. Topics of interest to the mothers were discussed and homemaking techniques presented. The objectives were both to assist the women in becoming better mothers, and to build a support unit for the public schools. The mothers sponsored fundraising activities for the schools and, when necessary, protested for improved educational facilities and curricula.

The Alumni Association of the Colored High School in 1902 had begun to raise funds for a school library. Other groups and individuals financially supported the efforts of teachers to provide meaningful instruction. Of equal concern were school facilities. During spring 1912, Laura J. Wheatley investigated the sanitary conditions in and around the school at Druid Hill

Avenue and Moore Street. She found a high rate of tuberculosis in the area and numerous problems in the school, including insufficient fire exits. Appalled, Wheatley called the black women of Baltimore to mount a unified protest.

As a result, the Civic Aid Association was formed, with Wheatley as president. The group visited the school board to acquaint its members with the conditions of the schools. Wheatley cited as one example of the inequity in the school system the fact that while $1,500,000 in loans for school buildings had been secured recently, no funds were being spent on schools for Afro-Americans. The Civic Aid Association solicited the support of the city's African Methodist Episcopal ministers. As a result of the agitation, Mayor Preston visited a number of schools in October 1912. In early November, a school board committee appeared before the city's Board of Estimates to request funds for a new Colored High School.[22]

The Colored Citizens' Equitable Improvement Association of East Baltimore joined in encouraging the mayor to approve the request for a new school building. The joint group effort proved successful, as Paul Lawrence Dunbar School (later to be a senior high school in East Baltimore), with twenty-four classrooms, teachers' rooms, manual training and cooking rooms, and an assembly hall, opened in September 1916. No longer did students from the eastern section have to travel across the city to pursue studies beyond the elementary level.[23]

A movement began in 1917 to equalize the salaries of black teachers, in order to stabilize the teaching staffs. In 1918, Maryland state law fixed the minimum salary of black teachers classified at the third grade at $30 a month; whites were to receive a minimum of $400 a year. The second-grade certificate carried a minimum of $35 a month for Afro-Americans and $450 a year for whites. The first-grade certificate qualified a white for at least $500 a year but a black for only $480 a year. In 1920 the state legislature voted a minimum salary for black teachers of $65 a month.[24] In 1924 a Defense League was founded to push for the equalization of salaries for teachers of Baltimore's Douglass High School. Mass meetings were held, with little effect.

That same year, however, the City of Baltimore passed a law prohibiting discrimination in the pay of teachers on account of their sex. In 1925 the city attempted to raise the salaries of white but not black female teachers. In an effort to combat the proposed city action, a power struggle ensued between two black groups. Laura J. Wheatley, now president of the Baltimore Federation of Colored Parent-Teacher Clubs, called a mass meeting in early May 1925 at Bethel A.M.E. Church. The federation, with ten thousand members, had branches at twenty-seven schools. Three topics were on the agenda for the meeting: (1) efforts to merge Morgan State College and the Teacher Training School; (2) promotion of the supervisor of colored schools to a superintendency; and (3) equalization of teachers' salaries. On 23 May 1925, Wheatley met with the Board of School Commissioners at a special meeting to discuss the topics raised at the mass meeting. A delegation from the Defense League also came but was told to leave because the meeting was not open. When the president of the board announced that proceedings would not begin if all remained, Wheatley stated that her delegation would leave so that the Defense League could present its concerns. However, the league's representatives left and protested outside the building.[25]

The actions of the Afro-Americans at the meeting unfortunately showed the inability of some local groups to develop cooperative strategies before presenting concerns to people who were generally unsympathetic. The Defense League, after filing a petition in the Superior Court of Maryland, gained a temporary injunction that stopped payment of $50,000 to the white female teachers. Judge Robert F. Stanton of the circuit court previously had ordered the city to distribute the funds to the white teachers but indicated that if the Afro-Americans won their suit, the city would have to provide funds for equalization.[26]

The Jeanes Fund

Because not all rural areas had energetic, well-trained, self-sacrificing teachers, other mechanisms had to be devised to provide quality education for rural children. Anna T. Jeanes, a white woman, made it possible for rural schools to develop and for the teachers in the areas to receive additional training. In 1905, she gave $200,000 to the General Education Board, to be spent under the direction of Booker T. Washington of Tuskegee and Dr. Hollis Frissell of Hampton. Impressed by the programs of Hampton and Tuskegee, Jeanes later gave $10,000 each to Washington and Frissell to pay the salaries of teachers in extension work and to help build rural schoolhouses. In 1907, before her death, she gave $1,000,000 more to create the Fund for Rudimentary Schools for Southern Negroes, to be directed by Washington and Frissell. The fund's purpose was "assisting and maintaining, in the Southern United States, community, country, and rural schools for the great class of Negroes to whom the small rural and community schools are alone available." To prolong their life, the funds were invested in various states.[27]

Virginia E. Randolph, who served as the first Jeanes teacher, was largely responsible for designing the Jeanes program's format. A black teacher at a rural school in Henrico County, Virginia, Randolph (1876–1958) was born of slave parents in Virginia and attended Bacon School and the Normal Department of Armstrong High School in Richmond, Virginia. At the age of sixteen, she began teaching in Goochland County, Virginia, then moved to the schoolhouse in Henrico County at nineteen. She became supervisor of the Jeanes Fund in 1908, at age thirty-two.

To prevent tension in her local community, Randolph was responsible to the local superintendent and school board rather than to the Jeanes Fund; the county supervisor provided Randolph's salary. Randolph's tasks included introducing industrial studies into the twenty-two rural schools in Henrico County and supervising the work of these schools' teachers. During the eight-month 1908–1909 school term, Randolph made 190 visits to the twenty-two schools and began the formation of school and home improvement organizations. Each scholar (pupil) was required to give five cents a month toward fundraising activities, generally some form of entertainment. From the outset, pupils, teachers, and the community actively participated in the program.

Randolph believed that the responsibilities of a teacher began in the primary grades and continued throughout the pupil's education. The teacher was, in fact, a model. She had to be concerned with cleanliness and health and maintain a neat and attractive schoolroom. The standards Randolph imposed were those she herself had adopted when she began her teaching career.[28]

Combining academic and industrial work, Randolph instructed her teachers to increase manual training from three to six hours a week. The schools furnished foodstuffs, prepared them, and sold them in the community; the proceeds went into a treasury. Of the $331.49 collected or earned, $108.81 was spent, and the remainder was reserved for stoves and cooking utensils for the next school term. These commercial activities helped teachers and students develop a sound business sense.

The female teaching staff in Henrico County accomplished much, as excerpts from their reports show:[29]

> Fenced in the yard, granolithic walk, set out hedges, trees, and rosebushes, white washed the trees and fence, taught sewing, needlework, carpentry, and shuck mats. Amount collected during the term, $50.05, Expended, $10.95. Balance in treasury for next term to fix up kitchen, $39.10.

> White washed trees, taught domestic science, sewing and carpentry, kept the yard in good condition. Amount collected, $23.00, Expended $12.63. Balance in treasury, $10.37.

Planted trees, flowers and hedge, taught sewing and paper cuttings. Amount collected, $10.00, Expended, $4.00. Balance in treasury, $6.00.

Taught sewing and paper cutting, could do no improvements on yard because property did not belong to the county. Amount collected, $5.00, Expended, $2.00. Balance in treasury, $3.00.

Set out hedge, built a large pavilion, white washed the trees, planted flowers, taught domestic science, sewing, fancy work, laundry work, paper cutting, mats, and carpentry. Much interest is being manifested in the school garden. Amount collected, $25.00, Expended, $10.00. Balance in treasury, $15.00.

Enclosed the school with hedges, set out trees and flowers, taught sewing, making mats, and carpentry. Much interest is being manifested in the school garden. Amount collected, $22.23, Expended, $6.63. Balance in treasury, $15.60.

Local citizens cooperated in the teachers' efforts:

The Chairman of Varina Board, Mr. S.C. Freeman, knowing how hard the teacher and patrons were working to build up their school, sent a good many workman that he employed at Curls Neck Farm, to the school and fenced in the yard, put up the belfry and bell, graveled the walk, built a porch, made benches and set out hedges; free of charge. He also assisted many of the other schools whenever called upon. Taught sewing and needlework. Amount collected, $5.30, Expended, $1.50. Balance in treasury, $3.80.[30]

After the first year, James H. Dillard, president and general agent of the fund, proposed that a modified form of the Henrico County Plan be implemented in other states. As of 5 June 1909, with all that had been done, the fund had expended only $14,011 for teachers' salaries; $1,965 for buildings and equipment; and $470 for the extension of the school term. By 1913 there were 120 Jeanes teachers in 120 counties in eleven southern states from Maryland to Texas. The teachers were trained in some phase of industrial work, domestic or vocational. They visited the county schools, taught lessons, planned programs with the regular teachers, and organized parents' clubs and community groups. The extension and supervising teachers submitted monthly reports of their activities. Soon applications from many states were requesting money to hire personnel to implement the objectives of the Henrico County Plan.[31] Local black newspapers also praised the efforts. Table 4 indicates the expansion of the Jeanes program by 1921.[32]

In time other philanthropies — the Phelps-Stokes Fund, the Peabody Fund, the Southern Education Board, and the General Education Board — helped to pay the salaries and expenses of the Jeanes teachers. White rural agents were assigned to work in Alabama, Arkansas, Georgia, Kentucky, North and South Carolina, Texas, and Virginia.

Table 4. Operations of the Jeanes Fund, January 1921

State	Counties	Supervising Teachers	Schools Visited	Pupils in Schools Visited	Salary Paid through Jeanes Fund	Salary Paid from Public Funds
Alabama	26	27*	378	33,906	$ 1,217.80	$ 991.83
Delaware	3	3	40	1,914	150.00	110.00
Florida	3	3	31	3,930	125.00	65.00
Georgia	27	28*	415	26,043	1,077.75	712.25
Kentucky	19	15*	117	5,753	620.00	944.50
Louisiana	16	17*	173	16,963	700.00	660.00
Mississippi	26	27*	378	33,906	1,217.80	991.83
North Carolina	43	44*	605	57,969	1,476.33	2,780.17
Oklahoma	1	1	9	400	62.50	62.50
South Carolina	24	24	440	45,945	1,230.00	840.00
Tennessee	22	21	195	19,214	620.00	1,196.50
Texas	15	15	115	7,745	821.45	451.05
Virginia	43	47*	643	45,593	1,343.72	2,405.28
Totals	265	268	3,568	306,211	$10,231.05	$12,613.58

*Including state supervising teacher

Source: "Supervising Teachers," James C. Napier Papers, Box 2, Special Collections, Fisk University Library, Nashville, Tennessee.

The path was not always smooth for the Jeanes teachers. Black parents wanted their children to have the educational training which would allow them to become something other than farmers and unskilled laborers dependent upon southern whites. They objected to the curriculum, which they saw as designed to meet not the needs and goals of Afro-Americans but those of whites. The Jeanes teachers had to win the support of parents, principals, and local teachers, however, since implementation of the new teaching methods required greater community involvement in the educational programs.

Once the Jeanes teachers overcame the initial objections of local residents, their efforts were generally successful. Through the extension of activities beyond the schools, the communities became involved and thus grew more concerned about the welfare of the schools. The changes in the curriculum not only provided solutions to common problems of rural people, but also helped the children see the relationship between what they learned in school and their daily lives.

Extension Activities

The work of the Jeanes teachers formed part of a broader movement being implemented by many institutions and school systems throughout the South, but particularly in regions near colleges like those we have discussed. When industrial education was officially declared part of the curriculum for Afro-American students in Fulton County, Georgia, for example, the teachers there voluntarily extended their duties to include greater community involvement. Cooking, housekeeping, sewing, handicrafts, manual training, gardening, and canning were all subjects which lent themselves to community activism. Clubs were organized for children and parents, especially mothers. Black people in Fulton County raised over $1,000 for improvement of the schools.

In 1913, Camilla Weems was hired by Spelman Institute to teach industrial work in the Fulton County schools. Her work was concentrated in the schools just outside the city limits of Atlanta. Weems first met with all of the county teachers and residents of the black communities. She noted that only a few of the Afro-Americans in the area were farmers; most worked in factories or held public jobs. Some of the residents were truck gardeners who supplied Atlanta markets with fresh vegetables, poultry, and dairy products, but few of the residents had personal gardens at home. Therefore she took gardens as her first project. When the schools opened in September 1913, school gardens were begun with the cooperation of the teachers. In spite of the lack of tools and funds, six gardens were soon planted on land near the schools.

Success with the school gardens led to the planting of home gardens. Weems, the teachers, and the recently formed Mothers' Clubs worked with the families to show them how not only to sell the products but also to save some for personal consumption. Girls in eleven of the school communities were organized into canning clubs. The Board of Education was so pleased with the progress of the clubs that in 1915 it offered a prize for the most canned items.

The county, which became fully involved in the efforts initiated by Spelman and Weems, made it mandatory for every child to learn the rudiments of sewing, handicrafts, basketry, mat making, and chair caning. For all of the activities, the children used readily available natural materials. Seven of the fifteen schools supervised by Weems installed cooking stoves. The children raised money for three, and the Mothers' Clubs raised money for the other four. Food was contributed by the families, and cooking lessons were given in kitchens built by the students. The boys made furniture for the kitchens; girls made tablecloths, towels, and curtains; and mothers donated most of the utensils. Where kitchens were not available in the schools, mothers opened their homes for lessons. Manual training lessons enabled the boys to build furniture for the schools and generally to improve the facilities. Home Makers' Clubs for children reinforced the skills which were taught and demonstrated the need to attain specific skills.

Mothers' Clubs, organized in ten school, extended their activities during the school vacation months. Some activities raised money to establish playgrounds and acquire materials for sewing. Club meetings included literary programs and discussions of economic matters, school work, handicrafts, and ways to improve the home. The constitution developed for the Mothers' Clubs stated as their objectives "the betterment of home life, the training of children, and the improvement of the community in every way possible."[33] The teachers assisted in implementing the objectives, even after 1925.

The concept of Mothers' Clubs and Home Makers' Clubs as extensions of public education was viable in the cities as well. In Baltimore during summer 1918, 1,333 girls, 1,064 mothers, and 675 boys enrolled in 228 clubs. The teachers and supervisors visited 1,392 homes, offering canning demonstrations in many. In Alabama, the Home Makers' Clubs were aided by the General Education Board and state authorities. During 1920, 15,000 women and girls enrolled in the Alabama clubs. As a direct result of the Clubs' formation, local black citizens in the state contributed $43,000 for school improvements and activities.

Private Schools

As we have seen, public school systems in the South often did not provide the educational opportunities needed by certain groups of black students. In such cases, individuals, groups, and religious organizations sometimes took it upon themselves to develop private institutions to meet special needs. Some of these were in rural areas; others provided schooling for the handicapped.

Mt. Meigs, Alabama. Georgia Washington, former slave and an 1892 graduate of Hampton Institute, in 1893 founded a private school for black children, the People's Village School, in Mt. Meigs Village, Montgomery County, Alabama. The community was fifteen miles from the city of Montgomery and twenty-eight miles from Tuskegee. In a cabin rented for two dollars a month, Washington began her school with four small boys as pupils. As the school's name suggests, it became a community project. By 1900, residents had been responsible for building on the school grounds a church and a three-story building which accommodated three hundred people. In 1900, a twenty-four-acre school farm was acquired. The land company which had enticed residents to the community disbanded in 1902, dividing the remaining acreage among the residents. To ensure greater economic security for the community, seventy-five men organized a work team in 1903 to build a communal cotton gin.[34]

By 1910, fifty families owned at least a home site, totaling three thousand acres of land. "Buy land" became the motto of the community. When the school began, only two families owned homes. Through Washington's encouragement and under a plan developed by the Mt. Meigs Negro Farmers' Union, members of the union paid a monthly fee which was to be used to purchase a plantation. Once acquired, the plantation was divided into lots and sold to individual families.[35] The school and the programs it sponsored became the nucleus of the community.

Both school and community flourished. By the 1905–1906 school year, the largely female staff was instructing students in seven grades. The curriculum was designed to build upon skills the students learned as they advanced from grade to grade. For example, students in Grade One were taught gardening skills, which were complemented in Grade Two with nature study. The curriculum also offered special industrial emphases for girls and boys. By the time the students reached the seventh grade, they were required to apply their skills in carefully supervised educational experiences. A cause-and-effect approach to history avoided memorization.[36] In the teaching of geography, pupils were introduced to familiar geographical concepts and

14

Fig. 14. The People's Village School opened in 1893 at Mt. Meigs Village, Montgomery County, Alabama. Georgia Washington (*foreground*) was the founder and principal. *Courtesy of Hampton University Archives.*

Fig. 15. Georgia Washington (*left front*) encouraged graduates of Hampton Institute to fulfill their responsibility to the race by teaching at the People's Village School, Mt. Meigs. *Courtesy of Hampton University Archives.*

15

regions and then made aware of other nations and areas of the world. The geography curriculum included the West Indies but did not list Africa as a continent to be examined.

The school's academic progress was not always matched by financial stability. In a 1906 letter to Dr. Frissell at Hampton, Washington wrote that she had no funds to pay the teachers and that one teacher was threatening to sue her. Her letter sought advice as to the best way to handle the situation.[37] Enough funds were raised to pay the salaries that year, but the situation recurred. In 1908 the staff included six female teachers and one male teacher, who were responsible for eighty male students and ninety-five female students between the ages of twelve and twenty-one.[38]

As of 1910, there were 800 black boys and girls of school age in Mt. Meigs Village and only 36 white children. That year the state paid a total of $675 for the education of all the white children but only $750 for the education of the 800 black children. Of the 800 children, 208 attended Mt. Meigs. The 123 families of the children paid $836 in tuition, $86 more than the state allocation. In that same year, the boys twelve and fourteen years of age raised one bale of cotton on one acre. After paying farming expenses, their profit was used to pay for clothes, tuition, and books. Through various personal enterprises, half of the children raised the money they needed for educational expenses.[39]

During the last term of the 1914–15 school year, the teachers again went unpaid. Washington, in her twenty-second annual report, called that year the "hardest period of all the twenty-two years that I have spent at Mount Meigs. The teachers had to go without their salaries for as long as two and three months. This was very embarrassing to me. Nevertheless, the teachers were extremely kind and patient."[40] Apparently, the teachers were as dedicated as Washington; in spite of the late payments, they remained and worked to further the growth of the school.

The hard work and personal sacrifices produced excellent results. By 1923, the school had expanded greatly. Additions to the physical plant — two teachers' cottages, a two-story building for the children who boarded, a five-room cottage for teaching domestic science to the girls, and a one-room cottage for teaching carpentry to the boys — resulted in increased enrollment and an expanded curriculum. The school term of nine months was divided into seven winter months and two summer months. The 184 students were divided into nine grades, six on the elementary level and three on the junior high level.[41]

After completing the ninth grade, the best students were encouraged to further their education. Of 5,000 students taught at the school, 125 completed the elementary course of study; of 90 graduates who attended other institutions, 32 became principals or teachers, 2 became physicians, and 3 worked in extension services. After thirty-two years of the school's existence, community changes were evident, too: "Better homes, better farms, better roads, and in many respects better people." Yet work still needed to be done, and the founder and teachers had no doubt as to who would be instrumental in completing that work: "The girls are the real homemakers and need special training of all kinds in order to change present conditions."[42]

As Washington's letter to Dr. Frissell and other alumni correspondence make clear, many graduates maintained contact with their former schools. The expertise and guidance of faculty and administrators were considered invaluable as alumni engaged in their professional careers. The institutions, too, welcomed and encouraged these ongoing contacts, which informed the institutions of the accomplishments of their graduates and allowed them to cite these accomplishments as proof that they were fulfilling their missions. The success stories also were used to convince philanthropists to contribute money to the educational institutions. More often than not, the worth of the institutions was measured by the calibre and professional activities of their graduates. Georgia Washington clearly understood that Hampton had a vested interest in her school and would assist in whatever way possible to guarantee the school's survival. However, because many of the black higher educational institutions were also struggling to survive financially, assistance was not usually in the form of money.

Also in Mt. Meigs was Mt. Meigs Institute, founded in 1889 by Cornelia Bowen, a graduate of Tuskegee Institute's first class. Begun with equipment given by Tuskegee, the institute was created to provide students a common school education including religious and industrial training. Seven teachers instructed 289 pupils; specialized subjects were taught to boys and girls. Bowen established farmers' conferences and mothers' meetings which were said to have reached two thousand people. Study leaves from the institute permitted her to further her education in New York and at Queen Margaret College in Glasgow, Scotland. She remained principal until 1922. In 1924, the State of Alabama assumed control of the school, renaming it Montgomery County Training School.[43]

Calhoun School. Another rural area in Alabama which prospered as the result of a land company was Calhoun, Alabama. Booker T. Washington selected the site where he saw Afro-Americans living in conditions under which they could not advance economically or educationally. In January 1892, he was partly responsible for securing incorporation for a school to service the community. Charlotte R. Thorn and Mabel W. Dillingham, both white, were cofounders of the school; both had been employed at Hampton. They hired two Hampton graduates, one of whom was Georgia Washington, to teach students ranging in age from six to twenty-eight. When the school opened, approximately two-thirds of the students could neither read nor write.

Because it was believed that community cohesiveness and economic stability would enable educational advancement to occur at a faster rate, residents of the area were encouraged to purchase land and build homes. However, since many of the residents did not have the resources to purchase land from the whites who owned it, cooperative land buying seemed the best solution to the problem. John W. Lemon, 1890 Hampton graduate and farmer-manager for the Calhoun School, developed a plan for buying the land and began to interest residents in the idea. The Calhoun Land Company was formed, and a 120-acre lot was purchased for $800 and divided among four families. By 1904, the land company owned plantations encompassing nearly 4,000 acres of land. That land was divided among eighty-eight families who paid a total of $27,400.[44]

Most residents of the community farmed, and when they began to realize profits from their farming, they were able to give financial assistance to the school. By 1908 the school employed twenty-five teachers to instruct 257 students. Rev. Pitt Dillingham assumed management of the school after his sister's death, but he resigned in June 1909. Thorn became principal of the school in 1910. As a community school, Calhoun offered classes from kindergarten to ninth grade and also included a night school program.[45]

The mechanisms of cooperative land-buying and the community school were used in other rural areas where education was seen as a means of addressing the needs of the "whole person." Not all areas were as successful as Calhoun, but where the experiment was tried, a greater sense of community did develop; more important, the residents were able to imagine and initiate an alternative to the conditions under which they lived.

Education of Handicapped Black Children

Offering special instruction, the Maryland School for the Colored Blind and Deaf was established in Baltimore in 1872. The state maintained the facility and provided free tuition and board for the students. The school closed for a time but reopened in September 1895.

In Nashville, because there was no state facility for the blind and deaf, one black woman began an effort to aid blind children. Susan M. Harris, of Fisk's Class of 1875 and one of the first three graduates of its Normal Department, assumed personal responsibility for and instruction of two blind children until a home could be located for them. In 1881, because of her success in working with the two youngsters, four others were brought. The state purchased a home, and Harris became principal of the Colored Department School for the Blind. She eventually trained others to work with the students. Harris personally canvassed communities to locate youngsters who needed educational training. Through her efforts, hundreds of blind students were enrolled in the school.[46]

Associations of Afro-American Teachers

Regardless of how the schools were formed, the populations they served, or the states where they were located, many experienced difficulties because they were educating Afro-Americans. As a result, in each state at the turn of the century, black teachers in the public and private sectors began to establish associations to publicize their concerns, to push for educational changes, and to persuade governmental authorities to respond to the educational needs of black children. In some cases, organizations merged in order better to address issues: in Virginia, for example, the Negro School Improvement League merged with the State Teachers' Association. Educational associations in various states sponsored similar programs and actively monitored the educational process on behalf of black children. More often than not, women were in the forefront of such organizations.

In time, the state associations combined to form a national organization. Because Afro-American educational issues required and deserved special attention, a call was issued in 1904 for all black teachers from the kindergarten level to college to meet and organize. The meeting was held in Nashville in August 1904. At the first meeting of the National Association of Teachers in Colored Schools (NATCS), twenty states were represented. The meetings rotated among different southern cities and sometimes were held in conjunction with other black educational organizations. NATCS published a monthly magazine, *The Colored Teacher*, to keep its members abreast of current trends in the field, innovative educational programs, and professional opportunities.

At the 1915 annual meeting in Cincinnati, Ohio, NATCS examined public and private schools. Those who presented papers and gave keynote addresses pointed to the unnecessary duplication of private and public schools,

Fig. 16. In August 1907, many noted educators, including (*left to right*) John Hope, Lugenia Hope, Margaret Murray Washington (*fourth*), and Mary McLeod Bethune (*fifth*), attended the National Association of Teachers in Colored Schools convention at Hampton Institute. *Courtesy of Atlanta University Center Woodruff Library.*

the need for better secondary schools and colleges in the largely unsupervised private sector, and the need for social service programs to involve students more directly in their communities.[47]

Only sixteen states were represented at the fourteenth annual NATCS session in New Orleans in 1917. Resolutions adopted at that meeting called for "direct representation of Negro patrons on all school boards; education of the Negro broadly as a citizen and not simply as a Negro; an impartial distribution of all Federal funds; a more equitable proportionment of all public school funds; and the placing of greater emphasis on education that makes for citizenship and the political rehabilitation of the race."[48] The resolutions echoed the concerns and petitions of black teachers in many local communities. By the end of the meeting it was obvious that the association was becoming a national lobby for broader educational issues.

At the 1923 meeting, J.A. Gregg, president of Wilberforce University, proposed that an accredited representative of NATCS be sent to the National Education Association, a predominantly white group. N.E.A. could serve as another forum and as a possible ally for the black educators as they sought to influence legislation and behavior. The NATCS incorporated under the laws of Washington, D.C., and established headquarters there. The staff consisted of a paid secretary and a board of five trustees. The association's purpose was "to assist in raising the standards and promoting the interests of the teaching profession and in advancing the career of education."[49] Through 1925, NATCS continued its efforts to influence educational policies affecting Afro-Americans and to improve the quality of education for all Afro-Americans.

Conclusion

Although black educators, parents, and community members agitated for change in the educational systems, they often met with overt opposition and obstinate blocks to progress. Even so, since education was seen as a major route to racial betterment, the black teachers, principally female, labored long hours to create educational programs within the schools and as extensions of the schools. They would not permit difficult working conditions or lack of adequate equipment to eliminate advancement and innovation. Although the focus during this period stressed women and their role in nurturing children, men were not entirely excluded. While it would have been easier for the women to see only the obstacles to quality education, they chose instead to concentrate on such positive factors as community involvement, community betterment, and enriching the lives of thousands of black children.

CHAPTER 5

Social Service Programs in Virginia: Focus on Hampton

Institutions of higher education such as those we have examined saw themselves as centers creating resources to transform the lives of the broad masses of oppressed Afro-Americans. Graduates, imbued with the Christian missionary spirit, the sense of having been given special gifts that carried with them special responsibilities, and an understanding of the common interests that bound all Afro-Americans together, set out to serve those less fortunate than they. Keenly aware of their small numbers, educated women, whether they became teachers or not, identified needs in their communities and strove to involve as many women as possible in the work of racial betterment.

Since the educational institutions we have looked at — Hampton Institute, Tuskegee Institute, the cluster of colleges at Atlanta, Fisk and Meharry in Nashville, Morgan State College in Baltimore — became centers of intellectual ferment for capable Afro-Americans, they also were especially effective cores of regional community work. In examining in more detail the work of women in the five communities around these colleges, we will also observe the development of human communication networks and programs of action that crucially influenced the lives of Afro-Americans genrally during the twentieth century. The social service efforts of black women in these five regions were designed to promote the development of both the individuals themselves and others to whom they felt linked by a vast heritage and a common present. The inescapable fact of racial discrimination by whites bound black women of many classes together in a common effort. Although urban and rural women's concerns differed in many ways, they shared a central preoccupation with education, health care, child care, family life, and housing. Using educational institutions and churches as bases of operation, the women brought together the three institutions which were the mainstays of black life in the United States — home, church, and school.

Let us begin by examining the social service efforts of women in Virginia, where Hampton's early influence was felt most immediately.

By the turn of the century, a small black middle class had become established in the town of Hampton, near the campus of the institute. "It is a rule established by their own custom and seldom broken, that no Hampton man shall marry until he owns a house and lot,"[1] observed a contemporary. To facilitate compliance with this unwritten rule, graduates of Hampton Institute founded the People's Building and Loan Association in Hampton, Virginia. Incorporated on 4 March 1889, the association had 636 stock holders by 1904. This venture provided homes for well-educated, affluent black citizens. Through association loans, 350 black familes had acquired homes in or near Hampton by 1904, and by 1915, 500 families had new homes. As early as 1899, an economic profile of Hampton's black population revealed five ministers, three lawyers, two justices of the peace, four notary publics, two doctors, one undertaker, and two contractors.[2] A number of the black businesses were located on the main street of the city. The black businesses and middle-class black citizens were called upon to give financial support to regional social service activities.

The Locust Street Settlement

Not all black females initially were willing workers in the struggle to improve conditions in the South. Janie Porter Barrett was cited in 1909 by Hampton Institute's Extension Work Committee as a "real power among the colored women of the country." Yet she was able to recall that during her years at Hampton, "I did not love my race! I didn't want the responsibility of it. I wanted fun and pretty things. At the Institute [Hampton], we were always hearing about our duty to our race, and I got so tired of that! Why, on Sundays I used to wake up and say to myself, 'Today I don't have to do a single thing for my race.'"[3]

Barrett had been raised in a house with whites because her mother was the nurse to the white children. The aristocratic southern setting and the white playmates were only a temporary part of Janie's world. When the inevitable question of social equality arose and when Barrett reached an age at which it was considered proper for her to leave, she was enrolled at Hampton Institute.[4] At Hampton she became more race-conscious and aware of the difficulties confronting all Afro-Americans. Hampton's curriculum and its involvement in the community had a great influence upon Barrett's attitudes toward her responsibilities as an educated woman. Although reluc-

17

18

Fig. 17. Janie Porter Barrett founded the Locust Street Settlement, which became known as "The Palace of Delight." In 1911, at a tea given in her honor by Jane Addams of Chicago, Barrett told of her community activities. *Courtesy of Hampton University Archives.*

Fig. 18. Janie Porter Barrett worked directly with girls' clubs until becoming superintendent of the Industrial Home School. Note Barrett's home (*left*) next to the settlement house. *Courtesy of Hampton University Archives.*

19

20

Fig. 19. Amelia Perry Pride (*second row, ninth from the left*), of the Hampton Institute class of 1879, taught public school in Lynchburg, Virginia for thirty-one years, retiring only to care for an ill son. These children were members of her last class. *Courtesy of Hampton University Archives.*

Fig. 20. In addition to teaching duties, family responsibilities, and civic commitments, Amelia Perry Pride, seated, established the Dorchester Home for destitute senior citizens in Lynchburg, Virginia. *Courtesy of Hampton University Archives.*

tant at first, she initiated social service programs for the young girls of Hampton. What began as a sewing class for a few girls in Barrett's home on Tuesday afternoons expanded into a club. The club sponsored classes every afternoon and evening for eight months of the year.

The club included persons of all ages and had as its objective "improving the homes and the moral and social life of that community." Boys, girls, and mothers, "classified according to age and need," were instructed in handicrafts, sewing, athletics, and quilt making. Other activities included discussions on homemaking, cooking classes for girls who were interested in or were working in domestic service, and a night school to prepare those who desired to further their education at Hampton.[5] Response to the club was overwhelming, and soon it became necessary to acquire larger quarters. In 1902 a committee of teachers and others pledged to pay the rent and fuel bills if a building could be located.

A house was duly purchased, and the Locust Street Social Settlement became the community center. During winter 1903, a kindergarten was added, and new classes were formed. Graduates of Hampton Institute and area women formed an auxiliary group which met on Sundays at churches to plan ways to raise funds and generally to support the settlement.

Special attention was given to developmental programs for women and girls. The women's club, known as the Homemakers' Club, had several departments which dealt with aspects of home improvement: child welfare, two divisions; cooking; industries; quilting; gardening; and poultry raising. The child welfare and quilting departments attempted to bridge age gaps to solve problems for the most vulnerable persons of the race, the young and old. In the first division of child welfare, talks were given on the care of infants and youngsters under six. The second division concentrated on children over six. A playground was established on the grounds of the settlement house to complete the program for children. Mothers of all ages, without their children, were treated to a day of relaxation and reflection through outings on Chesapeake Bay. Members of the girls' and women's clubs provided the food for the outing. During summer 1915, 2,200 mothers benefitted from the excursions.[6] Through the quilting department, senior citizens were given an opportunity for social interaction and for earning money. Grandmothers and older women made quilts to sell at a small cost to families. Some of the quilts were given to the Old Folks Home in Hampton for the "infirm colored women of good character" who resided there.[7]

In 1902, the auxiliary committee requested that Hampton Institute's Extension Work Committee supervise the Locust Street Settlement's activities. By 1909, the Settlement House was sponsoring five girls' and women's clubs which met every week and one which met once a month. Four clubs for boys were directed by senior students from Hampton Institute. Barrett also had begun to sponsor three annual events — Baby Day, Easter Field Day and Egg Hunt, and a Flower Show. Although each activity was designed for a particular age group, all of the events were made possible by community co-operation and participation.

Dorchester Home

During the late 1890s, Amelia Perry Pride, of Hampton Institute's Class of 1876, found herself appalled by the deplorable conditions in which elderly black women who did not have family to care for them were forced to live. Born during the era of slavery, many of the women had spent their early years in bondage. Thus Pride requested the aid of the more affluent black women in Lynchburg, Virginia, to establish an old folks' home. In winter 1896, Pride was able to elicit the support of approximately one hundred women. Dividing themselves into committees, the women provided fuel, food, clothing, and rent. Finally, through funds given by northerners, a building was purchased to house destitute black women until their deaths. As a consequence, residents of the Dorchester Home were no longer dependent upon their ability to scour for food and shelter. Since the first contribution came from residents of Dorchester, Massachusetts, the home was named after that city.[8]

Given the fact that Pride led the effort to establish the home while serving as a fulltime elementary school teacher, church worker, counselor to neighbors, and homemaker, her contribution is even more noteworthy. In 1904, after all but one of the elderly women had died, the home was sold and the proceeds from the sale used at the Theresa Pierce Industrial School, headed by Pride. The administration of a new home passed to William J. Calloway, who donated the property but utilized furniture from the old home.

In many instances, once black women responded to a specific community need and successfully implemented a program, a city or state government or other individuals later assumed control. As long as the original need was still met, the takeovers usually were not opposed; the skills and efforts of the women were simply directed towards another cause. As Pride stated in 1912, "My hands are full. All sorts of things I have to do."[9] Barrett's and Pride's involvement with the elderly is especially to be commended since Hampton Institute urged primary concern for those who were or would be fully productive members of the society.

Hampton Institute's Extension Activities

Hampton Institute and its extension programs, of course, worked closely with others in the community to promote social service activities by women in Hampton and the surrounding communities. Hampton's teachers and staff members both initiated activities involving community women and supported projects that originated in the community. The extension services included (1) community organizing, (2) publishing "how-to" guides in leaflet form, (3) educational exhibits at local and state fairs, (4) extension schools, (5) furnishing purebred livestock to local farmers, (6) employing the black farm demonstration agent in Elizabeth City County, (7) funding special supervising teachers, (8) traveling libraries, (9) a motion picture loan service, (10) publishing *Negro Progress Record*, the newsletter of the Negro Organization Society of Virginia, (11) support services for small public and private schools, and (12) a job placement bureau. Even though Hampton Institute's extension programs were principally staffed and funded by the institute with help from the Jeanes Fund, they could not have been successful without strong links to stable, capable, and influential community members.

One example of the close ties among Hampton Institute, extension services, and the black community was the Southern Industrial Classes. To assist black women in becoming effective homemakers and wage earners, these classes, employing seven paid black teachers or other workers and using volunteers as well, were organized independently in Norfolk, Virginia, on 20 April 1896. Sarah Evelyn Breed from New York was the superintendent, and Ellen Taylor, a Hampton graduate, was her assistant. A house was rented for sewing and cooking classes, but rooms in the public schools were used after school hours for the other classes.

Beginning in January 1900, as an extension service of Hampton Institute, industrial classes were established in the schools in Newport News, Virginia. Financed by Mrs. Collis P. Huntington of New York, the work was identical in aim and audience to the Southern Industrial Classes in Norfolk, except that the Hampton extension offered a sloyd class featuring elementary manual training with carpentry tools. Breed also served as superintendent for the Hampton classes. The two units remained distinct, but Hampton graduates and teachers worked with both. In 1902, the Southern Industrial Classes for Norfolk and vicinity enrolled 1,976; the Huntington Classes for Newport News and vicinity enrolled 807.[10]

To improve the organization of Hampton's neighborhood and missionary work, in 1908–1909 the area surrounding the school was divided into districts, and an Extension Work Committee was formed to oversee all activities. Each district was assigned a representative from Hampton: Little England, Marie Ulsamer; Lee's Corner, Ida A. Tourtellot; Bates District, Henrietta L. Graves; Hampton, the committee that supported Barrett's programs; and Phoebus, the Whittier Training School officers. In addition to the district work, women supervised three night schools, cabin work, jail work, poor house activities, the Pine Grove Homestead, song services, two Sunday schools, and the Locust Street Settlement.[11]

Hampton considered its night schools in Hampton, Phoebus, and Little England its most effective extension activity. Through the Locust Street Settlement night school, organized by Barrett in 1906, one student was attending Hampton Institute and two others were preparing to enroll. Between thirty and forty boys and young men in the Hampton District Night School were taught elementary subjects by five senoir male students from the institute. Plans for the school included expansion of the curriculum so that industrial classes could be offered to young men and women.

The district representatives became much involved in their respective communities, starting the night school in Little England and assisting extremely needy persons. Moreover, the "district visitors" forged strong links between Hampton and the communities, by keeping administrators fully aware of — and teachers and students active participants in — community activities. When Hampton Institute's women considered developing a campus club, the women's organizations of the communities indicated where their expertise and talents could be shared.

In addition to involvement with organized women's groups, the extension services developed activities for the youth of the neighborhoods. To this end, song services were held in Hampton, Buck Roe, and Phoebus, although Phoebus was the only area which had regular services. On Sunday afternoons at the Phoebus Baptist Church, the institute's Ethel Cooledge supplied the music which attracted youngsters from the community. Once a captive audience existed, one or two five-minute talks were presented on subjects such as health, temperance, education, cleanliness, proper amusements, and true religion. Plans for the 1909–1910 school year included a talk to stimulate interest in home gardens and musical performances by the residents.[12]

Home gardens, because of their potential for improving the health of the people, were planned as a major activity not only for Phoebus but also for Hampton. Care was taken to select six or more families, living reasonably far apart, to initiate the experiment: "These families are to be of the ordinary types rather than of our graduates, who are somewhat separated in location and in social standing from the masses."[13] Agricultural faculty and their students were to supply direction as well as seeds and fences when necessary. Barrett's flower show and gardens were recognized as proof that the institute's plans could succeed. The institute also encouraged raising vegetables and chickens as a supplement to the gardens.

Not all of the activities conducted in the communities were seen as positive ones. The administrators of Hampton Institute's extension services believed that even though the cabin work — self-help and social service programs for those living in one-room dwellings — appeared to have been fairly well initiated, "thus far undue importance has been given to the care of the old folks in the cabins and in the poor house and the prisoners in jail. We have been trying for several years to show that while the care of the unfortunates and of the abnormal is good missionary work, it is not the best. The most difficult and the most profitable neighborhood work is that for the normal, the boy, the girl, and the vigorous adult who needs direction in work and in play."[14]

A charity fund, contributed to by people at the institute, was kept in the school treasury and dispensed upon orders of the Neighborhood Committee. Limited funds, however, were expended by the institute for cabin work; dinners and gifts of fuel, costing a total of forty-eight dollars, were given during the 1909 Christmas season. Additional two to six dollars a month for fuel, and two to four dollars a month for groceries were allotted to some during the school term. Only one person received a weekly Sunday basket of food items, given personally by a staff member.

At times community residents did not fully appreciate the institute's intentions or its projects. Too much supervision of the Buck Roe Sunday School, for example, caused residents to criticize and withdraw. After the split, it was recognized that encouragement was a far better approach with some neighborhoods than near-dictatorial supervision.

Hampton Negro Conferences

Beginning in 1897, annual conferences brought together Hampton graduates and others to consider the plight of Afro-Americans as a race and to suggest ways to further their collective goals. Sessions at the Hampton Negro Conferences emphasized the needs of Afro-Americans who were or would be viable members of the labor force. At the first conference in July 1897, Fanny Jackson Coppin, principal of the Institute for Colored Youth in Philadelphia, was influential in forging the direction that industrial education and the conferences should take in regards to women: "One way to establish better relations with the white people will be to give them better cooks, better laundresses, better chambermaids, better housekeepers."[15] In agreement, some Afro-Americans asserted that an educational focus other than trades would cause Afro-Americans to lose respect for public officials, labor, and the home. This reasoning, which reflected the sentiments of advocates of industrial and manual training as well as of whites who feared intellectual Afro-Americans, maintained the industrial institutes and would have relegated too many Afro-Americans to positions of eternal servitude.

Proceedings of the third and other Hampton Conferences show the wide range of concerns voiced by women who had already become known among Afro-Americans as vocal, industrious, and innovative educators and social service workers. Women met in some separate sessions to discuss issues related to their roles as mothers, wives, and homemakers — for example, the proper dress for mothers, care of children, home ventilation, and preparation of foods. The men might have cooperated sooner if some of the discussions had been held in joint sessions. The invisible wall assumed to exist between men's and women's duties kept the two groups from working together on causes of direct importance to both.

Because black women held most of the teaching positions below the college level, at the Hampton Conferences, they also discussed problems confronting them as educators. At the 1899 conference, women presented papers which reflected their educational concerns but also questioned the roles and responsibilities of the educated woman; two papers were titled "The Burden of the Educated Negro Woman" and "The Educational Side of Sewing." Most of the discussion topics centered on industrial education, but some were designed to supplement the formal training of educated black women.[16] During the general sessions, the women were made aware of issues affecting the entire race.

Clubs for neighborhood girls and the dangers encountered by southern girls who migrated to the North were discussed at the first conference in 1897. Resolutions adopted at the 1899 conference greatly influenced the development of social service programs for women and strengthened those already in existence. It was recommended that social improvement societies be formed for girls, to give them a sense of the dignity and purity of womanhood and a knowledge of domestic industries; and for boys, "to inculcate [within the boy] respect for womanhood."[17] Barrett's work and that of the Coppin League of Chesapeake City, Maryland, were cited as examples of successful club work.

In 1902, under the general conference division of Domestic Economy,

Chairperson Rosa Bowser introduced the topic of domestic science. Following a pattern developed at the first conference, delegates at the 1903 conference presented papers dealing with the question raised in 1902. It was noted that opportunities abounded for black women in domestic service and that the compensation for those services was higher than ever.[18] One of the highlights of the 1906 conference was a roundtable discussion led by Janie Porter Barrett, entitled "How Can the Women Help?" The question was not fully answered, because the three hundred delegates were still searching for direction, but as the women continued to work and strategize, they did present some answers at future meetings. Each conference produced resolutions relating to education, religion, morals, sanitation, economic conditions, charities, corrections, land, and civic relations. The women's opinions were incorporated into the decisions and recommendations reached by the general assembly.

Virginia State Federation of Colored Women's Clubs

At the 1907 Hampton Negro Conference, the Virginia State Federation of Colored Women's Clubs was formed, with Janie Porter Barrett as president. Hampton Institute supplied stationery and other forms of support for the new organization. During the federation's 1909 meeting, the delegates were impressed by the accomplishments of the clubs organized by graduates of Hampton. Hampton's Extension Work Committee believed that Barrett's presidency and the organizing efforts for the federation by Laura D. Titus, worker with the Cumberland Street School (the only school for Afro-Americans in Norfolk), gave Hampton a chance to influence the leading black women of the state to change "their club work from the impractical efforts now attempted by so many women's organizations the country over to the practical work" represented by Hampton graduates.[19]

The activities of Hampton's Extension Work Committee were designed to centralize programs and projects in Hampton and surrounding towns. The Virginia Federation of Colored Women's Clubs also viewed itself as a centralizing body. Addie W. Hunton of New York, a delegate to the 1907 Hampton Conference, had prompted Laura D. Titus, later state organizer for the federation, to assemble the conference women for an initial meeting. In accord with the rules of the National Association of Colored women (NACW), ten clubs had to join the proposed federation before it could be recognized as a state federation and a member of the NACW. By November 1907, twenty-five clubs representing the southeastern part of the state met for one day at the Methodist Church in Hampton, Virginia. A number of clubs that had been functioning before the inception of the NACW now saw the possibility of expanding and enriching their programs. At the close of the one-day meeting, the federation decided to undertake one special project through a committee headed by Mrs. I.C. Norcum of Portsmouth, Virginia. The state project, an industrial home for wayward girls, would operate on a different level and with a different focus than the community work. The recommendation was unanimously accepted by the federation, and the first task was to raise funds.[20]

The idea for a home for wayward girls was not a new one. At the Woman's Conference during the 1899 Hampton Conference, Rosa Bowser had reported on the Negro Reformatory in Virginia. Of 1,259 black inmates, 66 were female. Bowser believed that a reformatory for women should be erected in order to "reclaim or save the youth of the race." She suggested that 1,382 acres of land available in Hanover County, with existing buildings and equipment, would serve as an excellent site. Nor, she felt, was this a task for whites to do: "It is for us to take the burden upon our shoulders and push the good work forward."[21]

Instead of a reformatory for women, the site in Hanover became the Virginia Manual Labor School of the Negro Reformatory Association of Virginia. John H. Smyth, former U.S. minister to Liberia, and Rev. J. Wesley Johnson went before the Prison Association for the State of Virginia in February 1897. They were able to secure incorporation in June 1897. The board of trustees had only black members, but the advisory board had white men, including H.B. Frissell, the principal of Hampton Institute. Smyth was empowered to purchase the site for the reformatory for $11,000.[22]

Smyth was given possession of the property in January 1899 and the first five inmates arrived in September 1899. The state legislature appropriated funds to maintain the property and erect additional buildings. The staff consisted of seventeen helpers; among them were four women, one a Hampton graduate. When Smyth died on September 5, 1908, the board of trustees permitted his sister-in-law, Elizabeth G. Shippin, a trained nurse who had served as matron and managed the reformatory during Smyth's illness, to continue as head. In spite of the establishment of the new reformatory, however, black women still believed that Virginia needed a home for delinquent black girls.

Some 1,200 women, representing forty-seven clubs, attended the federation's second annual meeting in Richmond in June 1909. There the federation reaffirmed its goal of establishing a home for "wayward colored girls." At the 1910 meeting in Norfolk, each club pledged ten dollars for the support of the home; the funds were collected at the June 1911 meeting in Roanoke. By June 1911, six hundred dollars had been raised for the home, and land was made available by local businessmen. The fact that the national meeting of the NACW was held at Hampton Institute in July 1911 provided additional impetus for the project; it had been difficult for many to travel to meetings in the North, but more women from the region were able to attend the national meeting at Hampton.[23]

On 19 January 1915, the Industrial Home School for Delinquent Colored Girls opened at Peake in Hanover County, Virginia, with two girls in residence. The site and three buildings had been purchased by the federation for $5,200 in 1914. A matron and farmer were employed by November 1915; the number of girls was then fifteen. The federation appealed to the state legislature and the community for $2,000 for a new building. The Virginia General Assembly appropriated $3,000 for 1915 and $3,000 for 1916.[24]

When Janie Porter Barrett was appointed superintendent of the institution in early 1916, it was estimated that five hundred black females were incarcerated in the state of Virginia. Only more money and expanded facilities would enable the institution to reach many of the five hundred before they became confirmed criminals. Constant appeals to the state for funds brought appropriations of $10,000 for 1917 and $20,000 for 1918. Because the legislature could and would provide additional funds and support, in 1919 the federation transferred the property to the state, and the school was renamed the Virginia Industrial School for Colored Girls. Barrett remained superintendent, but a governing board of trustees, with Mrs. Henry Lane Schnelz of Hampton as president, was appointed. Cottages and two new buildings were added to the facility, but livestock and farm implements were still needed.[25] Until after 1925, the school continued as the only institution of its kind for black females in Virginia.

Even though the federation chose to concentrate on projects on the state level, its very existence motivated women to continue the community work they had begun on the local level. For example, in 1907 the Portsmouth branch of the federation, led by Cornelia E. Reid, organized the Girls' Happy Workers' Club. Members of the club were involved in reading, domestic science, and art courses; the girls were also required to participate in some systematic charity drive. Assisting Mothers' Clubs, physicians, and ministers in what was termed a "war on tuberculosis," the girls provided food and plants to local tubercular patients.

The Portsmouth branch was also very concerned about the educational progress of local students who enrolled at Hampton Institute. After a survey of students revealed that when they entered Hampton or other institutions of higher learning, they fell behind at least one year because of their lack of preparation, the women raised money to teach manual classes and provided space for the classes. They structured the curriculum to ensure that literary subjects were taught along with the manual subjects. Largely through the initiative of the women, manual training was incorporated into the Portsmouth school system in 1910, and the school board elected to pay the expenses of the industrial school developed by the women. The program gained statewide recognition.

Because it was impossible for all interested parties to visit sites where successful activities were being carried on, the federation published guides for community improvement, homemaking, and club organizing. Several of the guides were printed in the *Hampton Leaflets* series. One leaflet, "Community Clubs for Women and Girls," written by Janie Barrett, Caroline D. Pratt, and Ida A. Tourtellot, embodied suggestions and principles adopted by state workers in the federal extension program described below. Acording to the leaflet's authors, women's clubs should aim "to make the individual, the home, and the community more useful in every way."[26] The women of a community should be brought together on one issue, and the club should broaden as the women's interests did. Suggested foci for organizing clubs were church or missionary work, old folks' homes, jails, schools, the poor, the sick, orphans, community improvement, welfare of children, and self-improvement. Domestic concerns such as sewing, cooking, gardening, poultry raising, house cleaning, and savings were considered part of self-improvement. Each step in the formation of a club, directions for electing officers, and the duties of officers and committees were clearly outlined.

For the formation of girls' clubs, "to make better women for the future from the girls of the present," it was recommended that some phase of "uplift," such as handicrafts, outdoor activities, housekeeping, or patriotic concerns, serve as the core. The authors stressed that for the girls' club movement to be successful, the organizers had to involve girls of the same age group, plan variety as a key element, and avoid the aura of church or school.[27] The leaflet was reissued in 1914, then revised and reissued again in 1916.

Federal Extension Programs

The Smith-Lever Agricultural Extension Act of 1914 provided for a national system of county agents who assisted farmers directly on their farms. Utilizing research data from the U.S. Department of Agriculture, county agricultural and home economic agents sponsored educational activities designed to further the agricultural interests of the nation. The extension services were conducted through the Department of Agriculture but were funded jointly by the states and the federal government. In the southern states, the agricultural colleges established by the Morrill Act of 1862, separate ones for black and white students, supervised the work of the agents.

Virginia was included in the extension programs of the federal government, which sponsored the development of clubs for girls and women. Lizzie A. Jenkins, a Hampton graduate who in 1915 was assistant district agent, was responsible for supervising the industrial teachers in thirty-six counties as they planned activities, gave sewing lessons and canning demonstrations, organized new clubs, raised funds, and set up exhibits which featured projects from the clubs and demonstrations. Jenkins' annual report for 1915 cited 2,155 actively enrolled club girls, and harmonious cooperation among superintendents, teachers, leagues, and clubs. The woman's club movement proved as successful as the club movement for girls. To be sure, some females hesitated to join the club movement until it was made clear that it was a free experience which would confer many benefits, but lessons in breadmaking, gardening, soap making, canning sausage, housecleaning, table setting, and care of small children and the sick produced visible results. In 1915, there were 955 active workers.[28]

In an account of her year's activities, Jenkins wrote, "During this year I have travelled 12,259 miles by rail, 1,200 miles by team [horsedrawn carriages], visited 200 homes, 50 clubs, talked with 1,000 club members, 20 superintendents, visited 145 schools, spoken at 50 other meetings with an estimated attendance of 15,339, wrote 814 letters, sent 159 circular letters and assisted with 23 county exhibits, as well as assisting with the exhibits at the Farmer's Conference." In spite of her impressive performance, she remained fully aware of the magnitude of the problems to be confronted and added, "It is true that I have not been able to do all I wanted done, but I feel that the outlook is promising."[29]

Individual whites, Hampton Institute, and the faculties of Virginia Normal and Industrial School, St. Paul School, Christiansburg Industrial School, Thyne Institute, Mannassas Industrial School, and Tidewater Institute all rallied behind Jenkins and the extension agents. In some cases, club activities also promoted interracial cooperation. Afro-Americans who were involved in the programs were generally viewed as productive, community-oriented citizens, and whites tended to support their projects financially.

In 1916, Jenkins became district black home demonstration agent in Virginia. This assignment was a dual appointment by the extension department of Virginia Polytechnic Institution at Blacksburg, Virginia, and the States Relations Service of the U.S. Department of Agriculture. Her performance remained impressive, as she supervised 336 clubs for 2,400 girls. During 1916, through her work and that of the local agents, 730 girls were able to earn money from their sponsored activities to help meet their school expenses, and 981 earned money for home expenses.[30]

In 1925, faced with increased responsibilities, Jenkins requested that a trained woman be hired to assist agents in the field. The director of home demonstration agents replied that the limited income of the program and other considerations made her request unrealistic. Unfortunately, as often happened, those who, because of their actual experiences, were best able to see the needs were not in a position to determine policies, hiring practices, and expenditures.

The Negro Organization Society

The frustration experienced by Afro-Americans in Virginia as they worked for improvement in all communities precipitated the formation of the Negro Organization Society in 1910, as an outgrowth of a Hampton Conference. H.B. Frissell had suggested extending the ideas and work of the conference beyond its narrow confines and appointed Robert Moton to head a committee to examine the feasibility of such a plan. In 1915, Moton wrote:

> The movement among colored people for better homes, better health, better farms, seems to have made an irresistible appeal to all the people of the state. Religious, benevolent, secret, and educational organizations of every character have joined in this movement. . . . The state-wide campaign for clean privies, clean homes, and clean lives has received help and support that was little dreamed of. The two races have been brought together on the ground of common needs of humanity. We have given white people a chance which they have long desired — a chance to help the Negro without compromise or embarrassment. They have met us more than half way.[31]

From the beginning, few women had roles in the Negro Organization Society, but they were very active in promoting the activities and philosophies of the organization throughout Virginia. Maggie L. Walker, Ora Stokes, and Ida N. Paey did serve on the executive committee during the organization's early years. As late as 1914, the committee was still attempting to chart the society's direction. In that year's meeting, Professor C.H. Blackwell, who wanted the primary focus to be the political life of the Negro, stipulated that members of the local branches should be registered to vote. Ida Paey urged that, regardless of the direction taken, Afro-Americans had to determine what they should do rather than complain about what others in their state did. The only other woman at the meeting, Maggie Walker, pledged her support to whatever was decided upon. During the second session of the executive committee on 29 December 1914, committees on health, homes, education, and farms were appointed to establish what needed to be done. Paey chaired the committee on homes.

As health problems were still a primary concern in black communities, the executive committee decided to concentrate upon the health campaign it had begun in 1913. On 14 April 1913, the society had cosponsored with the State Health Department a statewide Health Day. It had also assisted in the distribution of the "Health Handbook for Colored People," prepared by the Health Department. Dr. Roy K. Flanagan from the State Board of Health of Virginia, addressing the society in December, praised the society's health work and suggested that a nurse be hired to follow up its 1913 campaign. The society adopted Flanagan's suggestion. They also discussed fundraising for a proposed sanatorium for Afro-Americans. Maggie Walker proposed that a committee of three be appointed to confer with the State Board of Health to determine whether state authorities would permit black physicians to practice in the sanatorium. Her motion was approved and she was appointed to the committee.[32]

While the executive committee oversaw the administrative details of the health campaigns in later years, it still fell to women in the communities to carry out these programs. In cooperation with the Negro Organization Society, teachers, home demonstration agents, and club leaders scheduled health meetings in schools, Sunday schools, and clubs, where they taught the practical aspects of developing and maintaining good health habits. Clean-up Week, instituted as an adjunct to the health campaign, also had women in the forefront, as active workers and promoters. Often, the women were such willing workers because they saw the campaigns as extensions of programs they had initiated as early as 1895. Activities which in the past had been viewed by some as "woman's work" had culminated in statewide movements.

The Negro Organization Society became involved in two other areas which in past years had absorbed much time and energy of black women of Virginia. In 1915, the society began to place homeless black children or those charged with offenses in detention homes or private homes rather than in jail. The society, through the county supervisors, sought the cooperation of teachers in the placement process. In spite of the fact that women were consulted for the placements, the society appointed T.C. Walker superintendent of placement for the children, and Dr. J.T. Mastin, of the State Board of Charities, was paid $55 per month to supervise the affairs of the children. Dr. Mastin was responsible for the initial commitment of the children. A delegation from the society also participated in the selection of the site for the girls' home begun by the Virginia State Federation of Colored Women's Clubs.[33]

The society modeled its education program after the white Cooperative Education Association. During summer 1912 black Protestant pastors were asked to give a sermon on education once a month. Collectors supporting the society's drive for better schools requested one dollar for individual membership, five dollars for annual organizational membership, fifty cents for student membership, and two dollars for Sunday school membership. Elizabeth Cobb Jordan delineated three periods in the development of the educational programs of the Negro Organization Society:

> Period I: Improving, constructing buildings, lengthening sessions and increasing salaries of teachers.
> Period II: Improving instruction — model lessons being taught and the encouragement of in-service training.
> Period III: Development of the school as a site for community activities.[34]

Through cooperation with the State Teachers' Association and the School Improvement Leagues, the society was able to effect improvements in the education of Afro-Americans in Virginia.

About the activities of the Negro Organization Society, it was said that "the movement [for improvement of the race] had not sprung from any one man. It had come from frequent conferences of many men giving urgent, thoughtful consideration to the scheme." However, on a practical level the movement appears more to have begun with women who daily confronted situations that impeded the progress of Afro-Americans.

CHAPTER 6

Social Service Programs in Alabama: Focus on Tuskegee

Of the five regions treated in this book, Tuskegee, Alabama, was the most rural, a town surrounded by farms owned primarily by whites. The majority of Afro-Americans in the area sharecropped or hired out to work for whites on their farms.

Rural communities were generally isolated. Large expanses of land were needed for agricultural pursuits, and in rural areas the majority of black residents worked in agriculture. Therefore such residents' needs often were peculiar to the rural South. Class difference among black people, too, were more pronounced here than in urban areas. Groups such as the Tuskegee Woman's Club retained their elitist composition and sponsored some activities only for the formally educated. Personal attainments and social custom precluded full alliance of black women from all classes. Rural women were not as motivated to effect changes in the social structure, because in rural areas, the separation between Afro-Americans and whites was clearly defined and rigidly enforced. To challenge such customs might have endangered black lives, programs, services, and institutions.

Rural social programs emphasized industrial education and education for adults more than urban programs did. Education for both young and old stressed ways of adjusting to rural agricultural life. Educative activities usually were designed to discourage migration from the farms and the South. Those who were sent to schools in urban areas were expected to return to assist in the development of rural Afro-Americans in the South.

Unlike women in urban settings, women in rural communities such as Tuskegee and Mt. Meigs actually helped to create new communities and establish types of services considered commonplace in cities such as Atlanta and Baltimore. Rural women such as those in Tuskegee relied to a greater extent than urban women on federal and state funds and programs to implement their goals. As the populations in rural communities were not as large or affluent as those in urban areas, fundraising activities were not as successful. Limited funds, however, did not automatically dictate inferior programs. More often than not, people contributed goods and services rather than money to important causes. Since greater resourcefulness was required to obtain funds, people depended on and utilized more fully the natural resources available in the areas.

Tuskegee Negro Conferences

The Tuskegee Negro Conference provided opportunities for the women of Alabama both to learn skills needed in administering social service programs, and to hear what others were doing to combat the many problems of their communities. At Tuskegee on 23 February 1892, Booker T. Washington convened the first conference held mainly to discuss Afro-Americans and their concerns. Nearly five hundred persons attended. Washington announced that he would not submit reports of the conference for publication, because he feared that if he did so, open discussion would be hampered.

William T. Harris, U.S. commissioner of education, requested that reports be submitted to him. Washington replied that he would make certain that the typewritten reports were kept for future reference. Soon the annual conferences grew in popularity; eight hundred people came in February 1893, and nearly a thousand came in 1894 and 1895. Those attending felt that the conferences should be held annually in order to keep alive interest in continued progress and change.[1]

The Fifth Tuskegee Negro Conference in 1896 announced as its purpose "to show the masses of Colored people how to lift themselves up in their industrial, educational, moral and religious life."[2] The conference attendees defined two major objectives. The first was two-fold: to ascertain from those present the status of Afro-Americans, and then to seek solutions to the problems identified. The second objective was to determine how the educated could best use their talents to aid the masses. Philosophically and practically, both objectives were supported by black women.

The 1896 purpose and objectives implied important goals. Given the influence of Booker T. Washington and Tuskegee Institute in setting the educational philosophy for the conferences, it is not surprising that one conference declaration urged Afro-Americans to purchase land and improve their farming methods through crop diversification, dairying, fruit growing, and intensive stock raising. Those present were encouraged to stimulate interest in learning trades.

By 1896, the question of black control of their educational institutions was widely debated. Thus it is important to note that, while whites were present at the 1896 Tuskegee Conference and in some cases had been encouraged to attend, Afro-Americans held the leadership roles. The delegates did not plan for the Tuskegee Conferences to be ones at which people gathered to talk and then continued their lives as they had previously. Those who attended expected to take back to their communities techniques for improving the education and the lives of all Afro-Americans.

Delegates to the 1896 conference recognized that their declarations and the work of a dedicated few could not have the necessary impact unless more teachers and ministers moved into the country districts where conditions were worst. Many delegates felt that, to be of greatest value in these rural communities, college-educated men and women should be trained along industrial lines. Again, the Tuskegee philosophy was dominant.

The 1896 conference also declared that delegates should help Afro-Americans in their communities to do without mortgages and to discontinue living in one-room cabins. Parents were urged to exercise extreme care in the control of their children. Both to provide a more meaningful education and to assist parents in supervising their children, it was recommended that the school term be lengthened from three or four months to seven to eight.[3] The conference declarations helped to shape both the post-school activities sponsored by black female teachers and the curricula in some emerging black institutions. The conferences also served as an excellent forum for new ideas concerning industrial and general educational courses.

By 1896, the conference concept had become prevalent in the South; almost every state from Virginia to Texas held one or more farmers' and educators' conferences each year. In 1899, 150 farmers' conferences were held, based on the Tuskegee model. Their themes of thrift and hard work were simply transferred and applied to the educational conferences.[4]

The focus of the Tuskegee Conferences changed after 1900. Annually, and sometimes monthly, Afro-American farmers came from various parts of the South to display their products and to deliver talks on their farming methods. It was at this time that women began to play a lesser role in the proceedings of the conferences, then known as Negro Farmers' Conferences. In 1910, in conjunction with the conference, Tuskegee established a Department of School Extension to teach people how to improve themselves through the home, farm, and school, and to provide continuation work for "those who are engaged in teaching in the communities surrounding the school."[5]

In order to implement the instruction and recommendations of the conferences, Tuskegee Institute employed an agent to organize local communities, with improvement of the quality of life as the main objective. A two-week school for farmers, including women and girls, was initiated in 1912. Poultry raising, dairying, sewing, and cooking were some of the mini-workshops held.

At the 1916 conference, six lectures of twenty minutes each were presented for women, under the direction of Margaret M. Washington. During her address, "Improved Housing," Alice White, principal of Girls' Industrial School of Montgomery, Alabama, made a plea for simplicity in house furnishings. To emphasize her point, she indicated that she used furniture made from boxes in her home. Following this address, the women made utilitarian articles into decorative ones. Since care of the home was viewed as an integral part of women's work on farms, the women were shown how to select curtains and pictures for their homes, to prepare well-balanced meals from farm-grown items, to use proper table manners, and to practice domestic economy.

Some of the addresses at the 1916 conference appealed to both sexes; many were designed to demonstrate how the participants could continue to live on southern farms yet prosper. Cornelia Bowen discussed ways she had assisted farmers in diversifying crops. A Mrs. Mims illustrated Bowen's methods with an account of her farming activities near Selma. A settlement worker from Bessemer, Alabama, spoke of her efforts to secure houses for tenants, to encourage tenants to pay promptly, to encourage the landlord to repair and maintain the property, and to impress upon tenants the need to pay cash for items and to live within their means.

A highlight of the 1916 Tuskegee Conference was a lecture by Dr. Joseph Goldberger of the U.S. Public Health Bureau. Through an examination of the causes, cure, and prevention of pellagra, he hoped to make the participants more knowledgeable about a health problem which afflicted many Afro-Americans. Women suffered more from the disease, because the best food was usually given to the men of the household who performed the heavy manual and farming duties. Dr. Goldberger stressed that pellagra could be cured if diets were balanced, including milk, lean meat, peas, beans, legumes, and eggs.

Because of the declining southern economy, many Afro-Americans were not able to give their families the necessary items. With their meager resources, survival appeared almost impossible. The conferences continued to emphasize how the participants could fully exploit what they did have. Attention focused on home needs, health, crops diversification, racial problems, and the need for Afro-Americans to remain in the South.

In spite of the information and skills gleaned from the various conferences, many Afro-Americans were migrating northward. Josephine S. Calloway, wife of the head of Tuskegee Institute's Extension Department, outlined at the 1917 Tuskegee Negro Conference why Afro-Americans left: accumulated debts at home and the pull of opportunities in the North were at the base of the problem. In the South, floods and the boll weevil had destroyed what little income many had anticipated, while in the North, the European War had opened public work jobs for Afro-Americans and increased wages for all. More often than not, the men went northward first. Calloway advised wives whose husbands had left to maintain their homesteads. She realized that the extension services of Tuskegee would have to be broadened and strengthened in order to combat the loss of manpower, natural disasters, and increasing hopelessness in the South.

Tuskegee Institute's Extension Activities

Extension work had begun at Tuskegee in 1906 when Thomas M. Campbell, employed by the federal government to work with black farmers in Macon County, became the first black county agricultural agent. In 1914 the Smith-Lever Act improved extension services through formal agreements between the U.S. Department of Agriculture and land-grant colleges. The act consolidated federal and state funds and activities. Publications were added to field demonstrations so that residents could read about projects as well as participate in them. Tuskegee Institute became the official headquarters for the Extension Service in Alabama, Florida, Georgia, Louisiana, Texas, Mississippi, and Oklahoma. Using volunteers, the service worked with men, women, boys, and girls through local leaders who were supervised by county agents.[6]

From the beginning of Tuskegee's Extension Service, women were employed as local leaders and county agents to organize projects for girls and women. In 1914 the General Education Board gave funds for club work for black girls in ten Alabama counties. Funds from the Extension Service in Tuskegee were used for eleven clubs in Macon County. Because the experiment was new, no effort was made to raise local funds, and the work was placed under the direction of the state supervisor for Negro rural schools. Counties were selected where industrial teachers had been successful during winter and spring 1914. The Home Makers' Clubs for Negro Girls stressed three lines of work — gardening, domestic science, and sanitation.

A one-week conference was held at Tuskegee Institute to familiarize the new agents with their duties and to give them complete instructions for establishing clubs. The organizing efforts of the Tuskegee Woman's Club, to be discussed shortly, were used as models. Faculty from the institute conducted classes each day on topics such as children's diseases and nursing. Demonstrations were always provided with the lectures. At the conference, a monitoring system for the clubs was established, because the expansion of the Extension Service depended upon the success rate in the counties.

A community center was designated for each of the ten counties, with the stipulation that two of the ten would be visited each day by an agent, as part of the monitoring process. During July and August, each agent was to submit a field report to headquarters. Since the reports noted how difficult it was to locate garden plots for the girls to use, parents were requested to release land for planting and cultivation. During 1914, 1,500 girls joined, and average weekly attendance was 1,030. After an invitation was extended to parents to attend the meetings, 2,681 mothers attended during the season. Many community residents at first did not realize that the clubs were free and delayed joining. Home visits by agents helped to alleviate fears and misconceptions.

In fulfilling the objectives of the Extension Service, eleven agents in 1914 traveled 7,324 miles for weekly visits; held 743 meetings, demonstrations, and lectures; visited 1,623 homes; and supervised the canning of 7,272 jars of fruit and vegetables. At the end of the year, exhibits or rallies were held in the communities so that the residents could see the results of their activities and encourage participation by others. Samples of finished products were sent from each county to the state fair at Montgomery to be displayed at a booth in the Negro Building. A white man was so impressed by the display that he volunteered to loan ten acres of his land if similar projects were sponsored in his community during summer 1915. One of the superintendents expressed his belief that the success of the clubs was contributing to the general contentment of Afro-Americans on farms in the South.[7]

If not exactly "content," Afro-Americans were continuing to adjust to conditions and to improve them. Aiding in the adjustment process was the home demonstration work, established in Alabama in 1915 as part of the U.S. Department of Agriculture's Cooperative Extension Services. For the black farmers, Tuskegee again supervised the activities. Alabama was divided into northern and central sections, with a black home economics agent in each section. The agents were all women. During World War I, nine new agents were added, three in cities and six in rural communities. They established women's clubs which aimed "to make more efficient mothers and better families with higher standards of living, thus producing better citizens."[8] To be a club member, a woman had to plant and grow food in a garden, raise chickens, be or learn to be a good housekeeper, and attend some meetings. Club members kept record books which monitored their spending and profits; the books were inspected by the Home Demonstration agent during each visit, but independent thought and action were encouraged so that efforts would be sustained after the programs ended.

The clubs, started only where the girls' club work was well established, enrolled 221 farm women in eleven counties. Teachers and local women's clubs supported the agents' endeavors. Through the use of readily available materials and those purchased from profits, club members made forty-four fireless cookers, six iceless refrigerators, eight flytraps, and two wheeled trays. The agents also prompted many members to install cheap, simple water systems in their rural kitchens.

The duties of the agents were fully systematized by 1920. Table 5 outlines the full scope of objectives, activities, and desired results of the extension services for women and girls.[9] The outline emphasizes the three units which most directly affected the lives of Afro-Americans — home, school, and church. An effort was made to integrate social activities with educational ones and at the same time to promote creativity. Agents continued to be trained by selected educational institutions.

So productive were the services of the female agents that three black women held high-level administrative positions with the Extension Service as of 12 June 1920. Rosa B. Jones was state agent for Negro women, N. Juanita Coleman served as special agent of Negro movable schools, and Uva Mae Hester was rural nurse in cooperation with Tuskegee Institute and the Alabama State Board of Health. Hester's job was threatened on 24 September 1920, by a cutback in federal funds for the extension programs. Although her job performance was praised and the home economics and movable schools programs required a nurse, the only way for Hester to be retained was through the elimination of her travel allotment of $50 per month.

At the close of the first half of the 1921 fiscal year, it was apparent that federal funding would not be maintained at the level of earlier years. Ultimately, the success and survival of the programs would depend to a great extent upon community interest, support, and sacrifices.

The aftermath of World War I brought many economic shocks to the American public: the closing of wartime industries, an end to economic controls, inflation, and high unemployment rates. Recession caused a reordering of national financial priorities. Among the first projects to be eliminated or reduced were those which primarily benefitted Afro-Americans.

Afro-American women throughout the South found it difficult to secure funds for their programs. Responding to a request for funds from Lugenia Hope in Atlanta, Margaret Washington spoke of her own efforts to raise funds:

> Mr. Washington got your letter, I put it right into his hands. He has talked with me two of three times about it; he says that Mr. Rosenwald is very cranky on certain subjects; that is, he doesn't wish to give his money to city work at all, but to country work. Mr. Washington has promised me faithfully to keep his eyes open and see if he can get any help for you in any other direction. I am also looking out. I shall certainly keep right up with him and make him keep his promise even though he should be inclined to forget, which he is not likely to do.
>
> Mr. Washington looked all over the various funds here to see if there was anything from which he could draw but he finally decided that he ought not to try, for there are certain stipulations with reference to these funds that cannot be overstepped, but surely there will come a time when your work and mine will get what they need. I have this night school in town which costs me over Five hundred ($500.00) dollars a year and I have been trying to get Mr. Washington to give me something from Mr. Rosenwald's fund, but he says it is a city school. You know the town of Tuskegee, it is strictly country; people grow cotton almost in the streets here.[10]

In spite of limited financial resources, the black women agents continued to work with black women of the South. New clubs were organized in various parts of Alabama. The agents also maintained activities related to the care of the home and the prevention of contagious diseases. Representative reports show the agents' achievements:

> MISS M.L. SNIPES, LOCAL AGENT, Hale & Perry Counties, says, "I spent two weeks the month of July attending the agricultural short course at Tuskegee Institute where much information as well as inspiration was gleaned. Two weeks of August were spent assisting with the movable schools of agriculture. These schools were well attended and all attendants showed intense interest throughout all of the courses. Twenty-one demonstrations were given for the women, while the men were busy with their side of the program. Over, 1,000 people living in the communities where the two schools were held, attended. The homes at which the schools were held were greatly improved and their new appearance won the admiration of all who saw them. Already the people who attended these schools have applied for their return next year."

> MISS DAISY E. BRYANT, LOCAL AGENT, Madison County, states that "being a new agent just taking up my work July 1, 1921, I have spent a great deal of the time during the past two months visiting the club members in the various communities, giving some advice in planting fall and winter gardens, and incidentally get-

Table 5. *Outline for Rural Negro Women's and Girls' Clubs*

Object: Cooperation in Homemaking	Aim: To Reach All Women & Girls
SHE LEARNS BY	SHE STRIVES TOWARD AN IDEAL AND SERVES BY
Informal Discussions On:	*Personal Service:*
What am I going to do?	In the Home,
A Girl's at her best.	In the School,
A Girl's Budget.	In the Church.
Customs & Courtesies.	
First Aids to Beauty.	*Community Service:*
	Community Events.
Handicraft work, such as:	Community Sings.
Making a Fireless Cooker.	Christmas Tree Celebrations.
Making Fly Paper.	Other Celebrations.
Rural Nursing.	Parades, Drives.
Equipping a Rest Room	General Social Occasions.
in the Rural Church.	
Bottoming Chairs.	*Community Betterment:*
Canning & Drying Vegetables	"Clean up" Movements
and Fruits.	(Health Week).
Making Soap.	Gardens.
Making Bread.	Buying Equipment for Churches,
Preserving Eggs.	Schools, Rest Rooms, etc.
Making Rag Rugs.	"Fresh Air" Organizations.
Renovating the Home.	Charity Organizations.
Labor Saving Devices.	Hospitals.
Raffia Work.	Visiting Nurses.
Shuck Work.	Cooperative Clubs and
Bead Work.	Improvement Associations.
Stenciling.	
Sewing (Club Uniforms, etc.)	*National Service:*
Knitting.	Red Cross Activities.
	Cooperation with such Organiza-
Musical:	tions as:
Chorus Work	Anti-Tuberculosis Society
Glee Club	Children's Bureau,
Club Songs	War Saving Stamps.
Song Contests	

Table 5. (continued)

Object: Cooperation in Homemaking	Aim: To Reach All Women & Girls
SHE LEARNS BY	SHE STRIVES TOWARD AN IDEAL AND SERVES BY
Dramatics: Pageants Plays Stunts Charades	
SHE KEEPS WELL BY	SHE HAS GOOD TIMES
Athletics and Games: Basket Ball Volley Ball Track Meets Military Drill Hikes & Picnics Folk Games	*Parties for:* Lonely Girls Mothers Young Men Friends *Rallies for:* Community Clubs

Contests:
Drill Contests
Game Contests
Individual Contests of Skill
	Exhibits:
	To show results of Club Work in
	    Classes, Dramatics, Athletics,
	    etc.
	
	Fairs:
	To show results of Year's Work.
	
	Annual Short Courses:
	Tuskegee Institute.
	A. & M. College, Normal, Ala.
	    (Month of August.)

Source: "Cooperative Extension Work in Agriculture and Home Economics, State of Alabama: Outline for Rural Negro Women's and Girls' Clubs," 1 September 1920, Extension File, Box 4, Archival Collection, Hollis Burke Frissell Library, Tuskegee University, Tuskegee, Alabama.

ting acquainted. I have recently given one demonstration in planting fall gardens, one in applique work, one in cutting, basting and fitting skirts, two in canning tomatoes, one in canning beans, one in making apple jelly, one in cultivating the garden, one in treating chickens for scaly leg and one in making string handbags. Have held six meetings, including club gatherings, county fair association and rural schools.[11]

The agents met at Tuskegee for eleven days in July 1921, for a short course in agriculture for black farmers. During the roundtable discussions for women held at the Trades Building, the female agents reaffirmed their primary objectives and described problems they had encountered and possible solutions:

agents must make effort to do less individual work, that is, work must be done with groups rather than with individuals; that colored agents must cooperate with white agents; that one of the principal duties of the agent is to keep the people cheerful, to keep them encouraged in spite of hard times and never, under any circumstances, antagonize the landlords or plantation owners. Agents must help people to make the home a fit place in which to live and seek to improve the social life of the young people especially, by teaching them games, song and yells, and help in every way for community betterment.[12]

Through 1925 and after, the Department of Agriculture's extension services did assist southern black females in bettering their lives. As of 1934, fifteen states were participating in the federal extension programs; 350 people were employed as county home and farm demonstration agents, supervisors, movable school specialists, and clerical assistants.

The Tuskegee Woman's Club

It was largely through the organizational efforts of Margaret Murray (Mrs. Booker T.) Washington (1865–1925) that black women from all social and economic levels in Alabama, first in Tuskegee and then throughout the state, began to create their own social service programs. Born in Macon, Mississippi, Mrs. Washington was well acquainted with the South and its problems, and she understood the need carefully to plot her course so as to offend neither Afro-Americans nor whites. Her position as Booker T. Washington's wife made her views and positions more readily accepted by Afro-Americans and whites alike.

On March 2, 1895, thirteen women attended the first meeting of the Tus-kegee Woman's Club. Initiated by Mrs. Washington, its first president, the club proposed to promote the "general intellectual development of women." "I said nothing of my plan to Mr. Washington or to anybody else before-hand," she recalled in 1899, "because I was uncertain as to how the experi-ment would turn out, and I thought if I failed I should not want anybody to know it."[13] The club's membership was to be exclusive: "Those who are acquainted with the nature of this club know that in certain ways it is an exclusive club, taking in as members only those connected with the faculty as teachers and those who are indirectly connected, that is, the wives of the gentlemen teachers."[14] Meetings were held twice monthly on the Tuskegee Institute campus, and new teachers were encouraged to join.

By April 1895, membership in the group had increased and two other clubs, the Brooklyn Literary Group and the Women's League of Washing-ton, had requested branch affiliation. Susan B. Anthony, a national feminist leader, wrote a letter to the group, read at the April meeting, congratulating the members on their club movement. On 20 April 1896, the group decided to send J.M. Greene to the meeting of the National Federation of Colored Women's Clubs.

It was not until 1897 that the club became actively involved in com-munity affairs. In that year, a plantation settlement was founded on the Russell Plantation, eight miles from Tuskegee. It was formed in an "effort to adapt methods of University Settlement to needs of people living in poor conditions."[15] Ann Davis, a graduate of Tuskegee, moved into a cabin on the plantation and opened a school in 1898. Parents were requested to pay what they could towards the upkeep of the school; the county contributed fifteen dollars a month toward Davis' salary. Mrs. Washington was respon-sible for securing the county allocation for Davis because the tenants, many of them ex-convicts, simply did not have available funds. Household in-dustries were taught at the school, and the pupils raised farm products on the adjoining ten-acre farm. The school became part of the public system in 1906. For twelve years, members of the Woman's Club spent weekends working with the residents of the plantation. They taught Sunday school and organized boys' clubs, sewing classes for girls, mothers' clubs, and newspaper-reading clubs for men.[16] When the residents were able to main-tain the programs, direct involvement on the plantation ended, and time was given to other projects.

As early as 1901, Mrs. Washington started a public library and reading room, using her daughter's discarded books. The library was staffed by members of the Women's Club from 3 to 8 p.m. daily and all day on Saturday and Sunday. Books, magazines, three daily papers, and weekly and monthly papers were provided without charge to the residents.[17]

In 1910, when women were excluded from the annual Tuskegee Negro Conference, Mrs. Washington met with twelve other women. The Town Night School developed from this meeting. When it became necessary to keep the children occupied while their mothers were in class, a cooking class was formed for them. At the end of 1910 the Town Night School had eight teachers, two academic and six industrial. Along with basic reading, cooking, and sewing, such skills as carpentry, bricklaying, painting, and tailoring were taught. The cooking class met twice a week and was designed for women who were heads of families or were hired as cooks for whites. The Night School was listed in the official Tuskegee catalog as one of its extension programs.[18]

In 1912, Mr. Washington announced that Tuskegee was no longer able to support the Night School. The Woman's Club assumed responsibility for keeping the school open eight months a year. There were 103 night classes and 37 day or cooking classes. Enrollment included 140 boys and girls. The club paid the male head of the school $25 a month. Three persons from Tuskegee — one postgraduate, one student, and one teacher — taught at night without pay. Miss Nunn, a member of the club, taught sewing and other subjects at the school at least twice a week. The clubwomen collected and expended almost $300 in sustaining the school that year. There would not have been enough money for another year had additional donations not been made. Solicitations were made to the men of Tuskegee; George Washington Carver gave $25 and a Mr. Taylor $5.[19]

Despite the financial strain, the Night School curriculum was broadened to include additional academic subjects such as Negro history. The history course proved so beneficial that the women encouraged the teaching of Negro history in day and night schools throughout the county. For persons who could not afford much time or money, the Night School provided an opportunity to secure an education. Children of the town also became an integral part of the program and received educational experiences which reinforced what they learned in public school or, in some cases, substituted for public education.

In the early 1900s Woman's Club members began to visit Tuskegee homes to encourage residents to maintain a clean, orderly community and to teach the women how to attend to their homes. Enough interest was generated to form mothers' meetings. Discussion topics centered on the lives, homes, children, and needs of the mothers. Mrs. Washington believed that during the formative meetings, teachers from Tuskegee Institute and the area should spearhead the organizational process because they possessed the necessary skills. In order to avoid confining affiliations, the meetings were not held in homes or churches. Few officers were elected, generally just a president and a secretary.

Beginning the first Saturday in October 1912, mothers' meetings were held every week. Topics for discussion continued to include home management, child care, and marital concerns. The topics were selected to permit reflection and meaningful discussion. A new topic linked the women to a national movement, the campaign for woman suffrage. Political education was offered so that when women were granted the right to vote, they could participate as intelligent, informed citizens. However, in the rural areas political education was viewed as secondary to those activities and programs designed to improve the quality of life on an immediate, tangible, level.

The mothers' meetings were part of a national effort by women to improve the lives of Afro-Americans. By 1913, the *National Association Notes*, the official organ of the National Association of Colored Women (NACW), reported over five hundred groups in existence throughout the United States. It was recognized, however, that rural women especially needed more groups. Because of the success of the Tuskegee meetings, the editor of *Notes* invited Mrs. Washington to write an article providing simple instructions for the establishment of mothers' meetings and clubs.

The instructions delineated the plan of action used in Tuskegee. Topics for discussions suggested by Mrs. Washington included "Girls' Home Responsibilities, An Ideal Home For A Girl, When Shall A Girl be Permitted to Receive Her First Company, and Mother's Relation to the Teacher."[20] She recommended that topics be given to the women at least two weeks in advance so that they would have ample time to think seriously about them. In response to the article, Mrs. Washington received inquiries seeking more details. One was sent by Anne M. Evans, an investigator in the Women's Rural Organization for the U.S. Department of Agriculture. Mrs. Washington referred her to the NACW, whereupon Evans wrote back requesting data about the NACW.[21] Such exchanges promoted interchange among black and white women. Given the isolation of many rural women and the difficulty in maintaining quick, effective communication, any activity which fostered greater knowledge of programs and ideas was welcomed.

In time, the *Tuskegee Messenger* began to publish short accounts of the achievements of black women in the area. Through a variety of activities, the women's groups raised funds to support local outreach projects. Accounts of homes built by women without mates, savings accounts opened by women, and ways women supported their husbands in their endeavors became regular *Messenger* features. The success of the mothers' meetings was verified not only in such stories but also in visitations to the homes of the women by Woman's Club members. One of the products of the meetings was a women's restroom in the town, which was used as a model room for housekeeping instruction and as a retreat for the women from their normal responsibilities and problems. The women also began to provide supervised activities for boys and young men. Social and economic conditions in the South often made black males prey to hostile actions by whites. A town Sunday school, later a YMCA, was formed for boys only.

By 1913, the Woman's Club had established internal committees for specific programs. The majority of the committees focused on services for others. One, the Sex Hygiene Committee, presented materials which prompted extensive discussions and research activities to obtain additional information. They then shared their findings with other women in the community and with the female students at Tuskegee. The Temperance Work Committed also included female students; regular Saturday meetings were held on campus. The Humane Work Committee, to ensure kindness to dumb animals, and the Visitation Committee, to visit those in jail, concentrated on community activities.

The Social Service Work Committee was considered by the members to be the most important one. In 1913, that committee raised ninety dollars to finance its projects. The committee paid dental bills for one hundred children, purchased toothbrushes for twenty-five, and tended to the ill. In Greenwood, the committee established a reading room for boys between the ages of eight and eighteen, in connection with the Boys' Social and Literary Club. Ever mindful of social conditions, the women installed a curfew bell and held fresh air meetings. Their plans for the year 1914 included equipping a park for Greenwood residents.

Through the leadership of a Mrs. Woodward, selected girls from Greenwood and Tuskegee were invited to participate in a Big Sister Program, part of a national program of the NACW. One of the girls, Beatrice Reynolds, was "sistered" for seven years and graduated in 1913 from Vorhees Industrial School in Demark, South Carolina. After graduation, she was offered a position at that school. Ruth Hill was "sistered" for three years. She also attended Vorhees, but her dipolma was withheld because of "her lack of development." The Woman's Club planned to raise money to send Miss Hill to Hampton Institute for two years. During their educational experiences, the girls were provided with clothes, money, and affection.[22]

By 1920, membership in the Tuskegee Woman's Club had grown to 130. During the first twenty-five years of its existence, the membership requirements remained the same. All members were formally educated and were Tuskegee faculty members or wives of faculty members. The primary aim was still "to improve its members intellectually, morally and spiritually."[23] The club sponsored plays, held receptions for the male teachers, and developed study groups on national and international issues. The club members never forgot the need to develop and assess themselves while attempting to assist others.

The years from 1920 to 1925 were productive ones for the club. The Temperance Department organized meetings, lectures, and medal contests to prepare the community for Prohibition. Because of the women's efforts, many had taken the temperance pledge. The Temperance Department also campaigned against cigarette smoking and urged area merchants not to sell cigarettes to boys. A maid was hired to clean the railroad waiting room in Montgomery, Alabama. In a spirit of cooperation with whites, the maid was also instructed to clean the waiting room used by whites.[24] The women agitated not for equal facilities, but for clean ones. The women obviously were fully aware of the South's social limitations and of the 1896 *Plessy v. Ferguson* decision.

Alabama State Federation of Colored Women's Clubs

The activities of Mrs. Washington and the Woman's Club gained statewide attention, and in 1898 a statewide convention of black club women was held in Montgomery. Mrs. Washington was the principal organizer and first president of the Alabama State Federation of Colored Women's Clubs (ASFCWC). The federation sponsored projects similar to those of the Tuskegee Woman's Club but, because of its larger membership and financial resources, was also able to elicit support from whites, influence the allocation of state funds, and reach greater numbers of Afro-Americans. The federation developed two projects which served as examples for other state groups.

More often than not in southern states, young blacks, male and female, who were convicted of crimes, were sent to penal institutions for adults. In some cases, homeless youngsters were committed to the institutions because foster homes were not available. Mrs. Washington credited the NACW as the primary stimulus for the Alabama federation's creation of the Mt. Meigs Reformatory for Juvenile Negro Law-Breakers. The reformatory, organized to assist delinquent boys, became a state institution by act of the state legislature in 1911. The law provided $8,000 to improve the facility, and additional funds for maintenance. By December 1911, the state had assumed absolute control, and the governor had appointed nine trustees. The influence of the federation did not end with state control, however; the trustees appointed an advisory board which linked them with the federation. As of 1912, sixty-one boys were confined to the reformatory. The boys contributed a total of $497 toward their maintenance by picking cotton for neighboring farmers. Concerned that the boys not simply serve as cheap labor, the federation petitioned the trustees to build an annex to the main building to be used as a trades center. The women's watchdog efforts guaranteed just treatment and an education for an increasing number of boys: 87 in 1913, 202 in 1916, 300 in 1920. The reformatory, with seven buildings in 1920, employed teachers who prepared the boys to assume productive lives upon their release.

Cornelia Bowen, president of the federation in 1912 and the only female president of the Alabama State Teachers Association through 1925, chaired the federation's fourteenth annual meeting at a church in Tuscaloosa. In 1912, the Federation was composed of thirty clubs whose members were employed in various service fields; Bowen remarked that the federation was approved "by the best whites in the state."[25] The federation established a home for wayward black girls, the Mt. Meigs Rescue Home for Girls. At each annual meeting after 1912, the branch clubs gave funds to support the home. Other social and literary clubs in Alabama, not affiliated with the federation, also contributed funds. Among them were the Pierian Club for English teachers and the Handicrafters Club of Tuskegee Institute. The Mt. Meigs Home, unlike the Mt. Meigs Reformatory, was supported largely through private donations and funds raised by the federation. The girls also contributed through jobs held in the community or sales of items made at the home. The general objectives and programs of the home were similar to those of the reformatory.

By the time of the federation's 1925 annual meeting in Selma, the group had broadened its base, to fifty-three local organizations. The federation president indicated that $3,636.24 had been raised during the year to support the home and other programs.[26] The women had proven that they were responsive and responsible on local and state levels. Local, statewide, and regional concerns were similar; part of the success at state and regional levels can be attributed to models successfully implemented at the local level. The conceptual framework for the majority of state and regional programs had its origin in local communities.

CHAPTER 7

Social Service Programs in Georgia: Focus on Atlanta

Conditions in Atlanta

At the conclusion of the Civil War, Atlanta, largely destroyed by Sherman's army, faced a major rebuilding task. After Reconstruction, Afro-Americans found it especially difficult to survive there. Of 40,000 in Atlanta in 1900, one-fourth lived in abject poverty. Many were unemployed, and those who were employed received salaries ranging from $1.25 to $1.50 a month. Many, especially women, had to resort to picking up rags and papers from the streets to sell.[1] As the new century began, conditions for Afro-Americans worsened throughout Georgia. The literacy rate for the total population dropped from 92.1 percent in 1870 to 52.4 percent in 1900. Municipal ordinances against Afro-Americans proliferated as they flocked to urban areas, leaving behind their depleted farms.[2]

During the eighteen-month gubernatorial campaign of 1905–1906, the chief issue was the disenfranchisement of Afro-Americans. Hoke Smith, owner of the *Atlanta Journal*, and Clark Howell, owner of the *Atlanta Constitution*, were vying to become governor of Georgia. Many whites believed that the black voters of Atlanta were capable of ushering in a liberal state government which would be sympathetic to industry and to Afro-Americans. The candidates and their yellow journalism inflamed racial tensions. On 22 September 1906, ten thousand white men attacked the black community in the city proper. On 23 September, the white mob pushed into the suburb of Brownsville, where middle- and upper-class Afro-Americans lived. The black residents attempted to counter the attack, with little success. Much damage was inflicted on the black residential sections, and several lives were lost. The *Guardian* reported the events under the headline, "Bloody Massacre of Unarmed Colored People by Savage White Mob at

Atlanta, Ga."[3] Its editors charged that Atlanta newspapers had stirred the fears of whites and thus were responsible for the riot.

The riot intensified white efforts to keep Afro-Americans from voting. In 1908, to vote in Georgia one had to be a Confederate veteran or descended from one, possess good character and citizenship, read and write any part of the U.S. or Georgia Constitution, own forty acres of land or property valued at five hundred dollars, and have paid poll taxes since 1877. As was intended, the voting requirements deprived many Afro-Americans of the right to vote. For Afro-Americans, the political scene in Georgia, as in Alabama, Virginia, Tennessee, and parts of Maryland, remained bleak until late in the twentieth century.

Overt discrimination against Afro-Americans extended into the area of housing. Fifty white real estate agents in Atlanta agreed not to rent or sell property to Afro-Americans within areas determined by the Fourth Ward Progressive Club. A meeting of the mayor and representatives from the black community did not halt the restrictive covenant.[4] A housing segregation ordinance, fixing housing patterns, was passed in Atlanta by 1913. Atlanta strengthened its ordinance in 1916 by prohibiting Afro-Americans or whites from moving into neighborhoods occupied predominantly by one racial group. That ordinance was signed into law by Mayor Woodward on 12 April 1916.[5] Other cities in Georgia, including Augusta, Canton, and Savannah, also passed rigid segregation laws. However, because of the greater number of Afro-Americans in Atlanta, the laws were more stringent there.

Social and economic gains that had been achieved by Afro-Americans in Atlanta were threatened in 1915 by the revival of the Ku Klux Klan throughout the South. Some decided that the only way to escape the open hostility was to leave the South; an estimated 118,000 Afro-Americans left the city between 1 April and 1 December 1916. In January 1917, the *New York World* reported that New York had 10,000 new black residents from the state of Georgia.[6]

The Atlanta Conferences

Faced with the reality that local, state, and federal governments were not going to move quickly to resolve problems in the black communities, intellectuals, educators, and others began to search for ways to help the masses of Afro-Americans to survive and be productive citizens. Because of the complex of liberal arts institutions for Afro-Americans, Atlanta had black individuals with skills necessary to conduct systematic studies of factors affecting the quality of life of Afro-Americans.

Years before the racial strife of the early 1900s, the annual Atlanta Conferences had become a forum for the presentation of research findings and for discussions of specific topics relating to the black experience in the United States. Delegates met annually from 1896 through 1913, for a total of eighteen conferences. Although Horace Bumstead, a white serving as president of Atlanta University, chaired most of the conferences, the black delegates were determined that the issues discussed would relate directly to Afro-Americans.

The first Atlanta Conference, with the central theme "Mortality Among Negroes in the Cities," was held to initiate a thorough study of Afro-Americans in the cities. In 1895 there were 7.5 million Afro-Americans in the United States; of that number, one-sixth or 1.25 million lived in quickly-appearing urban slums. In Baltimore; Washington, D.C.; New Orleans; St. Louis; and Louisville, mortality rates for Afro-Americans were higher than for whites.[7] Many who presented papers on mortality were personally acquainted with the problems discussed, because they worked in urban areas. When it became apparent that a large number of illnesses, such as convulsions and gastroenteritis in infants, were caused by ignorance and poverty, the focus of the conference was altered to include education.

The second Atlanta Conference, in 1897, drew graduates of Atlanta, Fisk, Lincoln, Spelman, Howard, Meharry, and other Afro-American institutions. Among the delegates were men and women representing a broad spectrum of professions and interests: L.M. Hershaw of the Graduate Club of Washington, D.C.; Rev. H.H. Proctor, pastor of the First Congregational Church of Atlanta; and Adella Hunt Logan, Lucy Laney, Rosa Morehead Bass, and W.E.B. Du Bois, educators. The overall theme, "The Social and Physical Condition of Negroes in Cities," followed the 1896 conference topic. As a result of conclusions drawn from the papers and general discussions, the delegates expressed the need for kindergarten programs to establish a firm base for educational efforts in the cities.[8]

Kindergartens and Day Nurseries

Atlanta was one of the cities which did not have a kindergarten program for black children whose parents could not afford to send them to private schools. A model kindergarten had been established in Atlanta in 1884, under the auspices of the American Methodist Association, but had been discontinued because of lack of funds.[9] W.E.B. Du Bois presented a paper entitled "The Welfare of the Negro Child," and Gertrude Ware (later Bunce), the kindergarten training school teacher at Atlanta University, led the discussion on children left unattended while their mothers worked. After the discussion, Du Bois asked Ware to meet with the mothers at the conference and other women from the community to plan the development of free kindergartens for preschool children of working mothers.

As a direct result of the conference, the Gate City Free Kindergarten Association was founded; the first kindergarten opened in May 1905. The Cain Street Alley Building, used by the First Congregational Church for a Sunday school, housed the organization and kindergarten. The building was located on "Johnson's Row," a slum settlement on Cain Street. By October 1905, two other kindergartens had been founded, and in October 1906, the establishment of an additional two brought the total to five. All of the kindergartens were located in neighborhoods where residents lived at or near poverty levels.[10]

In spite of limited incomes, the residents provided money to rent the facilities and to purchase coal for fuel. The kindergartens were true community efforts that also drew support from persons and organizations outside the communities. Churches in the areas also assisted in the development of the kindergartens. The Presbyterian Mission, which housed one of the schools, supplied fuel and did not charge rent. The Leonard Street Orphanage, working to provide care for neglected children, gave fuel and money for rent to the last two schools which were organized. To provide needed nourishment for the children, milk was supplied by an anonymous friend, and bread was donated by a local bakery.[11]

During the first three years, approximately 150 children, an average of 30 children per center, enrolled in the program. By 1917, 3,000 children had received a better start in the educational process because of the free kindergartens, which featured structured learning and play activities. Only trained personnel who could properly motivate the children and at the same time teach them the basic skills they would need once they entered the public schools were selected for the staffs. Ware's choice was always a "strong Christian kindergarten teacher."[12] One of the first teachers hired for the schools was Ola Perry Cook, of Atlanta University's Class of 1905. She began work immediately after her graduation, at a salary of twenty dollars per month, and remained with the Gate City Association until 1928.

Until 1923, the bulk of the funds for general operating expenses was raised by the association's board. Gertrude Ware Bunce served as first president of the board, and Lugenia Bruns Hope was one of twenty active association members. Concerts, fairs, track meets, contests, and similar activities were sponsored as fundraising events. When Hope became president of the association, she actively involved the powerful Neighborhood Union in the fundraising drives. The association was chartered in 1920 and thus became eligible for selected public funds; in 1923, it became part of the Atlanta Community Chest. Private fundraising drives continued; in 1925 thirty thousand dollars in cash were generated.[13]

Even with the success of the kindergartens, many other children in slum areas were left unattended during the day because they either were too young for the kindergarten program or attended school only parttime. Beginning in 1918, day nurseries were established to provide supervised care and play for these other children. Alonzo F. Herndon was a black man who had become a millionaire through insurance and real estate. President of Atlanta Mutual Life Insurance Company, he gave the building, valued at $10,000, for the first nursery. He also donated two gallons of milk a day for years and paid the $480 annual salary of the matron for several years. In 1923, there were two day nurseries in different sections of the city: the Herndon Day Nursery at 539 Stonewall Street, S.W.; and the Elizabeth Burch Day Nursery at 166 Fort Street, N.E.[14]

Orphanages

The children who benefitted from the kindergartens and day nurseries belonged to intact family units. However, Atlanta also had a sizable number of younsters who for various reasons were without families. Black women developed institutions which provided care and instruction for groups of such children.

The Carrie Steele Orphanage is a symbol of the personal sacrifices and perseverance of one woman to help a few of the many. Carrie Steele was intimately acquainted with the hardships endured by orphans because, born a slave, she was orphaned at an early age. Serving as a volunteer probation officer in 1890 and working with underprivileged children reinforced her belief that orphans often fell prey to a life of crime. Determined to save some from the problems she witnessed, she decided to found an orphan home, using her personal funds. To acquire additional funds needed, she worked as a laborer in the railroad station, wrote and sold copies of her autobiography, sold her home, and appealed to other private citizens for money.

With these funds, she purchased four acres of land on the outskirts of

Atlanta. Into a two-room house on the property, Steele brought 5 orphans. At the 1898 Atlanta Conference, she reported that she had erected a three-story brick building to replace the house, a hospital, and a schoolhouse. She also reported that she had housed 225 children since the founding of the home and had kept some from being placed in a reformatory. Because of continuing financial difficulties, she arranged for the City of Atlanta to purchase the home and place its management under a "Board of Colored Trustees." However, she retained the right to name the institution. Pauper children from Atlanta and Fulton County were to be accepted in the home if funds for their care were paid by the local authorities.

When Steele married, the name of the home was changed to the Carrie Steele Logan Home. After her death, her husband continued the work she had started. He remarried but soon died, and his widow, Mrs. Logan Goodrum, assumed responsibility for maintaining the home. In 1908, C.C. Cater was serving as treasurer of the home. His first wife Mary, a graduate of Atlanta University, became interested in the work that even death had not been able to halt. She organized an auxiliary body of women to aid the trustee board and to raise funds. C.C. Cater became director of the home in 1910, and his second wife worked closely with him. After the death of her husband, Mrs. Clara M. Cater was elected manager and president by the board and remained in those positions through the end of 1925.

In spite of attempts from 1919 to 1928 to relocate the home, it remained on the site selected by Steele. The home was accepted as part of the Atlanta Community Chest in 1924 and that year received $8,160.75 to help defray operating costs. Alonzo F. Herndon "bequeathed in his will $1,000 for scholarships for older girls to continue their education in higher educational institutions outside of the city." Because of that bequest, some girls attended Tuskegee Institute, one graduated from the Forsythe State Agricultural School in Georgia in 1935, and one received training to become a public school teacher.[15]

Residents of the Leonard Street Orphanage also received educational experiences which permitted many of them to complete secondary school and college. Miss M.L. Lawson founded the home in 1890 for black girls between the ages of six and sixteen. The home, purchased from Spelman Seminary, was the principal site of the orphanage until 1926. Lawson served as director of the home until May 1903, when ill health forced her to turn the management over to Amy A. Chadwick, a white woman from the Northfield Bible Training School of East Northfield, Massachusetts. After her graduation from Spelman in 1914, Myrtle Scarlett, an orphan, joined the staff and became one of its outstanding workers. Unlike the Carrie Steele Orphanage, the Leonard Street Orphanage did not have a school on its grounds. Because of its proximity to Spelman and the shared religious views, children from the orphanage attended Spelman as day scholars from 1890 to 1928. When the orphanage opened, it was able to accommodate only fifty to sixty girls. That number remained fairly constant through the years and totaled approximately two thousand by 1925.[16]

During 1895–1925, neither the Leonard Street Orphanage nor the Carrie Steele Logan Home housed more than four thousand children in all. While that number might seem small, when the probable alternatives for the youngsters are considered, the number who were cared for takes on great significance. The residents of the orphanages were fortunate in that the personnel at both, because of their own backgrounds, were able to understand the needs and expectations of homeless children. The two institutions' concentration on the educational and religious development of their young charges produced a core of concerned, informed workers for the black communities.

The Neighborhood Union

Organization and Early Activities. Beginning in 1908, one woman's group emerged as the unifying force for social change and betterment in Atlanta. The movement originated because a woman in one of the neighborhoods who was often seen sitting on her veranda was not seen for several days. Later, she was found dying alone in her house. Lugenia Burns (Mrs. John) Hope heard of the incident and conceived the idea of a neighborhood organization to prevent such occurrences in the future. She called together women who lived in the section of Atlanta bounded by Ashby Avenue on the east, Walnut and Roach Streets on the west, Greensferry on the south, and Beckwith on the north. The purpose of the meeting was "to become better acquainted with one another and to improve the neighborhood in every way possible."[17] The members of the group were to be from "worthy" families residing within the above boundary. Eight women met at Hope's home on 8 July 1908, to determine whether settlement work was needed in the community. Committees were formed and charged with specific duties. The designated area was divided into sections, and each member was to bring to the next meeting the names of parents and the names and ages of children, "especially the girls between 8 and 22," from her assigned section.[18]

From the initial meeting, there was no doubt that this would be a working group and that Hope was a true leader — a capable organizer who was willing to work as hard and as long as those affiliated with her. Her personal notebook indicates that she spent much time before and after meetings and other activities reflecting upon the best procedures, strategies, and concepts to follow as the group developed into an activist organization challenging the social, economic, and political structures of Atlanta. At no time, however, was she unwilling to listen to others or incorporate their ideas.

Clearly, the black women of Atlanta saw the union as theirs. Additional women attended the second and third meetings. Hope appointed three committees to develop a name for the organization, by-laws, and a classification of the children.[19] Mrs. Stokes was chosen to chair the executive board. The classification report identified the target group for some of the early activities of the Neighborhood Union. In the area lived 77 girls between the ages of eight and twenty-two: 26 who were eight to twelve; 23, twelve to fifteen; and 28, fifteen to twenty-two. To finance the proposed activities, each member and mothers in the area would be taxed ten cents a month. A class in embroidery was planned after the business session of one early meeting.[20]

On 30 July 1908, two important phases of the Neighborhood Union's proposed plan of action were introduced. Using the classification data, members were to inform the girls in their sections about an embroidery class to be held at Hope's home the following week. Thus, the outreach program for girls began. The union's members taught the class, employing skills they had previously or had learned the week before. The members were also requested to research data concerning tuberculosis and be prepared to discuss their findings three weeks later. This request began the group's involvement in community health problems. The procedure was always for the women to expand their knowledge and then present needed information to others in the community.

As the women continued to meet during summer 1908, they formalized the union's structure and responsibilities and clarified the relationship they wanted to establish with other black women's groups. Group consensus determined that the union would not send photographs to the NACW national meeting, but instead would postpone affiliation for the time being.

A finance committee was appointed, and members agreed that they would not "beg" for money for their projects but would either raise or contribute the funds they required. At each meeting, the finance committee would report dues paid and monies collected, a practice that fostered cooperation in working toward financial goals.

Interest in the embroidery class induced the women to organize classes in cooking and dresscutting. Classes were enlarged to include people residing outside the districts, at ten cents a lesson. Lillian Alice Turner, a graduate of the Spelman Seminary Nurses' Department and of the Nurses' School of Provident Hospital in Chicago, gave the first demonstrations on care of the home and bathing the sick. Before the end of September 1908, the union was sponsoring a full schedule of classes on most aspects of home and personal care.

By the end of August 1908, it was clear that Hope's home would not accommodate the people who desired to attend classes. A House Committee was formed to investigate renting a store in the neighborhood, at West Fair and Mildred Streets. In a false start, the building was rented for five dollars a month, after some bargaining with the owner, but three months later he informed the group that he had sold the building and it would have to be vacated within one week. This setback—especially disappointing as the union had invested in furnishings for the store—could have dampened the new members' enthusiasm, but Hope again opened her home for meetings and classes, and her leadership skills bound the organization even more closely together.

During the conflict over quarters, the women continued to implement the union's objectives. To facilitate organizing the districts, directors were assigned to each previously delineated section. In response to questions by the new appointees, Hope outlined her view of their role. The directors would supervise district activities to ensure compliance with union goals and programs. They were also to spearhead financial and membership campaigns. Persons outside the district would be allowed to join the union by paying a membership fee of two dollars a year.

Members now made visits to the sick and shut-in, and demonstration lessons on bathing the sick were repeated. Having stimulated the residents of the district to a greater awareness of health concerns, the union held a general health clinic on 14 October 1908. Local doctors and nurses volunteered their time and services to make the clinic a success.

By December 1908, the Neighborhood Union had a full calendar of events. An oyster supper on 20 November 1908, with a ten-cent admission fee, had produced funds to support the events. On Monday nights, dress-cutting classes were held; Tuesdays, millinery classes; Wednesdays and Thursdays, art; Friday afternoons, classes for children (the playground at Spelman Seminary was available for their use); and Saturday nights, entertainment for girls.

The early months of 1909 were spent strengthening existing projects. Mothers' meetings continued on a regular basis; the union raised funds to purchase materials for its classes; and a dollar gold piece was established as a prize for the child who maintained the best home yard. Meetings and classes were held on a rotating basis at the homes of members until a suitable center could be found. Directors were requested to submit reports of their activities for a publication on the Neighborhood Union. T.B. Williams also requested an article for the *Southern Workman*.

By September 1909, an Investigation Committee was broadening the union's scope by reporting "everything that seems to be a menace to our neighborhood."[21] This new thrust was partly responsible for the decision to establish an advisory board composed of men. The board was not formed immediately, but the Investigation Committee did begin its tasks. To assist the committee, all directors were to canvass their neighborhoods for problems, especially those relating to diseases and sanitary conditions. The committee reported on 14 October 1909 the existence of "a house of questionable character on Roach Street."[22] Using what was to become a standard approach, the union petitioned the City Council for removal of the house. Before the petition was submitted, it was circulated in the community for signatures of those who supported the effort.

Possibly because of the new direction being taken by the union, Hope again recommended that names be solicited for the male advisory board. At a meeting in November 1909, after a formal discussion of the need for and composition of the board, it was decided to appoint eleven men "whose duty it is to assist the Union in stamping out anything that tends to injure the morals of the community."[23] To publicize the union and to interest others in its causes, a mass meeting was held on 10 December 1909, in the chapel at Atlanta Baptist College (Morehouse). Donations at the mass meeting added fifty dollars to the group's treasury.

December 1909 and the early months of 1910 were spent building the treasury for the purchase of a home. Each director was to raise a minimum of ten dollars. Printed cards authorized the solicitation and greatly aided the women in raising the amount designated for their sections. Private donations — one of fifty dollars came from the Club of Ten, white men, in the name of Professor Sales, former president of Atlanta Baptist College — increased the fund, but the major portion was raised by the women. The sale of thirty books purchased from Spelman increased the funds. As a fundraising incentive, a hat would go as a prize to the director who raised the largest sum of money. Because the union urged Afro-Americans to support other Afro-Americans, the union transferred its savings from the Georgia Savings Bank to the Colored Savings Bank. As of 24 June 1910, the union had a balance of $213.68 in the bank.

Support for black businesses in the community became one of the union's key objectives in 1910. Ads in the program for the Annual Inter-Collegiate Track Meet, held at Atlanta Baptist College as a benefit for the free kindergartens and the Neighborhood Union, featured black businesses, including undertakers, physicians, dentists, and Alonzo Herndon's Atlanta Mutual Life Insurance Company.[24] As an extension of the campaign to support black businesses, Hope called attention to the increasing number of Jewish-owned businesses in the neighborhood. In response to complaints, the union was to investigate one grocer, a Mr. Izenburg. Members of the union were requested "to remember their obligations to the race"[25] — that is, they were reminded to patronize businesses owned and operated by Afro-Americans.

Because of the union's expansion and its movement into highly sensitive economic and political areas, thought was given to incorporation as early as June 1910. A charter for incorporation, submitted to authorities in early 1911, listed Hope as president, Dora B. Whittaker as treasurer, and Maggie Williams as secretary. Monies for operation of the union, according to the document, were obtained from donations and offerings from members and "others interested in charitable work."[26] The charter revealed that the women were willing to extend their organization through the establishment of branch offices, but that the headquarters were to remain in Atlanta.

Once it became widely known that the union had applied for incorporation, the *Atlanta Constitution* commented on the group's work in an editorial, "Treating Negro Problem at Basis." While praising the union's efforts, the editor seemed more concerned with eliciting support from whites and quelling their possible fears and negative reactions: "The *Constitution* has many times pointed out, cooperation from the superior race is called for in the degree that the white man is inevitably affected by the progress or retrogression of the Negro."[27] The charter for incorporation was approved on 15 March 1911.

Because it still lacked a building, the union was forced to seek other facilities for selected activities. Some classes, such as the cooking class taught by Mrs. Kendall of Spelman College to sixteen persons on Tuesday of each week, could be held in private homes. Others, however, were best taught at other sites. Atlanta Baptist College lent its facilities for manual training, military tactics, and athletics for boys six to twenty-one years old. Sunday school classes, providing supervised activity for boys, were taught by young college men who served as excellent role models for the youths. Even with the additional programs for boys, more activities were needed in order to keep them from loitering in the streets. A wave of crime in June 1911 drew attention to the problem, as it became necessary to request police protection and appoint an investigative committee.

After an appeal to the president of the Atlanta school board, citing the difficulties created by the union's lack of a center, the union was granted permission to hold activities at different schools in the districts. In a letter to Hope dated 12 June 1912, William M. Slaton, superintendent of the public schools, authorized the Neighborhood Union to hold meetings in "colored school houses for civic purposes."[28] Approval to use the shcools had to be obtained three days before the activity. Slaton indicated that he approved the request because he believed that school buildings should be utilized as community centers for social welfare. The three public school buildings were open three days a week for settlement work. Instruction in the arts, games, and free play were held on two days, while Fridays were reserved for mothers' meetings and discussion session with the girls.

The use of the public school facilities solved some of the problems associated with lack of a permanent residence. This was extremely important because, by November 1912, the Neighborhood Union encompassed fourteen districts. During summer 1911, five new unions had been established, three in the Fourth Ward, one in Pittsburgh, and one in Summerhill. The union's core encompassed five departments: Moral Educational, Literary, Industrial, Sanitary, and Music. Table 6, giving the organizational elements of the Neighborhood Union,[29] illustrates the development of the group.

The membership was placed at the top because it was considered the most important component of the Neighborhood Union. The Board of Management was composed of the three leading officers from each union, for a total of eighteen board members; it had direct supervisory responsibility for all components of the union. Under the Board of Management were the units which functioned at the zone and neighborhood levels. The directors in charge of the districts were responsible for peparing monthly reports, organizing community persons, surveying the district for problems, and other related tasks. Each zone committee monitored the activities of the districts in its zone.

When Hope was again elected president of the union in December 1912, she agreed to accept the position only if an acting president were elected. She cited the pressures of her many obligations and the fact that she needed time to develop new unions. Even though she was president in name only, she continued as an active member. She headed one of three literary clubs for children between the ages of ten and twelve, spearheaded the development of a petition to the mayor for lights in the communities, worked to expand the number of public school centers to five for 1913, and still found time to organize unions in other parts of the state.

Even though the union had finally purchased a building for $1,200 in late

Table 6. Organization of the Neighborhood Union

Membership
↓
Board of Management
↓
Board of Directors

Neighborhood
↓
Committees of Neighborhoods
↓
Directors in Charge of Districts

Source: Lugenia Hope's Notebook, Neighborhood Union Box 5, Archives Department, Trevor Arnett Library, Atlanta University, Atlanta, Georgia. Used by permission of Atlanta University Center Woodruff Library.

1912, better quarters were sought in 1914. On 11 June 1914, the members agreed to purchase property at 41 Leonard Street for $1,800, at a 6 percent interest rate, with a down payment of $100 and $12 monthly payments. All members agreed to pay $1 for the first payment. For security reasons, someone from the Leonard Street Orphanage was to occupy the building until a suitable matron was employed or the building rented.

Purchase of the new center did not eliminate the programs held at neighborhood schools. What had started as a result of need had proved a highly workable and innovative concept. During summer 1914, the union organized three summer schools, two of them under direct union control. At those two schools, 446 children were enrolled and taught by a paid staff of nine teachers. The children attended school half a day every day for four weeks. During the previous summers, the schools had lasted six weeks, but the shortage of funds necessitated a reduction of the time in 1914. The summer sessions exposed youngsters to calisthenics, industries, and talks on good conduct, and singing groups were formed. At the end of the session, samples of the students' work were exhibited.

In 1913–14, involvement with other Atlanta institutions and social service organizations expanded. Demonstrations of classes conducted by the union and sessions of mothers' meetings were held as part of the Child's Welfare and Public Health Exhibit in December 1913. Over four thousand persons participated in the exhibit, which also publicized the union. Because of its specific interest in "wayward girls," the union assisted the Fulton County "Colored" Juvenile Probation Officer, Gary Moore, in placing neglected children in reformatories and orphanages or with families. However, in all of its work with city, county, and state organizations, the union insisted that its objectives not be jeopardized. In fact, in agreeing to assist the Associated Charities of Atlanta, the group clearly affirmed, "our method of relief in the neighborhood is to have each neighbor feel the responsibility of his next door neighbor."[30] Reports on the union's work in 1913–14 suggest the organizational strength which had developed:

> When families are in need, the director passes the word along and the present need is supplied. Two worthy families were cared for by the neighbors for a month, food and rent being looked after.
> Three families, victims of fire, were aided.
> Fifty-eight sick cases reported and aided.
> Money for rent loaned to family which was put into the street one cold Sunday night.
> One old woman sent to Almshouse.
> One district Neighborhood organized.
> One Neighborhood Union organized, and it has done excellent work; among other things it has made eight hundred fifty calls and conducted vacation school of one hundred ninety-six pupils.
> Two girls' clubs organized.
> One boys' club organized with twenty-five boys the first night.[31]

The Neighborhood Union reached a new plateau in September 1915, when the Neighborhood House was officially opened. Although the house was located on one of the worst streets of the city, where saloons were abundant and the crime rate high, the members immediately began to make it a community center. When young boys threw bricks at the door of the house because they had been ejected for improper behavior, thought was given as to how they could be made a working part of the center while still being made to realize that a few would not be permitted to destroy what was for all. Carribel Cole of New York was hired as director in charge of the house. In her previous employment as a physical education instructor and playground director, she had developed skills which proved useful in curbing the children's unruly behavior.

As part of the union's beautification program, a professor of agriculture from Morehouse College helped area residents to cultivate gardens on land near Neighborhood House. Two arc lights to be placed near the house were requested in 1917 from Z. Nespor, field secretary of the National War Department Commission. Even though they attempted to involve all persons from the community and to instill in them a sense of pride and accomplishment, the union members still felt that their work was being hampered by the "loungers and vicious people" who resided in the area.[32] In spite of those obstacles, seven additional neighborhoods were brought into the union; by 1919 there were nineteen zones.

Education. Two major campaigns attest to the Neighborhood Union's ability to work effectively with many segments of the community. The major objective of one campaign was "to work for better conditions of the Negro schools of Atlanta." As late as 1901, many whites strongly opposed any effort to establish more and better educational institutions for Afro-Americans. In that year, Georgia Gov. Allen Chandler made a public statement which expressed the attitudes of a large segment of Georgia's white population: "Do you know that you can stand on the dome of the capitol of Georgia and see more negro colleges with endowments than you can see white schools? I do not believe in the higher education of the darky. He should be taught the trades, but when he is taught the fine arts, he gets educated above his caste and it makes him unhappy."[33] Governor Chandler's remarks, although made in reference to institutions of higher education, were used by some whites to justify the inertia of public school officials at lower levels.

Because of the magnitude of the task ahead in working for better conditions in the schools, the union created a new committee, Social Improvement, in 1913. The members met regularly for about six months and investigated every school for Afro-Americans in Atlanta. Before the visitations, captains were given explicit instructions to follow as they collected data. The investigation revealed that the condition of the schools was generally deplorable. Because of inadequate facilities, many students were forced to attend on double shifts. Such shifts, of course, overworked teachers. Even with double shifts, classrooms were overcrowded. For the 1913–14 school year, there was a seating capacity of 4,102 in the schools for black children, but enrollment was 6,163. As a result, 2,061 students had to attend school in double sessions. Only ninety-seven teachers, the majority female, were instructing 6,163 students.[34] All schools except the Younge Street and Gary Street schools were found to have unsanitary conditions.

Once the Social Improvement Committee presented its findings to the union's Board of Management, it was decided that, if substantive improvements were to be achieved in the school system, other factions of the community would have to become involved. Committee members visited every influential white woman in Atlanta to solicit her support. Many of the white women visited the schools and confirmed the findings of the commit-

21

Fig. 21. In 1915, the Neighborhood Union of Atlanta purchased a house to serve as a community center and as headquarters for its many social service activities. *Courtesy of Atlanta University Center Woodruff Library.*

Fig. 22. The Neighborhood Union invited the community to an open house in 1915, to meet the staff and learn about the many services and programs of the organization. *Courtesy of the Atlanta University Center Woodruff Library.*

Fig. 23. Neighborhood Union open house in 1915. *Courtesy of the Atlanta University Center Woodruff Library*

22

23

Fig. 24. Day care for community children was one of the most important programs of the Neigborhood Union. Photo taken in 1915. *Courtesy of the Atlanta University Center Woodruff Library.*

tee. In groups of two and three, committee members also visited the mayor, all City Council members, and influential white pastors to plead for better schools for Afro-Americans. To gain cooperation from the black community, several mass meetings were held, at which a slide lecture was given depicting conditions of the schools. Placards were posted and black ministers were asked to rally their congregations behind the campaign.

A petition was prepared for presentation to the Board of Education, requesting (1) abolition of double sessions, (2) a school in South Atlanta, and (3) provisions for "feebleminded and defective children." The ultimate aim of the petition was to reduce crime and "to make of our children good citizens."[35] Annadel King, secretary of the Petition Committee, read the document to the Neighborhood Union's general membership at its meeting at the YMCA on 19 August 1913. At that meeting, captains from various churches reported on their visits to homes where children were out of school and indicated what they had done to bring the parents' attention to the fact.

The network established by the Neighborhood Union expanded, as more citizens became intimately involved in the campaign. Every opportunity was used to inform the people about their rights as taxpayers. Whether or not they owned property, all residents were still required to pay a personal tax which, Hope said, entitled them to certain public benefits. The campaign and home visitations also brought to the attention of the union children who were unable to attend school because of insufficient clothing or lack of vaccinations. Where clothes were needed, they were provided, and parents were told of sites where their children would be vaccinated.

To double-check the survey findings, the union appointed a committee of six to visit the schools on the first day of the fall term. Parents also were requested to visit. On 8 September 1913, the committee was to determine how many children were refused admittance because of lack of seats. Because the situation was so explosive, committee members were admonished not to interfere with the duties of the principal but simply to request that children who were to be sent home for any reason be sent first to them. Hope herself made the assignments for the first day visitations. Findings substantiated the union's earlier survey, and those data, along with pictures of the schools, were sent to the school superintendent, the Board of Education, the City Council, and the president of the Lady Board.

The union's meeting on 28 October 1913, heard reports on the status of the campaign. Walter Rich, a city councilman, had been distressed by the furor created by two groups of black men over the South Atlanta school question. In that district there was no public school, and 170 children were not receiving an education. After hearing statements by union members,

Rich agreed to push for the South Atlanta school. Mrs. Pickett, a white, attended the 28 October meeting to discuss how white women could advance the union's cause. A Press Committee was formed so that any statements which reached the public would represent accurately the intentions and actions of the union.

The well-organized campaign brought positive results and demonstrated the ability of black women to work together for the common good. The salaries of black teachers were raised; a makeshift school was established in South Atlanta; and black men joined to work for better schools. The union's Committee of Investigation of the Schools agreed not to disband "until better school conditions prevail for colored children."[36] The decision not to disband proved wise, for soon the women mobilized the community to protest a decision to drop the literary course after the sixth grade and substitute an industrial course only. Again the women were successful.

A census by city school officials in spring 1923 indicated that, of a school population of 52,000, 34,250 persons (66 percent) were white and 17,750 (34 percent) were Afro-Americans. By September 1923, it was estimated that 18,000 black children (33 percent of the total) and 36,000 white children (67 percent) were eligible to attend a public school. There were only twelve public school buildings for Afro-Americans; two more, David T. Howard and a junior-senior high school, were being erected. At the close of the school day on Friday, 28 September 1923, the twelve buildings had a total seating capacity of 4,887, but the total enrollment was 11,469 (64 percent of those eligible), even though students who were to attend the David T. Howard school had been told not to enroll. The buildings could seat only 42 percent of those who had enrolled. Further inequities existed: only 159 teachers were employed to teach the 11,469 pupils, making an average of 72 students per teacher. The shortage of facilities and teachers forced 9,028 children to attend a double session, 727 a triple session, and 898 a 2.5-hour school day plus recess. In the entire public school system, only 203 black pupils — less than 2 percent — were receiving a full day of schoolwork.[37]

On 29 September 1923, a letter was sent to the key public official of Atlanta deploring school conditions for Afro-Americans and asking for immediate redress. In collecting the data, preparing a letter, and sending it to public officials before the end of the next day, the union displayed the kind of vigilance that had made its earlier campaign successful. Nevertheless, the public school system of Atlanta maintained the dual system of education which sanctioned gross inequities between whites and Afro-Americans. Although some of the union requests were honored, agitation for improvements continued even after 1925. The school campaign had fostered community cohesion to sustain the residents as they combatted other evils. The campaign also reinforced the union's image as a group of dedicated women who were willing to challenge existing attitudes and programs.

Health. The Neighborhood Union's next campaign was to improve community health. In 1915, it was estimated that, nationwide, $300,000 was lost each year as a result of sickness and death among Afro-Americans. Of that figure, half—enough to provide houses and six months of schooling for every black child in the South—could have been saved with proper health education and care. The diseases most often fatal to Afro-Americans were diseases of infancy (27 percent of deaths), tuberculosis (18 percent), pneumonia (11 percent), heart disease (8 percent), Bright's Disease (7 percent), and diarrhea (6 percent).[38]

Medical personnel and others understood that, in addition to treating Afro-Americans' diseases, preventive medicine and health education must be offered. The executive committee of the National Negro Business League (NNBL) began a program to combat health problems before they arose. Organizations throughout the nation were called to participate in National Health Week. Many states had previously sponsored a health week or health days, but there had never been a national movement among Afro-Americans. The national efforts were to be linked, with Virginia serving as a model. The objectives, as defined by Booker T. Washington, founder of the NNBL, were to reduce the high death rate among Afro-Americans and to improve their health so that they might prosper in business, obtain property, and acquire an education. He noted that although Afro-Americans had in the past expressed differing opinions on other subjects, "There is no room for difference here."[39]

The plan of action for Health Week called for prayer for better health conditions. On Sunday, 21 March 1915, ministers would preach a special health sermon and structure their services to include discussions of health conditions. Each community would appoint a Clean-Up Committee to arrange the local program for Health Week. Specific duties for Clean-Up Week included cleaning the home, repairing buildings on farms, cleaning the toilets at schools and churches, and protecting the well or spring water.

The national Health Week campaigns continued through 1925. National contests were held and prizes awarded to the communities which demonstrated the greatest cooperation and progress. City committees obtained the support of local boards of education and health departments. The national impact was so great that the U.S. Public Health Service became involved. In 1922, Dr. Roscoe C. Brown, director of the services' work for Afro-

Americans, spearheaded the national efforts. The Health Week campaigns attempted to develop a level of health awareness among Afro-Americans which would last throughout the year. Some progress was made, but the health problems were in many cases only indicative of other social evils which had not been resolved. Poor housing led to poor health, which led to insufficient health care, which slowed economic growth, in a never-ending cycle.

In Atlanta, the Neighborhood Union's Committee of Investigation of the Schools had identified serious health problems among black schoolchildren. They found many who were unable to attend school or, if they did attend, to learn what was being taught. The union sponsored a meeting of leading Afro-Americans in Atlanta. A general committee was formed, including representatives from the social service departments of several black organizations. Hope served on the general committe, but Dr. A.D. Jones was elected president. Using the Neighborhood Union's neighborhood plan, the committee divided the city into sixteen zones in which a thorough investigation of health conditions would be conducted. The Atlanta Anti-Tuberculosis Association, founded in 1907, agreed to cooperate in the effort during summer 1914. The initial Atlanta Health Campaign resulted in the passage of ordinances "eliminating out-houses or 'priveys,' and discarded wells. Landlords and owners were required to provide cistern water, and garbage had to be removed regularly from sections where Afro-Americans lived."[40]

To sustain the health improvements, a health center was opened in June 1916, in a four-room building owned by the union; the center was the only one for Afro-Americans in Atlanta. Doctors and nurses volunteered time to staff the center and presented lectures on preventive health care. To involve the whole community in the health campaign, the union initiated an "Atlanta Clean-Up and Paint-Up Campaign." Schoolchildren conducted the survey of what needed to be done.[41]

By 1919, Hope held a fulltime position in the Colored Department of the Atlanta Anti-Tuberculosis Association. Drawing upon her experience with the Neighborhood Union, she organized the Afro-American community for an extensive Cleanup Campaign. In the sixteen fully operational zones, 143 chairpersons and subchairpersons were appointed. The 143 workers visited 5,406 homes, reaching 23,771 occupants. A special worker assigned to the visitation team reached 16,526 persons. During each visit, the occupants were urged not only to participate in the campaign but also to encourage others to join. The workers also gave preventive health care talks to schoolchildren and helped to organize courses to be offered at the Social Service Institute at Morehouse College in September 1919. The courses, designed for zone chairpersons and volunteer workers, included a child welfare course; a home nursing course taught by Ludie Andrews, head nurse of the Colored Department of Grady Hospital; a course in the care and preparation of foods for babies; and a course in community service taught by Gary Moore, the former probation officer who was soon to become the first director of the Atlanta School of Social Work.[42]

Realizing that many of the health problems could precipitate epidemics, Hope secured two positions for health education workers through the Anti-Tuberculosis Association. Carrie Dukes, a Spelman College graduate, was employed through the Neighborhood Union as the worker for Afro-Americans. A health exhibit in black neighborhoods in December 1919, during Mid-Way Carnival Week, concluded activities for the year.[43]

Under the auspices of the Atlanta Anti-Tuberculosis Association, the Neighborhood Union and other organizations participated in Negro National Health Week on 3–9 April 1921. In an effort to involve the community in the campaign for a sanitary city, the Colored Department of the association organized an executive committee composed of representatives from the Chamber of Commerce, life insurance companies, Atlanta Urban League, Ministerial Association, public schools, YMCA, nursing services, black colleges, and the Neighborhood Union. Several subcommittees were formed within the larger body to perform specific tasks. All of the zone chairpersons — those ultimately responsible for seeing that the work in the community was done — were women.

All activities for the week centered on the theme, "Burn, Bury, Beautify." A film, *Solving the Boy Problem in Beautifying Vacant Lots,* was shown in conjunction with lectures to over 2,400 schoolchildren who pledged to support the campaign. Three-minute addresses were also made to church congregations on Clean-Up Sunday, 3 April 1921. Distributed throughout the city were fifty thousand health leaflets and two hundred placards listing items to be buried.[44]

A boy squadron organized through the YMCA and a girl squadron from the public schools greatly assisted in the cleanup effort. Tasks included cleaning vacant lots, digging trenches to bury rubbish, and planting flowers. There had always been a shortage of playgrounds for black children in the city. After the boys had cleared several lots, two of the lots in one zone were designated as playgrounds. The responsibility for supervising and maintaining the playgrounds was given to the youngsters.

As the executive committee surveyed the work which needed to be done, its members observed that of 180 places reported as unsanitary in 1921, none had been among the 104 reported in 1917. In 1917, the major complaints had been of wells and surface toilets needing repair because of plumbing disorders. By 1921, the major complaints were lack of toilets and adequate water facilities. Of 180 places reported as unsanitary, 76 (42 percent) were cited because of lack of toilets and plumbing. Table 7 summarizes the major activities and the results in 1921.[45]

Conflict with the Urban League. Interest in the Neighborhood Union spread to other southern states and prompted the National League on Urban Conditions Among Negroes to attempt to persuade the union to affiliate. As it always had, the union refused to become affiliated with another group, but the league persisted. Eugene K. Jones, associate director of the league, requested that the union send data on its organizing efforts to women in other states via the league's headquarters.[46] In 1925, the union's refusal to affiliate with the National Urban League renewed the old tension between the two organizations and posed a threat to the union's financial stability. After refusing the league's affiliation request, the union was informed that it would be eliminated from the funding list of the Atlanta Community Chest. It was only through the efforts of Atlanta citizens, led by Mrs. Willie Daniels and Charlie Green, that the action was abandoned. The citizens were able to prove that the union was of value to the city and that statements made by the league's secretary were erroneous.[47] The manner in which the union met the league's attack reflected the members' experience in dealing with hostile, recalcitrant citizens and public officials. Their accurate financial records and documentation of program activities contradicted the false accusations.

Conclusion

The Neighborhood Union, free kindergartens, day nurseries, and orphanages in Atlanta emerged because black women were willing to provide for others. During the period 1895–1925, each organization, although created by women, involved the entire community. In time, because of the proven commitment and success of the women, the organizations also promoted racial understanding and cooperation.

Of the self-help and social service organizations in Atlanta, the Neighborhood Union assisted the most people and became the most noted. This success was not by chance. Hope's organizational and leadership skills, the level of commitment of the club members, the desire for betterment on the part of community residents, and the support given by other established

Table 7. *Neighborhood Union Health and Home Improvement Activities, 1921*

Activity		Results	
Homes visited	5,513	Houses repaired	40
People reached	23,513	Streets paved	2
Health pamphlets* distributed	582	Ditches filled	12
Posters distributed	80	Houses wired for lights	2
Report blanks and health hints		Toilets repaired	1
distributed	12,220	Sewers installed	1
Lime distributed (barrels)	25	Street lights installed	1
		Fences erected	2
		Houses painted	1
		Streets improved	20
		Concrete steps and	
		driveway	1

*Pamphlets: "Transmission of Disease by Flies" and "Malaria"

Source: "Report of Negro National Health Week—April 3–9, 1921," Neighborhood Union Box 14–B, 1914, 1915, 1916, Archives Department, Trevor Arnett Library, Atlanta University, Atlanta Georgia. Used by permission of the Atlanta University Center Woodruff Library.

organizations and white citizens contributed to the union's influence and its ability to effect change.

Even though the Neighborhood Union continuously expanded its objectives, it remained loyal to its orignial purpose. In Hope's words, the women realized that "the home was the basis of a people's development. Here fundamental lessons of system, thrift, law, and sacrifices are learned, and each community should try to bring its people together that they may discuss and apply these principles." Those women who worked for social betterment saw as the most meaningful result of their labor the fact that "in our neighborhood people own their homes, educate their children, and make further provisions for the continuance of prosperity in their own homes."[48]

The efforts of the Urban League to bring the Neighborhood Union under its control show that the union was accorded a great deal of respect and cooperation. It stands as an excellent example of what a self-help social service organization should be.

CHAPTER 8

Social Service Programs in Tennessee: Focus on Nashville

Social and Economic Conditions

As Lester Lamon notes, "The overriding feature of life for black Tennesseans in the early twentieth century was the separate community — separated from the recognized white mainstream partly by force and partly by choice."[1] Geographical, social, and economic factors helped to maintain this separation. The majority of the Afro-Americans in Tennessee in the early 1900s lived in rural areas; 48 percent lived in the western third of the state. Dependent upon farming as their economic base, most black Tennesseans continued to reside in rural areas through 1925.[2] However, Nashville, in the middle of Tennessee, received a great deal of attention because of its urban orientation and the activities of its black citizens.

According to Lamon, Afro-Americans in Nashville were relatively free from economic pressure. According to some leading black citizens of the time, this economic freedom did not represent economic strength and interdependence. Griggs, founder and editor of the black newspaper, *The Globe*, stated that Afro-Americans in Nashville and throughout the South were weak economically. He called for Afro-Americans to achieve economic unity by rejecting ideas of racial inferiority and dependence upon white paternalism.[3]

In August 1900, the National Negro Business League (NNBL) met in Boston, Massachusetts, to organize and to establish its programs. From the beginning, women were included as NNBL speakers and officers. The NNBL held its annual meetings in cities throughout the United States, attracting many participants. Local branches were organized as support for the league grew. The first Tennessee branch was organized by Nashville businessman

James C. Napier in 1902. The annual national NNBL meeting was held in Nashville in 1903. In 1908, the Business and Professional League was formed, with Andrew N. Johnson as the head. The group announced that it would cooperate with the NNBL but would remain separate.

Chapters of the NNBL in Tennessee grew to sixteen by 1909, with seven in East Tennessee, five in the central region, and four in the West. By 1910, there were three hundred local branches in thirty-one states. However, complaints about the League's and its branches' lack of effectiveness were heard as early as 1907. In Nashville, an editorial in *The Globe* was titled "Will It Sleep Always—Local Negro Business League Taking Rip Van Winkle Snooze." Several subsequent editorials and articles in *The Globe* challenged the black businessmen of the area to address problems and concerns unique to the black economic community.[4]

Partly in response to the challenges by *The Globe*, the Negro Board of Trade was organized in 1911 in Nashville to develop interest in commercial and industrial activities. The members included barbers, architects, bankers, and other businessmen. Their goals were to enhance the civil and social lives of Afro-Americans and to teach racial unity and cooperation. The organization proved successful and by 1925 had established Hadley Park and Napier Playground, secured funds for the Carnegie Library, aided the victims of the East Nashville Fire, and hired Elizabeth Kelly to work as a probation officer with delinquent children.[5]

When the Tennessee legislature began to enact new Jim Crow laws in 1905, Afro-Americans adopted policies and actions considered counterproductive by some whites and Afro-Americans. For example, a boycott of the public transportation system was organized in July 1905 to protest the new laws. To bring news of the boycott to the black populace, Afro-Americans founded a newspaper, *The Globe*. The climax of the boycott came on 29 August 1905, when sixteen Afro-Americans obtained a charter for the Union Transportation Company. When various problems forced the company to abandon the line during summer 1906, Afro-Americans had to return to the segregated system.[6]

Efforts to end segregation in other transportation systems also were made in the early 1900s. Because of the deplorable conditions of the waiting room used by Afro-Americans, Georgia Edwards of Chattanooga, Tennessee, filed a formal complaint against the Nashville, Chattanooga and St. Louis Railway in 1907. After a hearing, the Interstate Commerce Commission ruled that equal facilities must be provided for all patrons of the railway. The railroad lost on appeal, but enforcement of the ruling was lax.

Interracial Cooperation for Social Services for Afro-Americans

Nashville's self-help and social service programs for Afro-Americans fell into two distinct groups, those developed through interracial cooperation and those developed by black women. Of the five regions treated in this book, Nashville was among the first to attempt to remedy social problems by involving both whites and Afro-Americans directly. This attempt in Nashville reflected the personal philosophy, professional interests, and unflagging efforts of one man, Dr. George Edmund Haynes. As we have seen, Dr. Haynes headed Fisk University's Social Science Department. Despite the prevailing rigid racial separation, Dr. Haynes believed that cooperative efforts by whites and Afro-Americans were the key to economic and social advancement for black people. He saw white involvement as necessary, because only whites could insure justice for black citizens.

In 1908, social service projects with racially mixed founding bodies began to provide day care for Afro-American children. The Methodist Training School cooperated with the all-black Missionary Society of Capers Chapel to establish a Bethlehem House Settlement house in an impoverished neighborhood. Encouraged by its progess, Dr. Haynes in 1911 began to interest the black and white residents of Nashville in forming an umbrella committee to direct all social service programs for Afro-Americans. After a meeting of representatives from several organizations on 16 May 1911, it was agreed that a permanent, central committee of twenty-five persons would be formed "to coordinate all organizations among white citizens that aim for social betterment among Colored people, to start and develop needed agencies for uplift among Negroes, and to protect the community from well meaning but misdirected efforts."[7] The committee was to include representatives of the Minister's Alliances of the Methodist Episcopal (ME), African Methodist Episcopal (AME), and Baptist Churches; the Rock City Medical Academy; and the Principals' Association. Such a membership would, of course, include more men than women, even though it was clear that women became more directly involved than men in the actual development and operation of social service and self-help programs.

On 27 May 1911, in a letter to interested persons, Dr. Haynes outlined:

Suggested Steps That May Be Taken for Improving Conditions Among Colored People of Nashville:
1) efforts to secure library facilities; 2) improvement of housing conditions in Colored neighborhoods; 3) encouragement of work such as getting the children of the several Colored schools to take part in beautifying the grounds around the school building; 4) development of playground places and facilities; 5) provi-

sions for furnishing opportunities for vocational training for those already at work; and 6) a home for black working girls.[8]

The suggested activities clearly were those sanctioned by the National Urban League; Haynes sought to involve Nashville's Afro-Americans and whites within the proven framework of that national organization. The name of his group, the Nashville League on Conditions Among Negroes, points to its status as a chapter of the national body. In fact, to meet the demand for skilled leaders, the National Urban League had affiliated with Fisk University in Nashville, Atlanta Baptist College in Georgia, and Talledega College in Alabama. Graduates of the social science programs at these schools would receive additional training at the New York School of Philanthropy. By January 1912, the Nashville League on Conditions Among Negroes had as members representatives of the majority of black alliances, clubs, and associations in the city. Three principal goals in that year were to secure improved housing for black residents, to establish occupational training programs in the night schools, and to elicit greater cooperation between Afro-Americans and whites.[9]

The Bethlehem House Settlement proved instrumental in achieving the last two objectives of the Nashville League. When the Bethlehem House Settlement relocated to its new quarters at the corner of Ninth Avenue and Cedar Street in 1913, Fisk University became closely allied with the work at Bethlehem. During the first fifteen months in the new facility, two hundred families were aided by workers who accepted the responsibility as part of their Christian duties. The settlement also reported that 350 individuals were enrolled in mothers' clubs, cooking classes, sewing school, kindergarten, Campfire Girls, boys' and men's clubs, and Bible classes. There were four permanent staff members, all women, and a housekeeper, Sally Sawyer. Fisk students in field practicums for Sociology and Bible Study and those training for social service fields assisted the paid workers. The students conducted kindergarten classes, playground activities, and domestic science, art, and carpentry classes. Members of the all-white Woman's Council of the Methodist Episcopal Church-South, provided $1,000, a significant portion of the operating funds for 1914. The settlement was administered by a biracial board whose members were selected by the Woman's Council, Fisk University, and the Methodist Training School.[10]

Enrollment in the various activities of the settlement increased in 1914, and its program objectives were broadened. The Campfire Girls numbered twenty; fifty-four persons enrolled in three domestic science courses; average daily attendance was thirty children in the kindergarten and forty-six in the sewing school; approximately one hundred children attended the Sunday "Bible Story Hour"; and fifty boys participated in the junior and intermediate boys' clubs. As part of the outreach program, visits were made to two hundred fifty families when illness, death, delinquency of a youth, or other problems were reported. Staff members, along with the Joint Workingmen's Loan Fund Committee, helped two hundred black families to survive periods of unemployment; cooperation with the Charity Organization Society also brought relief for black families. As an integral part of the outreach program, a training course for social workers was structured around the experiences of the settlement."[11]

Also in 1914, two missionaries who were taking advanced courses at Peabody College were given fellowships of twenty-five dollars a month and assigned halftime employment at the settlement: Lula Crim, a former teacher at Payne and volunteer in Africa, supervised practicum students from Fisk, and Emma K. Olmstead, a former student at the Methodist Training School, worked with mothers and young women at the center.[12] With the new building secured, the fellowship program was expanded during the 1915–16 academic year. The Woman's Council provided one fellowship and the National Urban League another. Those fellows, Carrie L. Dukes and Forrester B. Washington, both Afro-Americans, were to live at the center with the three employees. Dr. Haynes anticipated that two other fulltime Fisk students would enroll in the social service course and begin practicum experiences, thus providing more assistance for the workers at Bethlehem.

With full administrative support from Fisk, student interest, and evident community need, Dr. Haynes planned to strengthen the social service course so that students available for the settlement and similar institutions would be better prepared. Undergraduates who chose elective courses in the Social Science Department were to receive fuller instruction. The program of supervised field experiences was refined to include exposure to juvenile probation, occupational assistance, and relief work.[13] The settlement, however, would still serve as the field laboratory. The National Urban League's philosophies and objectives obviously had been incorporated into Dr. Haynes' design for Fisk's Social Science Department. In fact, the 1916 Fisk University catalog indicated that the staff of the Bethlehem House Settlement and members of the Social Science Department at Fisk were to work directly with the Urban League: "The future aim [of that affiliation] is to bring the university into closer relation with the conditions among colored people in Nashville and to seek the cooperation of Negro colleges in other communities in developing this much needed phase of education."[14]

Most of the students who enrolled in the Social Science Department and took advantage of the practicum experiences at the Bethlehem House Settlement were black females. White females served as fellows, and the Woman's Council continued to support phases of the work; the Methodist Training School discontinued its support in late 1914. Because of the Bethlehem House Settlement's positive and enduring success, a branch settlement opened in South Nashville in 1918. In addition to providing many benefits to those who took advantage of the services, the Bethlehem experiment proved not only that interracial cooperation was possible, but that it was valuable to both races. The black female practicum students gained skills and became aware of sociological principles which made them more responsive to the needs of other Afro-Americans. Through the student involvement, Dr. Haynes was able to convince Fisk University administrators that the department he had created was a worthy one.

A fire on 21 March 1916, in East Nashville, affecting 2,500 black and white residents further convinced Fisk administrators of the need for the innovative department. After the fire, Fisk, through the Social Science Department, established a relief committee to assist those who had been left homeless and destitute. Fisk's senior class was dismissed from college responsibilities to join in the relief effort with black students from the State Normal School, Meharry Medical College, and Roger Williams University. Observers noted that many of the black students and teachers obviously had been trained for "scientific social work." White not only praised the work of the students but also invited them to their headquarters to confer until the work was finished.[15]

As a result of the cooperation during the crisis, the Public Welfare League, composed of black and white citizens, was formed. At a patriotic war service meeting sponsored by the Bethlehem House and the Public Welfare League in 1917, the two organizations were described as groups "emphasizing the patriotic necessity of constructive community work among blacks to prevent breaking up of families and increase of children appearing before courts, to resist the new dangers to health from inadequate food and fuel, and to prevent dangers that threaten the colored population."[16]

Programs Organized by Black Women

In spite of joint efforts by the races, many self-help and social service programs were initiated by black women only. Of these, two served as proto-

Fig. 25. After the East Nashville Fire of 21 March 1916, relief work to aid victims, under the leadership of Dr. George Haynes of Fisk University, encouraged interracial cooperation. *Courtesy of the Fisk University Special Collections and Archives.*

types for others; one used a multi-faceted approach, while the other concentrated on an identified need of a specific group within the black community.

The Phyllis Wheatley Club. Organized in 1895, the Phyllis Wheatley Club established its headquarters in the AME Publishing House on Public Square. During the club's early years, the members accepted as their charge assistance to the poor of Nashville and missions in Africa. Therefore, a Charitable Department was organized under the leadership of Mrs. Lewis Winter, to provide food baskets and other services for the needy. Clothing and shoes donated by merchants were also distributed among the poor of Nashville.[17]

Because of their similar goals and objectives, the Phyllis Wheatley Club sought affiliation with the National Federation of Afro-American Women and sent Emma J. Perry as its representative to the national meeting held in Buffalo, New York. In 1897, the club hosted the first biannual meeting of the National Association of Colored Women (NACW), formed from a union of the National Federation of Afro-American Women and the National Colored Women's League. The Wheatley Club continued its affiliation with NACW through 1925. It also remained one of the most active organizations of the City Federation of Colored Women's Clubs of Nashville.

As part of its social efforts, the club maintained the Phyllis Wheatley Room in Mercy Hospital. During the tenure of the third president, Ellen Tyree, the club work at Mercy flourished. Besides making garments for the sick, the women performed volunteer services for the hospital. However, during the presidency of Mrs. C.M. Taylor, the work at Mercy was discontinued, as the club concentrated upon obtaining a house to serve as an operational base. To save for the purchase of a building, the club opened its first bank account, at the Penny Savings Bank, a black establishment, with $68. In 1907, some of the funds were sent to a mission teacher in Africa. In the same year, through the designation of departments, the basic internal structure of the club was set. Members served in one of six departments: Temperance, Social Purity, Educational, Charitable, Mothers', Literary, and Industrial. As an outgrowth of the Charitable Department, the club in 1921 decided to purchase and maintain a home for aged women. That project, the club's priority goal, was completed by 1925.[18]

Day Homes' Club. As in other southern cities, in Nashville many children were left unattended at home while their parents went off to work. To provide food and training for the children, Nettie Langston (Mrs. J.C.) Napier proposed the establishment of the second program, a Day Homes' Club. By early January 1907, Napier was the president of the day home, known as Porter Homestead, at 618 Fourth Avenue South. During a meeting of interested women on 14 January 1907, the club developed a constitution; elected officers; appointed Dr. Josie E. Wells, specialist in diseases of women and children, physician-in-charge; and decided to seek a woman to serve as superintendent of the home. Women willing to serve as vice-presidents for the city's wards would also be sought.[19]

Nettie Napier convened a mass meeting of black women in February 1907 to discuss the future of the day home concept in Nashville. Before discussing the key agenda item, participants reported on current activities involving women. Reports on temperance and education elicited much reaction. Dr. Wells, in discussion after the education presentation by Minnie Lou Crosthwaite, stated that even though there was opposition to women becoming physicians, young women should be encouraged to attend not only nursing schools but medical schools as well.[20] After the general discussion and reports, and after having carefully prepared the audience, Napier delivered a presentation on neglected children. She called upon those present to assist her and others in building the day home into a strong, effective organization.

Even though the meeting generated some interest, after eighteen months of operation, the day home was floundering. There were few active club members; accommodations were meager; additional furniture, clothing for the children, and fuel were needed; and the treasury was empty. Original plans for the home had specified that it would be open only during the day. However, when the irregular work hours of some of the mothers interfered with that plan, arrangements were made to keep ten to twelve children as boarders throughout the week. The new hours made it necessary to secure a new building. The need could not be met without sizable contributions.

Parents were charged $1.95 per week per child; if two or more children from the same household attended, the fee was adjusted so that the parents paid less for the additional children. Even with the fees paid by parents, monthly expenses often exceeded the home's income. The matron was paid $15 a month; rent was $20 a month; $8 to $10 were allocated monthly for the cook; $35 to $40 were spent monthly on food; and tons of coal were purchased for heating and cooking. In an article in *The Globe* on 30 October 1908, Napier wrote that the club had attempted to raise money through many means, but if more funds were not forthcoming, the day home could not survive.[21]

Clearly, funds were available in Nashville's black community to support programs. Lack of funds cannot be the reason the Porter Homestead was unable to survive. As we have seen, a combination of financial efforts and broad community involvement could achieve social service success in Nashville.

Millie E. Hale Hospital and Auxiliary. Although health problems were of concern to all black Nashville residents, on 1 July 1916, Millie E. (Mrs. J.H.) Hale decided that she would accept the challenge to provide better health care for Afro-Americans and established a hospital. Beginning with twelve beds, the Millie E. Hale Hospital grew by 1923 to include one hundred beds and a staff of three physicians and twenty-six nurses.

From its inception, the hospital attempted to provide more than medical assistance for those who came to the facility. The 1923 hospital report revealed that the fourteen-room house of Dr. and Mrs. J.H. Hale had been converted into a community center which housed a prenatal and baby welfare clinic and a free dispensary and clinic for adults. Institutes for women who desired to learn methods of community betterment and club work were also held at the center. Because Millie Hale was very interested in the physical development of the young, plots of land were purchased for playgrounds. Children were also admitted to free band concerts and open air moving pictures three nights a week. Moreover, 1,155 people received food, money, bedding, and coal; 400 sick people were provided with meals; nurses visited 7,687 homes to provide bedside care; and nurses were assigned to two medical dispensaries.[22]

The Millie E. Hale Hospital Auxiliary, functioning as a social service club, continued to implement the goals set by Mrs. Hale. With assistance from the hospital staff, the women served the black populace of Nashville through educational programs, home visitations, recreation, and relief. Health meetings were held; a monthly paper was published; the playground was maintained; and relief was given in the form of food, coal, and medical and surgical care. When necessary, money was also given to the needy. The accomplishments of the auxiliary were impressive. In 1925, the women placed five infants in suitable foster homes, arranged a picnic for seven thousand boys and girls, conducted cottage service for one hundred homes, trained twenty-five young women in social service skills, purchased an additional playground, organized boys' and girls' clubs, and assisted neglected wives in securing proper support.[23]

As the social service units of the hospital developed, so did its Nurse Training Department. By 1925 twenty-four women had graduated, and twenty-five, from various states, were enrolled in the program. The three-year nursing program included a course in social service and internships. Millie Hale, a graduate of Fisk University and herself a registered nurse, served as the department's superintendent. Practicum experiences for the student nurses were offered at the Millie E. Hale Hospital and received recognition from the American College of Surgeons. Meharry Medical College students provided some clinical work at the hospital's free outpatient clinic. The hospital officially closed in 1938, and Dr. Hale became head of the Department of Surgery at Meharry Medical College. Many of the social services of the hospital were maintained, however, because of the impact they had had on the black community.

Conclusions

In 1925, it seemed on the surface that interracial efforts had moved the races closer together in Nashville. Organizations with interracial memberships still existed, and programs produced by interracial efforts still operated. However, the black community was still largely separated geographically, socially, politically, and economically from the other people of Nashville. Black residents, many in substandard housing, continued to live in segregated neighborhoods. The more affluent Afro-Americans generally resided in Fisk University Place, a planned community developed in 1907 by the Abraham Lincoln Land Company, in the area around Fisk University. Afro-Americans could purchase land for one hundred dollars down and fifty cents a week, with no taxes or interest payments. A free deed was given in case of the buyer's death. When the lots went on sale, only seventy to one hundred remained unsold on the first day. *The Globe* carried a banner headline, "Like Forest Fire—Negroes Purchase Land in New Fisk University Place."[24] In 1925, economic and social status continued to separate groups of Afro-Americans; but all Afro-Americans remained apart from the larger society.

By 1925, Nashville had 89 churches and 115 ministers. In an effort to bridge the gap within the race, the Methodist Episcopal Church erected a magnificent social service building and gym; an outdoor tennis court and playground were also part of the facility. A trained staff of social service workers, principally female, supervised the programs housed in the building. Many black professionals rendered service to the black residents. In the city were fifty-two physicians, nine undertaking establishments, eight printing plants, and forty-eight barber shops. Afro-Americans also had established two large banks, thirty-five groceries and meat markets, and seventeen drug stores. Three publishing houses owned, operated, and controlled by Afro-Americans employed hundreds of Afro-Americans as bookkeepers, stenographers, and skilled and unskilled laborers. The publishing houses, valued at $1,500,000, furnished religious literature to black churches and organizations throughout the world.[25] The statistics appear impressive, but Nashville's black lower socioeconomic class was much larger than its middle class.

No matter how limited, the advancement that could be noted in Nashville's black population proved that interracial cooperation could produce positive results for the black community and the city. However, the cooperation was between middle-class individuals of both races, working for those who were considered less fortunate. The cooperation provided services for individuals but did not to any measurable degree affect racial segregation, which was still the rule in 1925.

Credit must be given to Dr. Haynes for his pioneering efforts to create strong connections between a national organization, an educational institution, the black community, and the white community. Without a doubt, a good deal was accomplished because of his perseverance, ideas, and ideals. Nevertheless, black women still constituted the principal implementors of those programs affecting the quality of life for black Tennesseans. Given the varied needs of the black community, the women's approaches provided more involvement by more women, greater public exposure for community concerns, and more positive results.

CHAPTER 9

Social Service Programs in Maryland: Focus on Baltimore

During the antebellum period, Baltimore at times had the largest free black population in the South. Having served as a gateway between the Lower South and the North, after the Civil War the city attracted many Afro-Americans who hoped to advance socially and economically. Because of the great numbers of Afro-Americans there and the prevailing white prejudices against them, many migrants and residents found that the city was not the haven they sought.

Still, Baltimore was the most cosmopolitan of the five regions discussed in this book. Blending northern and southern characteristics, Baltimore presented confusing inconsistencies. Despite what appeared to be significant gains for the black population, segregation and discrimination were commonplace. There as throughout the South, Jim Crow laws created two separate worlds which could meet only when the meeting was essential to whites. On the other hand, in Baltimore alone among southern cities, the black community was able to defeat a transportation segregation bill in 1904, although it was continually presented anew to the City Council during the next twenty years. An examination of Afro-American efforts in the fields of suffrage, health, and social services will suggest some of the ways in which women, and indeed all black citizens, faced conditions that in some ways differed but in other ways resembled conditions elsewhere in the South.

Suffrage and Racial Stereotyping

After the Reconstruction era, most black males in the South were systematically denied the right to participate actively in the political process. Women were generally excluded from the polls both before and after Reconstruction. As women throughout America began to agitate for the right to vote, many of the black male arguments concerning the appropriate role of women reemerged. It might seem that black women then would have had to struggle with complex questions concerning the relative importance of promoting the vote for women generally versus continuing to work for both black male suffrage and their own rights as Afro-Americans and women. Such questions did receive some consideration by the black female intelligensia but were not subjects of continuous public debate. At no time did feminist views, largely articulated by white women, become more important than racial issues. It was not a matter of choice for black women; they understood clearly that advancement as women was meaningless if not accompanied by racial advancement. This is not to suggest that concerns unique to women were of no importance to them, but racial issues were of greater importance. More often than not, the women found time, energy, and resources to respond to both gender and racial concerns.

In general, Baltimore, Maryland, was exceptional in its attitude toward black male suffrage. Although even here some whites tried to deny black men their political rights, the city by and large differed from the rest of the South. In 1909 a suffrage amendment was introduced in the Baltimore City Council which would have excluded black males from the polls. Afro-American women rallied to support the men, holding a mass meeting at Grace Presbyterian Church, at which several resolutions were passed. It was decided, first, that the women would urge the men to marshal forces against the disenfranchisement amendment and the Democratic Party and, second, that the women would locate unregistered men and teach them how to "manipulate" the ballot. Mrs. E.J. Cummings headed the group of sixty-five women who implemented the registration campaign. The amendment was defeated by approximately ten thousand votes, but the women formally organized themselves into the Woman's Civic League to prepare to defeat the amendment if it were presented again in 1911.[1]

After the 1909 success, Baltimore's black women began to debate their own suffrage. At its November 1911 meetings, the Du Bois Circle reached a consensus that women should have the right to vote. After a bill to require educational testing as a qualification for voting was presented to the Maryland legislature in 1912, black women requested that the test be applied to all. They saw the testing as a means to bar them from voting. Mary R. Burkett, in an editorial in the *Afro-American Ledger*, stated that she was a suffragist but realized that Baltimore, wanting southern trade, could not permit whites elsewhere to believe that its Afro-Americans were treated equally or given privileges not granted to other southern Afro-Americans. Women were not granted the right to vote in Baltimore, but, like other women in the South, they continued to petition for inclusion in the political process. State laws allowed women to vote in the 1912 presidential election in California, Colorado, Idaho, Utah, Washington, and Wyoming. When women in Kentucky were permitted to vote in school elections, 190 black women registered.[2]

In 1912, *The Crisis* openly advocated women's right to vote and published the following argument in its August 1912 issue:

> Women are workers; Women should vote.
> Women are taxpayers; Taxpayers should vote.
> Women have brains; Voting needs brains.
> Women organize, direct and largely support
> the family; Families should vote.
> Women are mothers of men; if men vote, why
> not women?

The editors felt that arguments for the right of men to vote also apply to women, especially black women.

The Crisis devoted its entire September 1912 issue to the suffrage question. Adella Hunt Logan argued that it was important for women to be involved in politics because of the effect political actions had upon their lives. Women could best judge selected governmental services because they were the principal consumers of such services. If women were granted the right to vote, they could use the ballot to advance the interests of society. Logan pointed to the wise use of the ballot by black women in western states and the active involvement of some women in the National Woman Suffrage Association.

Mary Church Terrell expressed opinions similar to Logan's and suggested that intelligent black men would not oppose the vote for women. The sex of the voter was not important to her so long as any eligible Afro-American was disenfranchised. Black women and men continued to debate the question of suffrage until the passage of the Nineteenth Amendment which enfranchised women.

When it became necessary, black men and women were able to put aside gender differences in order to address problems that concerned all members of the race. From 1917 to 1925, black men sought the support of women in defeating state and national legislation which appeared to affect only the men. Wisconsin was one of the first states to attempt to pass a law to prohibit and felonize intermarriage. On 23 January 1923, Arthur Copper sponsored a similar bill in the U.S. Senate. James Weldon Johnson, national secretary of the NAACP, telegraphed Hallie Q. Brown, president of the National Association of Colored Women, asking that black women rise up against the bill. Johnson felt that the bill, by implication, demeaned black women. Since most intermarriages were between black men and white women, the implication was that black men preferred white women to black women. Brown, using the wording of Johnson's telegram, sent a memo to the presidents and other officers of state NACW chapters. Both the Wisconsin and the federal bills were defeated.[3]

Other joint efforts enabled members of the race to accomplish a number of goals. A campaign to eliminate racially negative images from public view began with an attempt to clarify the name by which all Afro-Americans should be known. As early as 1904, Fannie Barrier Williams, an educator and a noted clubwoman, asked whether Afro-Americans needed a name other than "Negro". "Colored," "Negro," and "Afro-American," were used interchangeably. Dr. W.E.B. Du Bois suggested "Negro," while Dr. A.R. Abbott of Toronto stated that "Afro-American" was new and distinctive.[4]

Regardless of the name to be used by the ethnic group, women felt that whites demonstrated great discourtesy when they refused to address black women by the titles "Miss" or "Mrs." in print or speech. Even more appalling was whites' consistent use of negative caricatures of Afro-Americans on public billboards, in magazines, and in food product advertisements. In 1914 the NACW campaigned to protest the caricatures.[5]

Black women also protested the erection of the "Mammy Statue," by sculptor George Julian Zolnay, in Washington, D.C. The statue was to memorialize the "mammy" by having her hold a white child while her own child cried by her side. According to Mary Church Terrell, black women were aghast at the idea. Nevertheless, the *Baltimore Sun* reported that Mrs. A. Moore, Jr., daughter of a former slave, had given a site in Berryville, Virginia, on which to erect a church built in honor of "black mammies." The *Baltimore Sun* labeled the proposed church "a noble and a worthy monument." The *Afro-American Ledger* suggested that the church be built with the skills of the black sons lynched in the South. The statue was not erected.

Health

Tuberculosis was the most dreaded disease of the early twentieth century. The alley districts of southern cities often were labeled "lung blocks." Each city's black population geared up to meet the onslaught of the disease, but found itself unable to control its spread, due to lack of funds, facilities, and trained personnel. The few black physicians in each city were not permitted to practice in the white hospitals. Some black institutions helped develop hospitals or treatment centers for black residents; none, however, established separate tubercular treatment centers. In most states, the centers for tubercular patients were operated by the state government, and they never had enough beds to meet the needs of ill Afro-Americans. For example, the Hospital for the Insane in Nashville, Tennessee, was remodeled in 1918 to provide additional beds. The three-story building for the black insane had a patient capacity of three hundred, but the tuberculosis building was able to provide care for only sixty black patients.

In Baltimore, each house in the Afro-American districts reported at least one death from tuberculosis. As late as 1925, in or near Baltimore only two medical units provided care for black tubercular patients — Baltimore City Hospitals and the state sanitorium at Henryton, Maryland. Baltimore City Hospitals admitted black children and provided them with school classes under the direction of the Board of Education. Henryton had 110 beds but admitted only a limited number of patients from Baltimore, since it served the entire state. On 1 April 1926, 92 patients were confined at Henryton; the men's ward was full, and ten men were on the waiting list.

In spite of these efforts to provide adequate medical care, the *Baltimore Sun* reported in January 1925 that approximately one hundred thousand Afro-Americans in the city had to have decent housing, because the formerly confined diseases were spreading to whites and had become epidemic.

Provident Hospital, which had opened in June 1844, attempted to provide medical care to Baltimore's indigent Afro-Americans. The physicians at the hospital sustained all the expenses and solicited money from the city and state to improve the facility. A free dispensary, providing medicine for ten cents if the patient supplied the bottle, opened on Biddle Street in 1909. However, a maternity department for poor women and funds for the children's department were still needed. Until 1937, the hospital, owned and managed by Afro-Americans, was not staffed or equipped to handle tubercular patients on an inpatient basis.

To meet the need for trained personnel, Provident Hospital established a Nurses' Training School. The first trained black nurse in the state, Lillian Jeanette Henry, graduated in 1898. A Nurses Training School Relief Association was organized in 1913 to raise funds to ensure the continuation of the school. Baltimore, by 1923, had twenty graduate nurses, primarily alumnae of Provident's school.

The Baltimore Clean-Up Committee, as part of the national Health Week activities, gave residents hints on preventive medicine and suggestions for improving their diets and maintaining clean, orderly homes. The committee also publicized problems which contributed to the spread of disease and pointed out that schools for Afro-Americans were generally old, congested, and plagued with rats. One particular school, No. 116 on Druid Hill Avenue, was located in the center of the infamous Biddle Alley District. The committee recommended that city officials provide better policing of the unpaved, crowded alley districts, open the alleys, and make new residential sections available to Afro-Americans so that congestion in the alleys could be relieved. Their recommendations were not heeded.

Social Service Programs of Black Club Women

Independent Order of St. Luke. As early as 1867, Mary Prout, an ex-slave, teacher, and one of the most progressive black women in Baltimore, founded the Independent Order of St. Luke to aid the sick and provide proper burial for the dead. Through its Juvenile Department, the order broadened its program to include some social concerns and programs for youth. From Baltimore the order spread to other southern states; the most noted chapter was formed in Virginia. Maggie L. Walker joined the Virginia chapter at fourteen years of age; by 1900 she was president. That chapter grew to a membership of twenty thousand by 1907, began publication of the *St. Luke Herald Newspaper*, and formed the St. Luke Bank and Trust Company in Richmond, Virginia.[6] The Baltimore chapter also prospered. Because of its basic goals, however, the order remained a self-help rather than a social service organization.

Johns Hopkins Colored Orphan Asylum. In the years immediately following the Civil War, other black women in Baltimore established clubs and facilities to assist others. One major area of concern was care of homeless or delinquent children; often the asylums were established for girls only. One of the earliest asylums was established during the Civil War by the will of Johns Hopkins. Managed by a group of women, the Johns Hopkins' Colored Orphan Asylum, located at 519 W. Biddle Street in East Baltimore, was restricted to girls in 1892. The girls, aged two to eight, were trained in housework and then "bound out" under the asylum's supervision until they were eighteen.[7] The home was also supposed to provide educational opportunities for the children. However, in June 1925 the *Afro-American,* in an article titled "Johns Hopkins University Perverted Its Funds," charged that the home had never met the requirements designated by the benefactor. During the period 1895–1925, similar accusations were partly responsible for the establishment of alternative facilities by black women.

Of the alternative facilities, three were established or maintained by active black female church workers and were largely supported by contributions from the black community. Their founders and staff also included educational opportunities in the goals of the homes.

Roman Catholic Orphanages. The St. Frances Orphan Asylum and Academy for Colored Girls, at Chase Street and Forrest Place, was founded by the Roman Catholic Oblate Sisters of Providence in November 1829, for the education of "colored girls." The Oblate Sisters of Providence was a religious order for Afro-American women established on 2 July 1829, by Father Joubert, a Frenchman who came to Baltimore by way of Haiti. Other branches of the order existed in Philadelphia and New Orleans, and in other nations. By 1909, under the leadership of Sister Elizabeth Lange, the order had increased from the original four women to ninety.

The asylum opened in 1866 and accepted "whole or half-orphans" aged three to ten. An effort was made to place the children in suitable homes. However, those who could not be placed remained in the care of the nuns until they were able to live independently.[8] The sisters believed that the orphanage and school helped them fulfill their mission as a "religious community of black women to devote lives to education and service of people." The orphanage eventually disbanded so that the nuns could devote their time to the school. Many of Baltimore's affluent Afro-Americans sent their daughters to be educated at the all-girl school which stressed the importance of Catholicism.[9]

The St. Elizabeth Home for Colored Children had objectives similar to those of the St. Frances Orphan Asylum. Begun by a black woman in a house on Mulberry Street in West Baltimore in 1879, the home was subsequently managed by the Franciscan Sisters, a white order. By 1910 the home was headed by Mother Mary Leonard, O.S.F., and staffed by ten women. The home claimed that it was the only institution in Maryland which accepted black children as young as four weeks old, suffering from lack of food and proper care, and the only one in the United States which accepted black infants. Some of the children, after residing in the home for a period of time, were returned to their parents. Once old enough, the girls remaining in the home were taught sewing, cooking, washing, ironing, and general domestic work and were "sent out to service when possible."[10] During the year 1910, the home housed 366 youngsters. By the end of the year, 51 had been returned to their parents; 10 had been transferred to other institutions or adopted; 8 had been sent into service; 216 remained at the home; and 81 had died, half due to marasmus or gastroenteritis, and 4 due to pulmonary tuberculosis. Of the 4 tubercular deaths, 2 were girls in service. In the 1910 annual report, the director stressed the need for additional funding; the state had given $1,275, the city $3,646, and the Indian and Negro Mission Fund $700 and a home in the country.[11]

Day Nursery Association. Many child care programs were developed in the city in 1895–1925. Children who resided with their parents but were in need of clothing and food were assisted through the organized activities of black women. In 1908, a group of women under the leadership of Cornelia Anderson sought funds to purchase a building for a day nursery. That same year, the Day Nursery Association for Colored Children began operating in temporary quarters. The nursery closed for a period of time because of inadequate facilities but reopened on 15 October 1912, in a building purchased by the association at 953 Druid Hill Avenue. Friends of the Day Nursery Association held a rally to help pay off the mortgage.[12]

Sarah Collins Fernandis, a black social worker who was a Hampton Institute graduate, was appointed director of the new nursery. The program was planned to provide care for children of working mothers, engage in social settlement work, establish clubs for both sexes, and organize cooking and sewing classes. The day nursery offered a full schedule of structured educational and recreational activities, and hot lunches, at a cost of two cents per day, were served to the children. Fundraising campaigns later contributed to the revenue of the nursery and helped to ensure its continuance.

Baltimore Colored Empty Stocking and Fresh Air Circle. After the devastating city fire of 1904, the Baltimore Colored Empty Stocking and Fresh Air Circle was formed "to bring sunshine and joy into the hearts and lives of Baltimore's dependent children." During winter 1904, the circle provided coal and clothing for black families in the city so that youngsters would not contract illnesses associated with deprivation. Aware that even more needed to be done to aid the children, the women in 1904 also began to provide Christmas treats; toys and food were distributed in the early years.[13]

In 1908 a dual-purpose fundraising activity was held. Concerned that many Afro-Americans had negative self-images, Richard H. Boyd had founded a company in Nashville, Tennessee, to manufacture Negro female dolls for children. Many black women praised the dolls because they felt that the dolls conveyed positive images of women. On 28 November 1908, in Baltimore, the Afro-American Newspaper Company displayed the first Negro doll to be seen by many. The doll was to be given to the person who guessed its name. Chances were purchased for one cent, with the proceeds to be divided between the Fresh Air Fund and the day nursery for colored children on Druid Hill Avenue. The award was to be made by a committee of women on 1 January 1909. If the name was not guessed, the doll was to be raffled, and those proceeds also would be given to the two organizations.

Another major activity of the circle for 1908 was a citywide campaign to obtain clothing for children. The contributions which poured into the collection headquarters at the Colored YWCA enabled the women to distribute gifts to over 1,300 children who assembled at Zion AME Church on 24 December 1908. The children, many accompanied by their teachers, were entertained by members of the Junior Empty Stocking Circle, who also assisted in the gift distribution. From 1904 to 1911, the annual affair was always held at a church in the city.[14] During those years, 8,525 needy children received gifts; children who were not economically deprived were taught responsibility to care for others.

Because the circle's members recognized that the deplorable living conditions endured by many children were partly responsible for their illnesses and lack of social adjustment, they decided to provide temporary relief for them during summer months. On 17 July 1905, the circle purchased a 10.5-acre farm fourteen miles from Baltimore, to serve as a retreat for the youngsters. The total cost was $1,750, of which $750 was paid in cash. Between 1905 and 1911, 1,078 youngsters spent one week each at the farm.

To support their projects, the women appealed to Afro-Americans for financial assistance. Ida R. Cummings, a teacher and president of the Empty Stocking club during its formative years, led the appeals for funds. Money was needed to meet the general operating expenses for the farm and to pay off the mortgage. Through a fundraising rally at Bethel AME Church on 1 March 1912, $600 was added to the treasury. Donations from members and sympathetic citizens paid the balance of the mortgage on 24 June 1912; the remaining funds were used to purchase a horse.[15] Nevertheless, financial difficulties continued to plague the circle as its efforts expanded. The summer session of 1912 closed early because of a lack of operating funds. The Colored YWCA again lent its support in raising the money needed to clear the outstanding debts. The *Afro-American* printed numerous articles and editorials, eliciting continual giving so that the farm could reopen in 1913. The Charities Endorsement Committee of Baltimore sanctioned the work of the Colored Empty Stocking and Fresh Air Circle in 1914, certifying to whites that the circle was worthy of their contributions. Despite some donations from whites, the majority of the circle's funds continued to come from the black community. The *Afro-American* announced the opening of each year's campaign for funds and called upon its readers to give more than they had in previous years. In 1925, the summer excursions included crippled children.

Interracial Cooperation

Because many Afro-American groups were sponsoring activities to benefit the race, public appeals for funds were constantly being made. In 1902, the Charity Organization Society, composed largely of black women, held a public meeting to define the needs of Baltimore's poor and to coordinate programs in the various sectors of the city. In 1912, however, an interracial effort was made to federate the philanthropic efforts to benefit Afro-Americans in Baltimore; the advisory board was all white.[16] Because the two races were able to work together successfully, a precedent was set for future interracial ventures.

Black women of Baltimore also were willing to work with white women to alleviate some of the problems caused by poor housing conditions. One such combined effort created the Women's Cooperative Civic League. In 1911, appalled by the lack of a city plan, insufficient parks, inadequate school facilities and curriculum, and a police force which was under state jurisdiction, five white people met at the home of Mr. and Mrs. Francis M. Jencks. From the meeting developed the all-white Women's Civic League. The league, with an advisory board of men, had five basic objectives: (1) cleaner and better paved streets and alleys; (2) abatement of noise; (3) a suitable supply of clean, wholesome milk and water; (4) improvement of the public schools and fuller utilization of the school buildings; and (5) creation of public sentiment to achieve the other objectives. The league incorporated and joined the state Federation of Women's Clubs.[17]

Shortly after the league was founded, its members realized that if the entire city of Baltimore was to benefit from league programs, Afro-Americans had to be included. Therefore, Sarah Collins Fernandis, director of the Day Nursery Association, was requested to invite a group of black women to meet with Heller Jones of the league. The group met on 28 October 1913, to discuss ways to improve the community through interracial cooperation. The permanent Women's Cooperative Civic League was established in November 1913, with Fernandis as president, Margaret G. Hawkins as vice-chair of the executive committee, Hannah Smith as treasurer, and Mrs. D.A. Brooks as secretary.

The advisory committee, composed of both black and white women, met once a month to "informally discuss the problems which confront the colored people and possible ways in which they may be assisted in meeting these problems wisely."[18] The problems identified in 1913 included: lack of temporary or detention homes for delinquent black children, care for the retarded, a sanitarium for tubercular children, and a truant school; the poor condition of school buildings; and improper city zoning.

Under the leadership of Fernandis, the 35 charter members of the Co-operative League established their headquarters at 953 Druid Hill Avenue. The Cooperative League's activities were modeled after those of the Women's Civic League, although, except for the joint advisory committee, the memberships remained distinct. The membership of the Cooperative League grew to 130 by 1914.[19] In that year, the group began to sponsor Flower Marts to raise funds. The first was held on the lawn of Bethel AME Church, and subsequent marts were held at Perkins Square. Coupled with the Flower Marts were neighborhood beautification programs.

Others were concerned about the stability and maintenance of Baltimore neighborhoods during the period before World War I. At the Second Annual Conference of Colored Public Health Associations in Baltimore in March 1916, a major discussion was held concerning the poor housing for Afro-Americans. Mrs. A.L. Horner, a member of the Women's Civic League, reported that she owned apartments with land for gardens, which accommodated twelve families. She stressed that while the apartments represented a financial venture for her, she was also seeking to provide good housing for her tenants. Similar decent low-cost housing was mentioned by other discussants, but there was still an acute shortage of both row and detached houses. Hugh M. Burkett, a black realtor, said, "The real estate market for colored people is at a standstill, although there are hundreds of colored people ready and anxious to purchase. But where will they buy? The segregation ordinance which was aimed at the colored people, has as a matter-of-fact proved a boomerang and hit the white property owner harder than the colored purchaser."[20]

For homeowners and renters, the Cooperative League continued throughout 1917 to install gardens and flower boxes. Clubs were organized in Public Schools 107, 112, 113, and 116 to implement the program. However, with the approach of World War I, Baltimore, like the rest of the nation, focused its attention on national issues.

Sarah Fernandis, as president of the Cooperative League, supervised the local Food Conservation Campaign among Afro-Americans. She asked the Women's Civic League members to request that their cooks sign food conservation pledges. She recognized that even though the pledges were sent to the homes of white women, the task of conserving food supplies was primarily the responsibility of their black cooks. In contrast to the food conservation program, which required that citizens make personal sacrifice, from 1918 to 1920 the league also aided citizens by selling Army surplus food and blankets to Afro-Americans. Part of the $10,000 proceeds from the sales was contributed to the colored branch of the Red Cross to help meet Maryland's quota of $1,200,000. The Cooperative League also donated the proceeds from its annual outdoor fete at Perkins Square. The Flower Marts were discontinued during the war.

The Cooperative League's advisory committee convened in 1920 to assess conditions in postwar Baltimore. "The winter has been a very severe one," wrote Margaret G. Hawkins in her "Annual Report of the Women's Cooperative Civic League" in March 1920, "and when we take into account that the active workers in this branch of the League are women with practically no leisure, but with heavy household and sometimes added business responsibilities, we trust that the amount of work accomplished by them will not be measured so much by the concrete examples of their work as by the self-sacrificing and earnest spirit they put into their endeavors to show that women of their race are as anxious as any to meet life's responsibilities."

The advisory committee noted that the condition of streets and alleys was "rather uniformly worse in sections where the colored people lived,"[21] and cited poverty and lack of spokespersons to intervene on their behalf with City Hall as major reasons for the conditions. The Cooperative League created six committees to implement its objectives: Refuse Disposal, Smoke Abatement, Home Gardens, Milk, Eduation, and Zoning. The officers began to teach members ways to apply pressure on municipal authorities to secure the needed services.

The Milk Committee made the Health Department fully aware of the "deplorable conditions which existed in the small shops which dispensed milk to the colored residents of the city." The Education Committee in 1923 conducted a nutritional experiment providing free milk to preschool children through a clinic set up for the purpose at 1220 McCulloh Street. A committee of volunteers worked during the summer under Vivian J. Cook, the new executive secretary of the Cooperative League, and visited the children's homes to evaluate the experiment's effectiveness. The committee also became interested in the welfare of handicapped children. During summer

1923, the league paid expenses for handicapped children to attend the Fresh Air Circle's farm.

In 1924, the league directed its two hundred members to concentrate their activities in specific wards. The primary goal was to organize the residents in Wards 6, 12, 14, 17, 19, 22, and 27 for community activism. Housing, health, and neighborhood beautification were the issues used to motivate the wards to action. By February 1924, five wards were fully organized. Ward 14 was given special attention because it contained the seven worst blocks in the city; here filth, abandoned and dilapidated houses, and diseases prevailed. During Negro Health Week, the league, in conjunction with the Health and Street Cleaning Departments, endeavored to improve these conditions.

After World War I

Afro-Americans worked and sacrificed to support their city and nation in the struggle for democracy overseas, hopeful that the end of the war would bring democracy to them. Instead, the end of World War I marked the beginning of drastic changes and adjustments for black Baltimoreans. The proportion of Afro-Americans in Baltimore had remained fairly constant until 1920. But between 1920 and 1930, the number of Afro-Americans increased five times more rapidly than the white population. Between World War I and 1928, the average increase of Afro-Americans in the city per decade was 29.5 percent. Most of the newcomers came from rural Maryland, seeking better economic and social opportunities. Instead, at the conclusion of the war many lost their jobs and faced harsh, overt discrimination.

In 1920, Afro-Americans constituted 14 percent of Baltimore's population but were receiving 39 percent of the relief given by the Family Welfare Association. In 1922, 772 black families were receiving assistance.[22] Existing data does not indicate the number who applied but were rejected, or the number who did not apply but could have qualified.

Baltimore was eighth among the country's largest cities in 1923 and seventh in terms of manufacturing. Called the "Gateway to the South" in commercial circles, Baltimore offered plentiful, cheap labor. The majority of black workers held unskilled or semiskilled positions. During World War I, the plant labor force grew from 600 to 22,000. "In its industrial development Baltimore is northern," one commentator said, "in its social customs it is more southern than Virginia, for example."[23] Many Afro-Americans who had migrated to the city before and during the war found themselves

Table 8. *Afro-Americans Employed in Baltimore, 1923*

	Women	Men
Professional Service	533[1]	660[2]
Entrepreneurs	177[3]	750
Managers and Foremen	14	162
Clerical Workers	249[4]	538
Skilled Workers	674[5]	2,260
Semiskilled Workers	1,940[6]	1,833
Domestic and Personal Service	22,640[7]	10,796
Unskilled Workers	328	12,094
Unskilled Laborers	0	9,512
Laborers		491
Farm Laborers		114

[1] 396 teachers; no dentist, doctor, minister
[2] Including 53 teachers
[3] Restaurant owners, milliners, retail dealers
[4] 79 clerks; others saleswomen and bookkeepers
[5] 661 dressmakers; 13 tailors
[6] 343 in food industries; others in manufacturing
[7] 12,333 servants; 7,716 launderers not in laundries

Source: "Negroes at Work in Baltimore, Maryland," *Opportunity: A Journal of Negro Life* 1 (May 1923): 12.

unemployed after the war. Because more black women than black men lived in the city, in terms of sheer numbers, women were hardest hit by the economic reversal. Table 8 presents an economic profile of black workers employed in 1923.

Racial discrimination accounted for the inability of many Afro-Americans to secure skilled positions at good pay. At the same time, many remained at the lower end of the economic scale because they were unqualified to seek better positions. The majority of women still worked in the fields considered most appropriate for them — fields which generally did not pay reasonable wages or offer opportunities for advancement.[24]

As a result of Baltimore's geographical location, its urban character, and the infusion of northern ideals, the city's self-help and social service programs for Afro-Americans exhibited unique qualities. White Baltimoreans provided the impetus for the creation of a major black woman's group and the implementation of selected services. Whites, however, promoted the interaction between the races and the implementation of services primarily because of anticipated benefits to whites. Major fundraising activities succeeded in involving a cross-section of black citizens; the economic strength of the city and the support of the black press stimulated giving to worthy causes. Religious groups, including orders of black and white nuns, developed programs to care for and educate the young. The varied programs initiated by black women made it possible for many Afro-Americans to share the benefits of Baltimore's growth. This was possible in part because of the passage of laws more favorable to the black residents; laws which were enacted because black residents became involved in the political process. These factors all contributed to the survival of many programs which continued to meet the needs of specific groups in Baltimore's black population.

CHAPTER 10

Developing a National Organization of Afro-American Women

Early Years

While laboring to relieve economic, social, and political inequities in their communities, black women also were aware of national issues and concerns. Many realized that only race separated them from white counterparts who were engaged in various reform efforts. As a result, some black women sought inclusion in national women's organizations having objectives similar to those they had identified; they hoped through combined effort to produce more immediate benefits for all. However, their attempts to join white organizations in 1899 and 1900 met with rejection and, at times, overt hostility.

In 1887, white women had formed the General Federation of Women's Clubs (GFWC). Josephine St. Pierre Ruffin, an Afro-American, attempted to attend the GFWC convention in Milwaukee in 1889 as a delegate but was denied admission. Four years later, Hallie O. Brown requested that an Afro-American be appointed to the Columbian Exposition's board of managers. She was told that there was no organization of black women to support her request.[1] Such incidents induced black women to work toward the creation of a national women's organization for Afro-Americans.

In June 1892 a small group of black women organized the National Colored Women's League in Washington, D.C. The incorporation document of 11 January 1894 indicated the league's objectives: racial and social progress, formation of a national organization from similar local organizations, "industrial and educational purposes, and educational and improvement of Colored women and the promotion of their interests."[2] Those signing the document were Helen A. Cook, president; Charlotte F. Grimké, Josephine B. Bruce, Anna J. Cooper, Mary Church Terrell, Mary J. Patterson, Evelyn Shaw, and Ida D. Bailey—all women noted for their racial activism. Beginning their programs in Washington, D.C., prior to incorporation, the women established a model kindergarten, a training class, a sewing class, a day nursery, and a course in kitchen gardening for girls under eighteen. They also financially supported a young woman who was attending the Manassas Industrial School. As an adjunct to the league, a Woman's Protective Union was formed to push for reforms needed in the District of Columbia.

Impressed by the progress the league had made, on 9 October 1894, the National Council of Women (NCW) invited the league to join the council. The league was requested to send representatives to the council's convention to be held in Washington, D.C., from 17 February to 2 March 1895. The league formed a large committee to invite black women from other organizations and leagues to attend the NCW convention. The Woman's Era Club of Boston, founded by Ruffin in March 1894, voted not to send delegates to the convention;[3] it was to affiliate with the NCW only after the black women's groups had formed their own coherent national body.

In early 1895, James W. Jack, president of the Missouri Press Association, wrote a letter to Florence Belgarnie of England, secretary of the Anti-Slavery Society, deprecating the capability and character of black women. To combat such attacks and to combine strength, Ruffin issued a call to all black women to attend the First National Conference of Colored Women of America, to be held in Boston on 29 July 1895. According to Margaret Murray Washington, forty women "went up from every section of the country, eager to prove that with equal opportunities to make a living, equal chances for an education, we were not unlike other women of other races."[4]

During the Boston meeting, the association was named the National Federation of Afro-American Women, and Washington was elected the first president. Some of the delegates proposed that the newly created federation form a union with the National Colored Women's League. However, because some felt that the federation was not national in scope and since this was its first convention, the league did not immediately agree to join the federation. Both groups held annual conventions in Washington, D.C., during July 1896. The National League of Colored Women, as it was then identified, held its first convention from 14 July through 16 July at the Fifteenth Street Presbyterian Church. The federation held its second convention 20–22 July at the Nineteenth Street Baptist Church.[5]

During the first day of the federation's convention, a committee of seven from the league and seven from the federation met to discuss the two groups' goals and differences. Terrell chaired the joint committee, which recommended that the groups merge to form the National Association of Colored

Women's Clubs of America (NACW). After much balloting, Terrell was elected the first president. After consolidation, the association encompassed fifty clubs with five hundred members in various states.

The early years of the NACW were spent primarily defining basic directions and mediating differences which arose among members. The 1897–99 issues of the *National Association Notes,* the NACW newsletter, indicate that internal conflicts between the two founding groups had not been fully resolved. The Woman's Era Club made public its intent to withdraw from the NACW until properly elected officials were installed.[6] In spite of the accusations and conflicts, Terrell remained president until 1901; during her tenure, the NACW defined objectives which were realistic, purposeful, and lasting.

The association not only operated national programs, but also constituted the first cohesive national network of black women. The structure of the organization facilitated communication: local clubs at the base, then state federations, regional federations, and at the top the national body. Information and influence flowed freely from bottom to top as well as in the reverse direction.

By 1913, the NACW was affiliated with organizations in Canada, Liberia, and Madagascar, as well as in thirty states in the U.S. Although most of the members were educated, middle-class women, reform for the masses was seen as the basic goal. Mother's clubs, day nurseries, kindergartens, and schools of domestic science were among the many programs implemented to effect reform. So that all members could be kept abreast of local and national programs, Terrell organized biennial conventions, to be held in cities where there were large numbers of active members. At the new organization's first convention in Nashville, in 1897, Harriet Tubman, then seventy-six years old, spoke of her work as a Union scout, providing much inspiration for the delegates.

In 1901, the NACW was granted affiliation with the National Council of Women. Mrs. A.A. Granger, president of the white Georgia Federation of Women's Clubs, stated on 21 April 1902, at the General Federation's convention, that if black women were permitted to join their national body, the Georgia Federation would withdraw its membership. The Tennessee Federation of Women's Clubs indicated it would not. After the 1902 General Federation meeting, an anonymous letter was sent to selected white women, as well as to Ida Wells Barnett and Fannie B. Williams, warning black women to stop trying to gain admittance to the General Federation; Barnett had held a racially mixed meeting of club women at her home in Chicago. In spite of this continued rejection by the General Federation of

Women's Clubs, white and black women had begun to work together on selected issues. The NACW sent delegates to the next convention of the National Council of Women in order to keep abreast of the activities of the white women and to share their experiences in club work.

Major Programs

Affiliation with the NCW did not alter the programs and objectives of the NACW; the group kept in sight its slogan, "Raise the standards and purify the atmosphere of the home." The NACW membership continued to grow; at its 1912 convention in Hampton, Virginia, 10,908 members were reported. Margaret Murray Washington was installed as president, and officers came from across the country. Between 1910 and 1912, the women had collected $32,425 for their activities, and in 1912 the NACW owned property valued at $113,832. Their programs concentrated on "reformatories, old folk's homes, social settlements, nurseries, working girls' homes, study of civics, needlecrafts and domestic science, development of social uplift work."[7] In order to implement their national objectives, the women created departments to carry out their activities. Among the departments were Young Women's Work, headed by Nannie H. Burroughs of Washington, D.C.; Humane Departments, headed by Mary F. Handy of Baltimore; and Rural Conditions, headed by Adella Hunt Logan of Tuskegee.

At the tenth biennial convention, held 6–10 August 1916 at Bethel AME Church in Baltimore, Maryland, twenty-eight departments reported on their progress and activities. Mary Talbert was elected over Hallie Q. Brown on the second ballot, 231 to 130 votes, to succeed Washington as president. Ida R. Cummings of Baltimore was elected vice-president.

During the convention questions were asked, programs launched, and statements made which clearly demonstrated that the women were concerned about and willing to work in many areas not traditionally considered part of their domain. Present at the meeting was an NAACP representative, Miss Freeman, who had investigated a lynching in Waco, Texas. The assembly agreed to send a petition protesting such occurrences to President Woodrow Wilson, and seventy-five dollars were collected and given to the antilynching fund of the NAACP. Moreover, Washington urged the women "to study carefully and strive to understand the question of suffrage." She also urged them to cooperate with the National Negro Business League in promoting "Railroad Day," as a means of striving for better railroad accommodations for Afro-Americans, especially for those living in the South.

The NACW board reported in 1916 that it had received fourteen applications from leading white women for affiliated membership. The requests were honored for such women as Jane Addams, Mary Austin, and Zonale Gale because it was felt their affiliation would be motivational for Afro-Americans,[8] and because acceptance reaffirmed that black women were not opposed to working with whites on common causes.

During the 1916 convention, it was also agreed to lift the $4,000 mortgage from the Frederick Douglass home in the Anacostia section of Washington, D.C., so that the house could serve as NACW headquarters. The agreement crystalized efforts begun in 1897 to make Cedar Hill for Afro-Americans what Mt. Vernon was to white Americans. A committee was appointed to advise and assist the trustees of the Douglass Home; a special act of Congress had created the Frederick Douglass Historical Association to supervise the maintenance of the home. The NACW, in soliciting support for the home, designated all black women to serve as the support unit for the effort. In the campaign to raise $15,000 to restore the home and its grounds, every woman's club was urged to mobilize boys and girls, and schools and Sunday schools were asked to designate special days when each child would donate one cent toward the cause.[9] By February 1918, all indebtedness of the home was cleared, and the proposal was again made that the house become the permanent NACW headquarters and a repository for materials relating to the Afro-American experience in the United States. Although the headquarters proposal was not realized, the women continued to provide funds to maintain the home. On 15 February, 1925, a national one-year drive was launched to raise $10,000 for upkeep of the home. Sallie W. Steward of Evansville, Indiana, spearheaded the drive to create the Mary B. Talbert Memorial Fund.

In 1922, Ida Wells Barnett wrote in an editorial in *The Woman's Forum* that the NACW, the only national body for black women, was not as responsive to the needs and concerns of its constituency as it should be. To support her criticism, she cited the manner in which the Dyer Anti-Lynching bill was discussed and the amount of time allotted to the NAACP and its causes at the 1922 Richmond convention. Delegates did not have enough time to present local program reports or concerns. Barnett, noted for her activism in the anti-lynching cause, indicated that senators who supported the Dyer Anti-Lynching bill, not NAACP representatives, should have made the convention presentations. On 14 August 1922, members of the executive committee did meet with Senators Shortbridge, Lodge, and McCormick. Afterwards, during an audience with President Harding, Hallie Q. Brown read an appeal for a federal anti-lynching bill. According to Barnett, more needed to be done.[10] The comments and writings of a progressive reformer such as Barnett often challenged the NACW leaders to rethink a plan of action and consider other approaches.

The years 1924 and 1925 were crucial developmental ones for the NACW. On 5 July 1924, in a letter to Nannie H. Burroughs, Washington indicated that there was conflict among the national leaders of the NACW. Before the biennial convention in Chicago in 1924, Hallie Q. Brown had held a meeting of selected women; Washington had not been invited. Washington asked Burroughs to assist her in keeping the organization free from internal strife. Burroughs agreed.[11] If internal conflicts disrupted the effectiveness of the organization which had grown to include one hundred thousand members, gains made by the women would be lost. With the election of Mary McLeod Bethune as NACW president in 1924, much of the disquiet was quelled, and the programs of the organization were broadened.

Bethune, having served for twenty years as president of Bethune-Cookman College, brought to the office vast administrative skills and the ability to structure innovative programs. Beginning in 1924, she managed to rally the women behind several key activities. A $50,000 scholarship fund was proposed; $12,000 had been contributed by November 1924. Addie W. Hunton chaired the Department of Programs and Literature, whose four aims were: to observe events historically significant to the race, to encourage the study of literature by and about Afro-Americans in order to develop a new level of racial pride, to foster the study of race relationships and literature with the belief that peace was founded on understanding, and to participate in all programs making for citizenship recognition. The aims were indicative of the organization's efforts to give Afro-Americans on all levels as much knowledge and preparation as possible for moving toward equality in American society.

Bethune's five-point program for 1926 made it clear that the NACW would continue to address unresolved problems and strengthen its membership base. The five goals were: completion of efforts to raise $50,000 for the scholarship fund; raising the remainder of the $10,000 Mary B. Talbert Memorial Fund; revision of the organization's constitution; induction of thirty thousand women into the organization from other organizations and sororities; and establishment of a national headquarters.[12] The fourth point was crucial for the continuation and viability of the organization. Bethune, like previous presidents, recognized that the true strength of the NACW rested with the cadres of female workers who made up hundreds of clubs throughout the United States. In order for the national programs to be successful, women in their individual communities had to raise funds, implement the national objectives, and keep alive a national unifying body.

Three Levels in the Structure

The national organizational structure remained in effect through 1925. Washington, in a 1917 speech at the Nashville Women's Club, identified the three key elements of club work: individual or city work, state work, and national programs. The city federation, she said, should be composed of clubs of city women at work in various sections of the city but with one ideal. The state federations were to work on projects for the betterment of all in the state.[13]

On the state level, the Georgia Federation of Colored Women's Clubs serves as an excellent example of how women supported national goals and at the same time attempted to respond to the specific needs of citizens in their state. Organized in 1902 with the motto, "Not Be Ministered Unto But To Minister," the federation established a state home for delinquent girls in Chatham County, assisted in raising funds for the Mills Memorial Hospital, volunteered over four thousand hours of services during World War I, participated in activities designed to obtain the vote for black women, and protested overt acts of discrimination. The members still found time to assist in the development of the club movement in their communities, region, and nation.[14]

On the regional level, the Southeastern Federation of Colored Women industriously implemented its programs and activities. In 1900, with Margaret Washington as president, the federation made the development of kindergartens its primary activity. This project was selected because the group believed that work with young people was the best way to prevent them from having serious problems later. Seen as the first step in organizing the black women of the South, the kindergartens would have mothers at their core. There would be an "organizer for the Southern States who will promote the formation of mothers' clubs throughout the South, the object of which shall be the establishment and maintenance of kindergartens for all classes of colored children. Each state will, in time, have an organizer who will act under the general agent." Also to be appointed was a "financial representative of the work who will go through the country, North and South, setting forth the plans of the association and securing such financial aid as will be necessary to supplement what the colored people themselves can do in the matter."[15] The kindergarten effort was aimed at those living at the poverty level and was to be chiefly financed and implemented by Afro-Americans.

Participation in International Organizations

The NACW's success among black women was due in part to its commitment to improve the general status of the race. The link between black women in the United States and other women of the diaspora was one concern which the NACW addressed during the 1920s. Even before the 1920s, black women throughout the United States had sought ways to broaden their understanding of international affairs and the conditions under which other peoples of color lived. Now, to influence international affairs and to help improve life for black people in Africa and the Caribbean, NACW members joined the International Council of Women and formed the International Council of Women of the Darker Races.

The International Council of Women (ICW) had been organized in 1888 by white women as an outgrowth of the General Federation of Women's Clubs. Frances Willard served as the first chairperson. The ICW formulated a broad program during its formative years and held congresses in 1888, 1893, and 1902 to discuss issues of international importance, particularly international suffrage.[16] A principal goal of the ICW was to unite women throughout the world to speak out on issues affecting all people, but esecially women.

Mary Church Terrell represented the NACW at the 1904 ICW congress in Berlin, Germany. Upon her return, *The Voice of the Negro* published her article detailing the trip. In 1920, Mary Talbert and Dr. Mary F. Waring served as the NACW's representatives to the congress in Christiana, Norway. Talbert was one of five women chosen to address the body and to present a resolution. Thus, she became the first Afro-American to speak before the House of Parliament in Norway.

Talbert's overseas experience was marred when, because of her race, she was refused admittance to the dining hall operated by the YWCA at the American Woman's Club in Paris. On 19 January 1921, the NAACP issued a statement protesting Talbert's treatment. On 27 January, Dr. W.E.B Du Bois wrote a letter of protest to Mrs. Paul Gaston Darrott, chair of the national board of the YWCA.[17] The discriminatory act indicated clearly that although black women were active participants in the ICW, they were not to receive the same respect and amenities as white women.

Because black women had seen that they faced some obstacles solely because of their race and that there were problems unique to them as a group, in 1920 some members of the NACW founded the International Council of Women of the Darker Races to disseminate information regarding peoples of color and to help instill racial pride in such peoples. The original members were fifty American women of color and fifty foreign women of color. Mary Church Terrell and Addie W. Hunton were vice presidents, and Maggie Walker, Mary McLeod Bethune, and Nannie Burroughs were members of the executive council.[18]

In 1900, H. Sylvester Williams organized and hosted a Pan-African Conference at Westminister Hall, London. Anna J. Cooper, author and educator, addressed the delegates, demonstrating that women were willing to cooperate in achieving international goals. How best to achieve those goals was the key question.

Some believed that the only way to solve race problems in the United States and at the same time assist African nations in their economic and political development was to emigrate to the African continent. In October 1901, the Emigration Society was formed in Nashville, Tennessee. The founder, Dr. William Heard, argued that Africans were moral, that white men had committed crimes against black women, and that the only solution to the race crisis in the South was emigration. To encourage migration, the society combined techniques used by earlier emigration groups with new methods. Through an agreement with the government of Liberia, each black American who moved to Liberia would receive twenty-five acres of land. To provide transportation to Liberia, the society formed a company to purchase steamships. To finance the venture, the company sold shares for $5 each. Each vessel cost $10,000, and the passage to Africa was to cost $45 or $50. By 1902, there were local emigration clubs throughout the South, with a total of five thousand members.[19] An editorial in the *Afro-American Ledger* on 22 February 1902, entitled "Emigration Will Not Help," expressed a view opposite to Dr. Heard's. Although in the early 1920s Marcus Garvey's campaign for emigration to Africa had enticed many more black Americans than Heard did, the majority of black Americans still believed that other methods must be employed to effect changes for black Americans and Africans.

In a more intellectual approach, W.E.B Du Bois organized a series of Pan-African Congresses. The first was held February 1919 in Paris. The sixty delegates were West Indians, Africans, and Afro-Americans. Jessie Faucet attended the 1921 congress as a representative of the NACW. During the thirteenth biennial session of the NACW in Richmond, Virginia, in 1922, Faucet reported her impressions of the congress. Other NACW members made presentations at the NACW 1922 convention that clearly reflected objectives of the International Council of Women of the Darker Races: Adelaide Casely-Hayford of Sierra Leone, West Africa, gave a lecture-demonstration on Africa; Fannie R. Givens of Louisville, Kentucky, president of National

Historial Art League of America, presented a lecture based on a six-month stay in Africa; and Mary Talbert reported on her trip to Norway.[20]

In 1922, the International Council of Women of the Darker Races began to hold conventions separate from the general sessions of the NACW. The council's meeting in Washington, D.C., attracted representatives from Africa, Haiti, Ceylon, and the West Indies. A definitive statement of purpose was developed at the 1922 meeting: "The Council has as its object the economic, social, and political welfare of the women of all the darker races."[21] The stature of the elected officers attested to the significance given to the organization: Margaret M. Washington, president; Addie W. Hunton, first vice-president; Mary Church Terrell, second vice-president; Lugenia Burns Hope, third vice-president, Adelaide Casely-Hayford, fourth vice-president for West Africa; Elizabeth C. Carter, secretary; Marion Wilkerson, treasurer; and Nannie H. Burroughs, chair of the executive board. The principal activity for the remainder of 1922 was to be an investigation of the status of women and children in Haiti. Emily Williams was sent to Haiti to study women there; her trip was partially financed by the council, and her report was submitted to the general body at the 1923 convention.

On 5–8 August 1923, when the council met at the National Training School in Washington, D.C., three sections were organized. Mrs. C. Edward Dickerson was to chair the International Relationships Section; Lugenia Hope the Social and Economic Conditions Section; and Margaret Washington the Education Section. Three resolutions were passed and disseminated to the press: a commendation of Mrs. Casely-Hayford for her efforts to found a school for girls in Sierra Leone, a resolution to study the condition of women and girls in Africa, and a condemnation of the French government for its stand on racial discrimination in African nations.[22] The second resolution was crucial; no longer would the council be merely a fact-finding body. After studying conditions in Africa, the next step would be work to change conditions.

Unfortunately, the International Council of Women of the Darker Races never moved far beyond gathering data and proposing solutions. The international political arena was not receptive to black women who attempted to become involved in the internal affairs of colonized nations. Nevertheless, the women were able to expand their knowledge of peoples of color and to aid specific individuals or groups in foreign nations. The women also pressured school superintendents in the United States to order books about people of the diaspora. The council was especially concerned that black youngsters, as well as council members, be exposed to and understand the history and literature of their people.

To ensure that all of its own members were as well informed as possible, the council encouraged the development of study groups. Under the council's Education Section, Committees of Seven were formed in 1924 to "study conditions of the darker races of the world." Each community was to form a committee to study problems of Afro-Americans in the U.S. and Africa. Educational, social, religious and industrial concerns were suggested as broad areas from which specific topics could be selected. It was also recommended that the women read books about Africa and schedule visits from native Africans and missionaries.[23] Articles, letters, and minutes of club meetings show that the local committees took the suggestions quite seriously and worked to complete the recommended tasks. Janie Porter Barrett, in a letter to Washington, wrote that evenings were spent on discussions about the women of Haiti, China, Africa, and Japan. According to Barrett, the women in her group modeled their discussions after the ones held at Tuskegee.[24]

While the women labored to make the International Council of Women of the Darker Races a channel for their concerns about African peoples abroad and in the U.S., they maintained their affiliation with the International Council of Women. Mary McLeod Bethune and Hallie Q. Brown represented the NACW at the ICW's meeting in Washington in 1925. Because Afro-Americans would be in attendance, the Daughters of the American Revolution refused to allow the ICW to use the auditorium of Memorial Continental Hall. When it was agreed among the whites that Afro-Americans would not have open seating but would be required to sit in a segregated section in the gallery, the members of the NACW walked out. National black male leaders and the black press praised the women for their response to such an overt act of discrimination.[25]

In spite of the advances made by women in general, in 1925 black women still toiled under the heavy yokes of race and sex. Nor had the struggle for women's rights matured enough to embrace black women as a vital unit of that movement. Membership in traditionally white organizations did not guarantee greater inclusion, respect, or success. Organizations started by black women in response to their specific needs and interests were the most effective conduits for progress.

CHAPTER 11

Working Within National Movements

Black women who were actively involved in self-help and social service programs on a national level soon saw that their efforts would have more impact if they linked aspects of their programs with other national movements. Of the many social reform issues, two had special significance for black women: suffrage for women and temperance.

Suffrage

At the end of the nineteenth century, only white males had free access to the polls. Southern black men were largely disenfranchised and would remain so until after 1910. Poll taxes, property requirements, literacy and "understanding" tests, and terrorism were some of the tactics used to deny black men the right to vote. The late 1890s witnessed a wave of new laws designed to segregate the races and deny Afro-Americans legitimate forms of redress. The *Plessy v. Ferguson* "Separate but equal" decision of 1896, further isolated the race socially and politically. There were exceptions, however, as some Afro-Americans were granted the right to vote and were even elected to political offices in some states.

A movement to secure the vote for women, led by Lucretia Mott and Elizabeth Cady Stanton, began in July 1848 at Seneca Falls, New York. In 1869, Stanton and Susan Brownell Anthony founded the Woman Suffrage Association, a national lobbying organization. It was reorganized in 1890 as the National American Woman Suffrage Association (NAWSA). The new organization immediately faced opposition from men and women who viewed the suffrage movement as being counter to the best interests of home and family.

Beginning in 1890, women were granted the right to vote in certain states: Wyoming (1890); Colorado (1893); Idaho and Utah (1896). Nevertheless, NAWSA, under the presidencies of Carrie Clinton Lane Chapman Catt (1900–1904 and 1914–20) and Dr. Anna Howard Shaw (beginning in 1904), continued to agitate for suffrage for women in all states. Local black newspapers announced the national meeting of NAWSA, but black women generally were excluded from the decision-making body of the organization and were not recognized as a group to be included in the general deliberations. According to Dr. Shaw, however, the organization made no distinction based on race. As long as she was president, she said, black women would be welcome. NAWSA had no black members because none had applied, she said, even though some Afro-Americans had attended conventions and participated in programs in earlier years. In June 1911, NAWSA appointed two black women as captains of their district in New York; the black vote was dominant in that district.[1]

The Crisis pointed out in June 1912 that black women had not been and were not included in NAWSA because in the past black men generally had not been supportive of the right of women to vote and had assisted in defeating woman suffrage bills in various states. Moreover, NAWSA officers feared that inclusion of black women would lead to disruptions during their planned 1912 convention in Louisville, Kentucky.[2] In fact, the NAWSA convention in Louisville took a nebulous position on the question of involving black women.

At a meeting in Chicago on 9 January 1913, held to organize black women into a suffrage club, Belle Squire, a white suffragist, said, "This is the first time in the history of the suffragist movement, to my knowledge, than an attempt has been made to organize colored women for the cause. We have been narrow. We have been too prudish. But we realize now that we must broaden out for our mutual good."[3] Ida Wells Barnett, organizer of the Alpha Suffrage Club, affirmed that she too saw the voting issue as one shared by black and white women.

By 1913 women had been granted the right to vote in the states of Washington, California, Arizona, Kansas, Oregon, Montana, Nevada, and Illinois. In that year, NAWSA sponsored its first national parade in Washington, D.C. The local suffrage committee was reluctant to allow blacks to participate, but forty-one did and were treated no worse than the white female marchers.[4] The inclusion of black women in the national suffrage movement remained an issue as NAWSA expanded and as the Congressional Union, founded by Alice Paul in 1915 in a split from NAWSA, developed. Paul's organization, later known as the National Woman's Party, was more radical in its approach to woman suffrage, but even it did not envision black women as a necessary component. Black women remained on the fringes of the national movement.

In the hope of eliciting black male support for suffrage for women in New York, *The Crisis* published an editorial, "Votes for Women," in November 1917, explaining why the majority of black males did not support woman suffrage. Part of the explanation was that men resented the attitudes of the white suffragists. Also black men failed to recognize the new status of women in society and in industry: "Despite the fact that within his own group women are achieving economic independence even faster than whites, he thinks of these as exceptional and abnormal and looks forward to the time when his wages will be large enough to support his wife and daughters in comparative idleness at home."[5] The editorial pointed out that denying the black woman's right to vote was as bad as denying "the American Negro's" right to vote. White women could not be punished by denying them their right; in time southern white women would learn "political justice" faster than white men.

It was becoming increasingly difficult for southern white men to disenfranchise black women. Public opinion was against the use of physical violence to remove black women from the polls. The economic power men held over black women also was eroding. Black men were called upon to support the suffrage movement because of the possible benefits for the race as a whole. The practicality of the suggestion was demonstrated in a November 1917 election in New York, in which 75,000 black women voted; two blacks were elected to the New York Assembly.[6]

In spring 1919, the woman suffrage amendment had passed the House and was under consideration by the Senate. When NACW requested membership in NAWSA, Ida Husted Harper, NAWSA publicist, through Mary Church Terrell, asked NACW to hold its application until after the Senate vote. The black women agreed to do so. Through the direct intervention of President Woodrow Wilson, the bill passed the Senate on 14 June 1918. On 21 August 1919, Tennessee ratified the Nineteenth Amendment, making it a national law. Sex was no longer a criterion for voting, but race still was.

"When suffragists suggested to Alice Paul that the voting rights of black women would be a continuing vital issue, she replied that the year 1920 was not the time to discuss that question. Rather, she said, the suffragists should enjoy their new political power and make plans for other battles in the future."[7] In spite of the reluctance of white women to address their concern, some black women began to encourage others to register to vote. Mary Church Terrell, as director of Work Among Colored Women in the East for the Republican National Committee, used her position to promote black female voter registration.

Cases of rejection (one was in Hampton, Virginia) began to flood the headquarters of the National Association for the Advancement of Colored People (NAACP) in 1920. The NAACP became further involved in the issue when Mary Talbert was invited to speak at the National Woman's Party meeting on 15 February 1921. The New York representatives on the executive committee had voted unanimously to have a black speaker. Nevertheless, Alice Paul ruled that speakers must represent organizations with legislative programs relating only to women. It was therefore decided that, as a representative of the NAACP, Talbert could not speak because her organization related "to race, not to a sex."[8] Instead, Talbert was asked to recommend possible black women delegates for the Washington, D.C., meeting. She would be one.

During the 1921 NWP victory celebration in Washington, Mary Church Terrell visited Alice Paul to ascertain whether the latter supported enforcement of the amendment to secure the vote for black women. Paul refused to respond, so Terrell presented to the NWP Resolutions Committee the statement she had given to Paul. The committee's refusal to issue a clear statement of support for Afro-Americans left no doubt that black women themselves would have to assume principal responsibility for securing the ballot for their group.

During the late nineteenth century, the Republican Party had emerged as the dominant political party in the United States, and it remained that through 1925. It was through this party that black women began to emerge as a viable political force. Louise M. Dodson, director of the Republican Women's National Executive Committee, spoke to a thousand delegates at the NACW convention on 11 August 1922, in Richmond, Virginia. She stressed the need for black women to organize politically, to educate black voters, and to increase the number of voters. Mrs. George S. Williams, the first black woman appointed to the National Republican Committee and the first woman to speak at the 1924 National Republican Convention in Cleveland, Ohio, is credited with organizing the National Republican League of Colored Women. As of February 1925, the league had fourteen directors representing twelve states; Georgia, Mississippi, and Maryland were the only southern ones. Additional southern states were represented by committee members.[9] The standing committees were: Speaker's Bureau, Finance, Publicity, Law Enforcement, Campaign, and Education.

Although black women in certain states could vote, the majority of black women in the South were not permitted that privilege. Subtle and blatant actions were taken to deny black women (and men) what had been granted by national law. Because of their inability to influence political, economic, and social conditions through the power of the vote, black women in the southern states remained dependent upon their own skills, energy, and often money, to effect meaningful change. The refusal of noted national white suffragists to fight for black women's voting rights delayed their full inclusion in the political process. The right to vote became yet another cause for which black women had to fight on their own.

Temperance

In depicting alcoholic beverages as destroying homes and engendering loose morals, the temperance movement appealed strongly to black women, who in 1895–1925 emphasized developing and strengthening the home. However, like early suffragists, early warriors against alcoholic consumption did not readily include Afro-Americans in their organizations and programs. The temperance movement was largely the creation of middle-class white women who directed their energies toward reforming the lower classes, whom they often saw as the true abusers placing yet another burden on society. Although initiated before the Civil War, the temperance movement did not gain momentum until the early 1870s.

The Women's Christian Temperance Union (WCTU), with Frances Willard as its second president in 1874, in 1920 led the nation to the Eighteenth Amendment, the Volstead Act, and Prohibition. Asked at a WCTU organizing meeting if Afro-Americans would be involved, Frances Willard replied that "everything possible would be done for the colored people but that it would be separate and distinct from the work among white people."[10] The WCTU's temperance work among black women did not begin until 1881, with Jane Kenny as the first superintendent; in 1883 Frances E. Harper became the second superintendent.

Immediately after Kenny's appointment, utilizing churches and educational facilities as platforms for the WCTU, black women organized local chapters to combat drunkenness in their communities. Local newspapers supported the cause and continuously covered the progress of the movement. The *Afro-American Ledger* in Baltimore featured a column, "Temperance," which included statistics relating to the negative effects of alcohol and the pledges of women who would not marry a man who drank. Large numbers of professional women in southern states, readily supported the campaign. Della Haydn, an 1877 Hampton graduate, organized a State

Teachers' Temperance Union in 1888. It grew to include six hundred members in 1904.[11] The work among Afro-Americans was also furthered by national speaking tours conducted by the WCTU's national superintendents of work among colored people, Lucy Thurman, 1902–1907, and Eliza T. Peterson, 1909–1917. Black women also attended the national convention of the WCTU in large numbers. As a headline in the *Globe* on 15 November 1907, put it: "Thirty-Fourth Gathering—Woman's Christian Temperance Union—Immeasurable Good Accomplished—Prominent WCTU Workers in Attendance From Every Part of This Great Country. These Earnest Women, Colored and Whites, Are After Drunkenness."

Successes in the five states under study in this book heralded the impact of the movement upon the masses. Maryland was often cited as a state where excellent results were achieved. Maryland had an Anti-Saloon League in 1910, but the WCTU fueled its activities. In February 1912, Peterson traveled to Baltimore to organize Afro-Americans. She spent weeks assisting Baltimoreans to develop their campaign and spoke at local churches to motivate citizens. In 1913, Laura (Mrs. E.J.) Wheatley led the campaign during which five hundred persons appeared before the Board of Liquor License Commissioners to protest the existence of saloons on "two principal streets" inhabited by Afro-Americans. Of greater concern was the proximity of a school and churches to the saloons. The persistence of women such as Wheatley forced the closing of 163 saloons by September 1913.[12]

In spite of thousands of signed pledges, willing workers, and documented positive results, the temperance movement maintained separate organizations for Afro-Americans and whites. The chapters for Afro-Americans were easily distinguishable by the word "colored" affixed to WCTU. In black neighborhoods, black women and men continued the crusade until the passage of the Eighteenth Amendment on 16 January 1920. Even after Prohibition, the women continued to work with individuals to prevent backsliding and the consequent ruin of Afro-American homes.

The Young Women's Christian Association

Black Women Within the National Framework. Because the Young Women's Christian Association (YWCA) also sought to improve the quality of home life through the personal development of young women, black women were attracted to the organization. They were also interested in the "Y" because many of its national programs sanctioned the Christian principles that formed the core of black religion. In seeking membership in the YWCA, black women again were faced with a racial barrier in direct conflict with the professed doctrine of the organization. Black women could become members, but only in separate colored branches. To facilitate work among black women while adhering to unwritten segregation codes, the YWCA created administrative posts on several levels.

One of the first posts created was that of student secretary for work among colored women. Appointed by the national board of the YWCA in 1908, Elizabeth Ross (later Haynes) became the first to hold that position. Cecelia Holloway became student secretary when Ross married in 1910. At the time of Ross' appointment, fourteen chapters were in existence at black educational institutions. By 1910, fifty-two chapters existed. Because local chapters could be fully effective only if they were aware of national policies and programs, a series of student conferences was held in 1910 at Talladega, Claflin, and Tougaloo Colleges, and at Fisk University. During summer 1911, three young black female graduates of Radcliffe, Hartshorn, and Fisk received training at the National Training School in New York, designed to prepare them for service in the "Y." It was expected that these women would serve as role models for the undergraduate staffs in campus YWCAs and assist them in program development.[13]

The first colored student conference, held at Spelman 26 May to 15 June 1916, established the focus for all future student conferences. The seventy-nine delegates participated in a four-point program — Bible study, missionary and social work discussions, vocational discussions, and the technical council hour. During the technical council hour, the young women were taught how to implement the work of the "Y." To assist in their personal development, the delegates had a quiet hour, took trips into Atlanta, played games, or participated in informal talks during the evenings.[14]

Each year brought an increase in the number of conference delegates. In 1918, 105 came to Spelman. Of that number, 86 represented thirty-one schools and eleven colleges. The theme that year was "Christian Democracy."[15] Eva Bowles and Adele Ruffin presented lectures and led the technical hour discussions of war work among Afro-Americans. Eva Bowles was YWCA national secretary for colored work in cities — the highest YWCA post for a black woman. Before her appointment in 1916, Bowles had been secretary of the colored branch of the YWCA in New York.

As more young black women became involved in the YWCA, new chapters developed, and membership increased. The work among college students was most successful due to the need for social interaction on the campuses, the social service emphasis of the educational institutions, and the religious backgrounds of the students. More than ten thousand black students were active members in 105 southern chapters in 1924.[16]

Baltimore Branch. YWCA activities among more mature black women in the South occurred principally in urban areas. Because of its location and cosmopolitan character, Baltimore was one of the first southern cities to establish a YWCA chapter. Organized at the Madison Street Presbyterian Church on 3 January 1896, the founding chapter had seven members. Under the leadership of Mrs. S.A. Charity, the membership decided upon a benevolent emphasis for their projects. They stated, "No one must be made to feel that we are reaching down to them, but that we are reaching across to help them, with Christ between, and that all are on a level."[17] In order to reach others they began cooking and sewing classes. The sewing classes were held each Thursday from 6 to 8 p.m. In keeping with the organization's purpose, Bible classes were conducted each Tuesday. An Employment Bureau was established under the direction of Margaret Boisseau. By May 1896, the bureau had secured positions for twenty-three men and women. Operating hours for the bureau were 9 a.m. to 12 noon and 4 to 6 p.m. daily. A pamphlet detailing the "Y"'s purpose and programs was disseminated throughout the greater Baltimore area. A reading room for ladies was also made available to the general public.[18]

Because of the attention given to specific community needs, the newly formed "Y" chapter was soon highly respected. By the end of the chapter's first year, membership had increased to fifty black women. As the membership grew, the chapter expanded its program offerings and community services. One of the earliest innovations was the introduction of classes which were equivalent to normal school courses. Beginning on 4 January 1902, the classes met every Saturday at 1 p.m. Lecturers such as Mrs. M. Brandon Tull, missionary to South Africa, were invited to present free public lectures on timely topics. All of the supplementary activities were designed either to assist others or to enhance the personal growth of the members.

The Baltimore branch had officers who not only were capable administrators but also were willing to make reasonable projections for the future. From 1900 to 1902, Aletha Bowen was president; Martha E. Murphy was elected president in 1902. Both women were convinced that the membership should purchase the building where the headquarters were housed. Because of their foresight, a down payment was made on the property at 1216 Druid Hill Avenue in July 1902. Even though the thirteen-room building was located in West Baltimore where the majority of the black population lived, the programs were accessible to all black Baltimoreans. Of the total cost of $4,000, $1,500 was raised by 19 July 1902.[19] Whites assisted in the fund-raising effort, and Cornelia Anderson, leader of the Colored King's Daughter Circle, organized the Willing Workers in August 1902 to raise money to pay off the building loan.

Owing to the concerted fundraising campaigns, the mortgage was paid in full by June 1909, and the members had a bank account of $900. The growth of the chapter necessitated the hiring of a general secretary. Cora B. Jackson, a former teacher of English at the Baltimore Colored Hall and Training School, was hired August 1909.

According to Rev. George F. Bragg, one of Baltimore's most influential black ministers, the YWCA was the most conspicuous and comprehensive organization in the city in January 1912. Therefore he believed that the "Y" should serve as the umbrella organization for all black groups in the city. When Reverend Bragg's recommendations were published in the *Afro-American Ledger*, there was no doubt that they would be given due consideration by Baltimore's leading black and white citizens. The recommendations were:

1. The colored YWCA should have an elected board of managers to administer its affairs.
2. The headquarters should house all charities.
3. A board of control, with two or three representatives from each organization, should be formed; each group would maintain its own identity, but the board would solicit funds for all the groups.
4. Baltimore should be divided into districts with active members in each serving as field agents.[20]

Reverend Bragg believed that his recommendations were a way to gain the support of whites and at the same time motivate Afro-Americans to contribute funds in support of charitable goals. The "Y" did not become the mechanism for implementing the recommendations, but they were considered by the Charity Organization Society. The "Y" remained an independent, viable force in Baltimore.

Norfolk Branch and Migrants North. Unlike the Baltimore branch, the Norfolk Colored Branch of the YWCA did not begin as a recognized chapter. However, it too became known as a branch after which others could model themselves. The Norfolk history clearly demonstrates that the YWCA national board was willing to encourage affiliation with black women who had already created respected community programs with philosophies similar to theirs. The history of the branch is also noteworthy because it shows how several organizations in one community were able to cooperate to aid a specific group of black women, those migrating north.

As we have seen, in the period under consideration in this book, many southern black women decided that life and opportunities would be better in the North and began the journey to a new home. Many of these women encountered special problems en route. Between early spring and late fall each year, crowds of young women came to Virginia each week on the Southern Steamship Line. The weekly groups were referred to as "crops," and each "crop" was estimated to be productive for about five years.[21] Black men and women, as well as whites, promoted schemes to lure the women to the city with grandiose promises; Afro-Americans typically worked behind the scenes to establish "employment bureaus." Some of the women who went north to become servants became prostitutes instead. Migrants were required to sign contracts which gave the bureau the right to collect their wages until all of their traveling expenses had been repaid. Upon arriving in New York, where they were most often taken, the women found themselves housed in ill-kept quarters and given little food. "They find the company treats them as so many heads of cattle."[22]

A report submitted to the Hampton Negro Conference in 1898 declared, "By various sophistries many refined, educated girls, particularly mulattoes and fair quadroons, are secured for the diversion of young Hebrews (the identity of their offspring is easily lost among Afro-Americans)."[23] Similar practices existed in a number of cities. The conference participants were asked to speak out against the employment bureaus which corrupted the morals and endangered the lives of black women. Further, all females seeking work in the North should have a personal contact in the northern city and adequate traveling and initial living expenses before departing from the South.

After the 1898 Hampton Conference, a study was conducted of employment agencies in Richmond, Norfolk, and Lynchburg, Virginia. At the 1899 Hampton Conference, the Woman's Conference of Norfolk issued the following resolution:

> Because of the fact that many young women and girls who leave their homes in the South for the North are decoyed off by irresponsible agents, the Woman's Conference of Norfolk has passed the following resolutions:
>
> Whereas: It has come to our knowledge that girls and young women from country and city homes in the South are induced to go north to places of employment, and since it is evident that many of them are led into vile places by their helpless condition after their arrival,

1. Be it resolved: That we do all in our power to discourage this custom among our girls of leaving good homes in the South for uncertain ones in the North.

2. That we invoke the aid of the pastors of northern churches in behalf of those girls who are already in these cities or may hereafter go.

3. That we place circulars containing practical suggestions for these girls in the hands of the stewardesses of the boats which leave our cities to be given to young women travellers.[24]

Norfolk, Virginia, was a seaport town which became a stopover for girls migrating to the North. The black women and ministers of Norfolk wanted to assist those who came with limited funds and no lodging. Hattie A.V. Proctor was paid by the ministers to meet the girls as they disembarked from the steamers. When she could not house the girls in her home, Proctor located rooms for them. Laura D. Titus, of Hampton's Class of 1876, is credited with calling together a group of black women to support Proctor's work; that call eventually resulted in the establishment of the Colored Branch of the YWCA in Norfolk. Local women founded the Norfolk Association of Colored Women to function as the organizing agency for the relief service.

At the 1905 Hampton Conference, because the practice of exploiting young female migrants continued, it was determined that cooperation with northern agencies could ensure greater protection for those young women who still sought employment in the North. As we shall see, the effort to establish this cooperation led to the creation of an organization that eventually became the National Urban League.

In Norfolk, enough funds were collected by 1910 to purchase a nine-room house to serve as a temporary boarding home for the migrants. With one room furnished by the Colored King's Daughter Circle and four others furnished by private donations, the home began to accept boarders in July. By 1911 there were twelve beds, one dining room, a parlor, and a library. The girls were required to pay twenty-five cents per night for lodging and bath.[25] The home received a charter from the national board in 1910 but did not receive official status as a branch of the YWCA until 1913.

Soon the building became the meeting place for clubs, the center where community and special interest lectures were given, and the site for church socials. The services to the boarders were also extended; a matron was hired and an employment service for temporary work was offered. The "Y" did not establish an employment bureau for permanent positions because it did not possess a license. In Baltimore the license fee was $25 and in New York $40, but in Norfolk it was $125. The fee was high to act as a deterrent to unscrupulous agents who sent girls to the North without proper preparation and suitable employment possibilities.

Because some of the boarders stayed as long as two to three weeks in the temporary quarters, self-improvement activities were offered, with girls from the vicinity also invited to participate. During winter 1911, twelve to fifteen girls met one night a week for a serving class. In the spring, twenty-five girls enrolled in the cooking and sewing classes. Those girls planted flowers and vegetables during the summer months. Young women between the ages of 15 and 18 met each Friday afternoon.[26] Even with the involvement of girls from the community, however, the primary concern of the "Y" remained the young migrating women.

Travelers' Aid, the Colored Woman's Protective League, and the YWCA joined forces to provide shelter and counseling to the many who arrived by train or steamer. The League hired Ida Bagnall as dock agent when Hattie Proctor indicated that she was overburdened by her increasing responsibilities. The expansion of services also necessitated the move to a larger facility in 1913. A membership rally in April 1913 attracted two hundred new members.[27] The national board of the YWCA in 1913 recommended that the branch hire Gertrude James of New York as secretary for the employment unit, which had proven greatly beneficial to the young women and the community. Because most of the placements were in domestic service, classes were held to give the girls proper training and so enhance their job opportunities.

By the end of 1913, the Norfolk Colored Branch of the YWCA was an established public service organization. The ministers of the city remained supportive, but the women managed the "Y" and its many programs; new programs included Camp Fire Girls and Blue Birds. However, because the mythical golden opportunities in the North retained their allure, the "Y" still served as a haven for stranded girls.

Controversy in Atlanta. Pleased with the progress of many of its local branches, the YWCA began to coordinate branch activities more closely in 1912, when the first conference of black workers took place. The following year, in February, a conference of volunteer and paid YWCA workers was held in Baltimore. Instead of seeing the potential for growth and general advancement of the black YWCA branches as a natural and desirable result of the conferences, some southern white women began to feel threatened. From 1915 to 1918, the national board heard complaints about discriminatory acts and the inability of white and black women to cooperate on the regional level. Typically the "Y" relied on Eva Bowles and the black field supervisors to resolve all problems concerning the southern black branches. In 1918, Adele F. Ruffin was the black field supervisor for the South Atlantic states of Virginia, North Carolina, South Carolina, Georgia, and Florida. The racial tensions in the "Y" received national attention during a 1918 controversy. During the controversy, it became clear that black women were not willing to accept decisions made for them by either black or white "Y" officials.

Because no single organization could serve the myriad needs of all black citizens, proven and productive service organizations were welcomed in the black community. In Atlanta, however, the black club women firmly believed that they must have some input into decisions affecting their community. Beatrice Walker, a field worker for the national "Y" through the public schools and churches, in 1918 began an organizing campaign in Atlanta. The campaign's effectiveness was hindered, however, by lack of a community center to serve as home base. Adele Ruffin came to Atlanta, met with leading black men and women, spoke for a few minutes, and then left without responding to many of the concerns of those present. The work of the floundering colored "Y" was greatly hampered by the lack of branch affiliation, since the national YWCA board required a "joint relationship committee" to oversee the operations of newly founded branches. Even though three white women had been appointed to that committee, no Afro-Americans had.[28]

Soon Walker was reassigned to another locale, and Florence Kennedy replaced her. She located a building for the proposed community center but lost the bid for it before Ruffin gave approval. Further complications arose when Ruffin advised Kennedy to seek the assistance of Mrs. Hucles, head of the YWCA's black hostess house at Camp Gordon, in selecting another possible site for the center. Because she was not a resident of Atlanta, Mrs. Hucles requested the assistance of Lugenia Burns Hope and another leading black woman of the city. Both insisted that the key black women of Atlanta be consulted before a center site was selected. A representative committee was formed, and two site recommendations were made. Through haste, oversight, or deliberate intention, however, without consulting the committee, Ruffin decided which site would be selected.

Because Ruffin did speak with selected individuals regarding their choice, it can be assumed that she gave some thought to her decision. She signed the lease for the Piedmont Avenue house, which she felt was in better condition, without consulting Miss Kennedy. However, in spite of the signed lease, the local residents decided that the designated location was not suitable for girls' work. As part of her effort to retain control of the situation, Ruffin dismissed Kennedy and assigned Miss Frazier, Kennedy's assistant to the post.[29]

By this time, the persons who had been involved were outraged. Ruffin and Mrs. Archibald Davis, a white woman serving as president of the Central Association of the YWCA for Atlanta, planned a mass meeting. In an effort to avoid any further public disagreements with Ruffin, several people met with her on Thursday before the scheduled Sunday meeting to ask about the agenda. According to their report, Ruffin told them to attend the mass meeting to learn what the agenda was. Many of the women were not willing to accept Ruffin's insult and her attempt to dictate what should happen in their community. Once the mass meeting was held, they sent a resolution to the YWCA central headquarters stating that Ruffin was not the best person to work with the citizens of Atlanta, and requesting Kennedy's reinstatement.[30]

Discrimination by The National YWCA. The feelings of distrust and frustration generated by the Atlanta crisis had not disappeared before a distressing incident involving the YWCA took place elsewhere. Eva Bowles' duties required her to visit local YWCA chapters to assist in program planning and inplementation. Despite the fact that Bowles had spent many years of her life working with the "Y" on different levels, while performing her duties at the Denver office, she was barred from eating in the cafeteria. A headline in the *Denver Post* on 15 July 1918 reported the event: "Prejudice and the Color Line are Paradox Even in YWCA, Shown by Miss Bowles' Visit." Bowles did not protest the policy.

Catharine D. Lealtal, however, did object to the YWCA's internal discriminatory practices. Because of those practices, she resigned in December 1919 from the position of secretary of the YWCA's Department of Methods to become associate secretary of the New York Urban League. Because of "racial feelings in the South" the YWCA's national office had planned to reassign her to the Field Work Department.[31] Also contributing to her decision to resign was the fact that her requests for equal accommodations for black staff persons in Des Moines had not been heeded, and Bowles, the chief black official at headquarters, had not supported her protests. The policy was not changed.

Obviously, YWCA officials were able to ignore the Christian creed of the "Y" when it would require them to treat black women as equals. In keeping with widely accepted social standards, the YWCA was willing to maintain a dual internal structure.

Despite the organization's obvious deficiencies, many black women decided not to relinquish their YWCA membership. Instead they chose to influence policies and practices by remaining active members. Four black delegates attended a 1920 YWCA conference in Louisville, Kentucky. Lugenia Hope of Atlanta, Charlotte Hawkins Brown of Sedalia, North Carolina, and Millie Hale of Nashville were quite vocal during the meetings. Two key policies were formulated as a result of the conference. (1) The first YWCA chapter organized in a city would be called the Central Association. All others would be designated branches. Previously, regardless of founding date, only white branches had been permitted to become a Central Association. (2) An Interlocking Committee would coordinate the activities of all branches and serve as an advisory committee.[32] Each branch would be represented on the committee.

On 6 April 1920, shortly after the Louisville conference, the black women met to discuss the best course of action to take regarding the YWCA's work among Afro-Americans in the South. Several plans were outlines. H.M. McCrorey, Charlotte Brown, Marion Wilkerson, Francis Keyser, and Lugenia Hope were assigned the task of drafting an appeal that their requests be acted upon. Since "Y" secretaries were not permitted to visit the South Atlantic Field or to attend conferences in the region, the women wanted "Y" executives to have the freedom to visit their centers. They requested the addition of a black female representative to the YWCA national board. They also hoped to clarify statements made about the "Alley Girl" and branch relationships. Hope and Lucy Laney were to travel to either New York or Cleveland to meet with Bowles or other key national staff memebrs concerning their appeal.

At the national convention in Cleveland on 24 April 1920, some white southern delegates objected to the presence of the black delegates at the annual banquet. The YWCA officials maintained that the waiters were the ones who objected. An article in the Ohio *Advocate* stressed how ridiculous the statement of the officials was and charged them with having an "un-Christian attitude."[33] The *Advocate's* May 1 editorial entitled "Too much Paternalism in 'Y's," stated that the YMCA and YWCA work among Afro-Americans was a form of segregation designed to keep Afro-Americans from joining white brances. Because the black Board of Managers was not permitted to exercise full responsibility for the black branches, it was recommended that Afro-Americans have complete control of the black branches.[34]

On 3 July 1920, Hope, McCrorey, and Laney met with members of the YWCA national board, including Eva Bowles. Chairing her delegation, Hope submitted a statement on behalf of 300,000 black women of the South. Included in that statement were three questions: "1. What colored work can be done in centers having no white Young Women's Christian Association? 2. What form should the organization of colored women take? 3. What should be the relationship between the field committee and the local colored work?"[35] The answers to the questions were crucial because the report from the Louisville conference had indicated that only work permitted by southern white women would be undertaken among Afro-Americans. The report had created much alarm among Afro-Americans throughout the United States, because the majority of southern white club women clearly were not willing to alter or remove existing racial barriers.

Replies to Hope's questions were not given in haste. The board did not wish to lose white members, nor did it wish to continue to receive negative publicity because of its policies. On the other hand, the eleven black centers, eight of them branches, in the South Atlantic Field were fully operational, productive units of the YWCA with influential advocates who would not remain silent if reasonable answers were not given.

Rather than provide answers, the YWCA national board held an interracial conference in Louisville on 15–17 February 1921 "for the better understanding of the groups concerned and discussion of the possibility of further extending YWCA in the Southland among colored women."[36] Sixty-four delegates—thirty-three Afro-Americans and thirty-one whites—formulated the guidelines by which the "colored" branches would operate through 1925:

1. Training would be provided for "Y" workers.
2. Local associations would cooperate with the interracial commissions in their areas.
3. All work for the colored groups would go through the regular channels of the association. A subcommittee on colored work, composed of white and colored women, would be formed.
4. A committee of management of the local association, representative of the different groups and interests of the community, would be formed.
5. The committee on colored work would be organized by the local association.
6. Field conferences, camps, and local institutes would be held as often as possible for all who were interested.
7. Whenever possible, local associations would hold interracial conferences.[37]

Not all of the ambitious guidelines were strictly adhered to. However, they did provide a framework from which the women could begin to cooperate to strengthen the branches. Some of the guidelines were implemented immediately. Ruth Logan Roberts of New York was appointed to the national board; she was to work directly with Eva Bowles. Of more direct benefit to the black branches, a three-week training camp was held at Hampton

Institute for the eighteen local secretaries in the YWCA's Southeastern Section. Two-thirds were college graduates, and none had had previous technical training. After the three-week session, the women were eligible to attend a session at the National Training School in New York. College graduates were eligible to attend the regular nine-month course at the Training School, and in 1921 C. Vivian Carter of Baltimore became the first Afro-American to do so. As of 1 January 1923, 107 black women were holding secretarial posts in the YWCA.[38]

The War Effort

On 2 April 1917, President Woodrow Wilson went before Congress to request a declaration of war against Germany. From the original Selective Service draft of 18 May 1917, 8,848,882 whites and 737,626 Afro-Americans, thirty-six out of every one hundred Afro-Americans and twenty-five out of every one hundred whites, registered. Of those registering, 711,213 whites and 75,697 Afro-Americans were certified. Before the war ended in November 1918, 400,000 Afro-Americans had served. In an open letter to President Wilson in 1917, the College Alumnae Club, composed of black women, appealed to the president to give verbal support to all Afro-Americans who were supporting the war effort.[39]

The Women's Committee of the Council of National Defense defined ways in which women should support the war effort. Alice Dunbar, widow of Paul L. Dunbar, served as one of the field representatives during 1918, and Mary B. Talbert served as one of the national committee members. Talbert indicated that black women could make their contribution by encouraging black males to serve on active duty, buying Liberty Bonds, keeping black females from loitering at the Army campus, assisting the Red Cross, and producing and conserving food.[40]

Government Programs. Food production and food conservation were national issues which forced the Federal Government to intervene directly in the wartime activities of Afro-Americans. Americans were asked to save food, grow food, and to substitute for needed food items those not in demand overseas. In an article entitled "An Appeal to the Negroes of the United States," Herbert Hoover wrote, "The Negroes have shown themselves loyal and responsive in every national crisis."[41] It was expected, therefore, that Afro-Americans would adhere to the policies of the U.S. Food Administration.

To rally blacks behind the campaigns of the Food Administration, Ernest J. Atwell, director of its Negro section, said, "No racial group will benefit more if the ideals for which we are fighting are achieved; therefore, we ought not to let any other people do more in any direction in proportion to our means and opportunities."[42] Atwell, formerly head of the Business Department of Tuskegee Institute, had been a special representative of the Food Administration for some time. He began his duties as director by decentralizing the state programs. In states where there were large black populations, Negro state directors were appointed by the state's federal food administrator. Atwell visited seventeen states to help implement the plan to establish Negro sections.

The decentralization plan ended the Food Administration's Negro Press Section but provided for information to be sent to the Negro press through the Educational Division. More often than not, press releases were directed towards women, who were considered the primary conservers of food. Black women, particularly in the South, were encouraged to grow food for their families and to curtail their use of items necessary for the war effort. Only the use of milk, because of the nutritional needs of children, was not curtailed.

The YWCA's War Efforts. As early as 1913, the YWCA was assisting black females who did wish to work in industrial jobs. The industrial secretary of the YWCA national headquarters stressed three goals in working with black women: to place them in jobs, to secure more job openings, and to educate the public, particularly employers, about the value of hiring black women for industrial labor.[43] Mary E. Jackson was appointed by the YWCA's War Work Council as a "special worker for colored girls." In 1918 she prepared and disseminated a questionnaire designed to ascertain the involvement of black women in industrial work throughout the nation. Responding to the questionnaire, Eva Bowles stressed the need for white women to support their black coworkers. She wrote, "As the colored girl enters industry, we are brought face to face with two vital problems—her own adjustment to her new work, and her maintenance of standards of wages and time which have been attained after years of struggle."[44] From January to June 1919, the YWCA reported 1,734 black female applicants for jobs; 727 positions (85 percent more than in 1918) were filled.[45]

Within a segregated internal structure, the YWCA developed programs to ensure black female involvement in the war effort. As the first paid secretary for the Colored Branch of the YWCA in New York City for 1906–1907, Eva Bowles had paved the way for organized assistance to black women.

In 1913 she served on the YWCA national board as secretary of colored work in cities. Working with other YWCA officials, she organized a conference which would outline the approach to working with Afro-Americans in the war effort. With black and white women in attendance, the conference was held at Louisville, Kentucky, in October 1915.

A more definite plan evolved after the YWCA War Work Council, a committee of the national board, was organized in June 1917 to be "responsible for using resources of the YWCA to meet special needs of girls and young women of all countries affected by the war."[46] Helen P. Wallace chaired the Colored Work Committe of the War Work Council. The war work was divided into three sections: hostess houses in military camps, recreation centers, and industrial centers. In October 1917, Mary Belcher was appointed field war worker for the South Central Field, and Adele F. Ruffin was named field supervisor and war worker for the South Atlantic Field.

The War Work Council appropriated $200,000 for programs among black women; Theodore Roosevelt gave an aditional $4,000.[47] A total of sixteen black organizations or branches affiliated with the YWCA national board. The branches relied upon the central headquarters to direct program activities, ensuring the same quality of programming. The Committee of Management of Colored Women handled its own affairs, however, while maintaining contact with the white women of the Central Association. To implement programs and facilitate communication between black and white women, nine black female workers were hired initially.[48] As the program developed, additional black women were hired to staff the centers and serve as secretaries.

The hostess houses had a number of paid workers but also depended on the volunteer services of black women. The houses were located at or near military installations and were established to provide services for military personnel and, when applicable, their visiting families. Josephine Pinyon was the director of workers for black hostess houses. In August 1917, workers at the white hostess house in Petersburg, Virginia, asked for assistance. Pinyon went to the city to attempt to establish a "colored hostess house," because of racial prejudices and the inability of the black and white women to work together, she was unsuccessful. The first hostess house for Afro-Americans was opened at Camp Dix in New Jersey, followed by one at Camp Upton in New York.

The houses could not effectively serve their purpose without trained workers. Because of her widely recognized organizational skills, Lugenia Hope was hired to conduct the training of hostesses at the training site at Camp Upton. However, Emily Brown, a graduate of Hampton Institute living in Yonkers, New York, in May 1918 became executive hostess and head of the training program at Camp Upton and became responsible for fully developing and implementing the training program. Normally, those accepted as trainees were college or normal school graduates or possessed equivalent education and experience. In the eight-week course, the first four weeks were spent learning about the overall operation of a hostess house and the duties of the hostess; the second four weeks consisted of in-depth training in the area of one's choice. The need for trained workers was evident; Camp Upton had an average of five thousand visitors each week during the year 1918.

Eight houses for Afro-Americans had opened by the end of 1918. Personnel at the houses worked with local committees of women to ensure their cooperation. After Armistice Day, the houses were chiefly concerned with maintaining the morale of the men. As the men, some sick or wounded, began to return in 1919, the housing problems faced by visiting relatives were greatly mitigated by the hostess houses.

In keeping with its original goals, the YWCA also sponsored centers for young black females during the war. Josephine Pinyon organized the first center during her visit to Petersburg, Virginia, in August 1917. The centers developed as a result of requests in 1917 from the U.S. War Department Commission on Training Camp Activities and from the YMCA Committee for Women Workers to provide some type of guidance for girls living near Army and Navy training camps. The centers were named "Girls Reserves and Recreation Centers." The Reserve movement was part of a national and international thrust: "The object of the movement is to give girls through normal, natural activities, the habits, insights and ideals which will make them responsible women, capable and ready to help make America more true to its best hopes and traditions."[49] The Reserves assumed the functions of the YWCA's Patriotic Leagues in fall 1918.

The YWCA's recreation center component followed the club work format which had been established previously for white girls. The participants at the center were required to be in grade or high school or, if employed, under eighteen. From 1 November 1918 to 31 October 1919, the YWCA War Council expected to expend $200,000 to establish recreation and industrial centers throughout the U.S.[50] Crystal Bird of Boston was appointed the national girls' work secretary for colored girls. Through her efforts and the involvement of black females working on the local level, recreation centers were established in Atlanta, Georgia; New Jersey; North Carolina; Ohio; Virginia; and the District of Columbia. To direct the centers' activities, thirty-nine black girls' workers were hired.[51] In conjunction with the centers' programs, the first YWCA camp for black girls in the United States opened in 1918 at Harrod's Creek, Kentucky. By the end of 1919, forty-five recreational and industrial centers had been established in forty-five communities in twenty-one states and the District of Columbia. There were 112 paid local workers, 3 field workers, 9 persons serving on the headquarters staff, a student secretary at the headquarters, and 42 branch secretaries. The clubs enrolled twelve thousand black females.[52]

The YWCA's wartime work with black females was one of many programs developed through racial cooperation. The YWCA, because of its resources and international reputation, provided the framework within which black women could assist black military personnel and their families at the hostess house. However, because the programs for Afro-Americans were forced to operate in a rigidly segregated system, the majority of the accolades for implementation and success must be given to the paid and volunteer black workers. The goals and activities of the Girl Reserves and Recreation Centers were in many ways extensions of the clubs founded by black women before World War I. Thus, the "Y" provided national link to local communities, where club workers and leaders could share existing skills and commitment.

The Circle for Negro Relief. The Circle for Negro Relief was organized in 1917 as a war relief organization. Originally developed to aid soldiers and their families, the circle reorganized in 1919. In 1920, a health program was established "to meet the critical need for health education and Public Health nursing service in the neglected rural districts of the South."[53] In addition, a national Public Health Nursing Scholarships Fund helped black women to receive training.

The circle was the only national organization actively developing programs to improve the health of Afro-Americans. It was able to pursue this effort when it received five thousand dollars from the National War Relief Committee from remaining funds. The local communities of Fort Valley, Georgia; Palalka, Florida; and Mt. Meigs, Alabama, were required to subsidize the public health nurse assigned by the circle. Through special gifts, the circle was able to pay the tuition of two persons in public health education courses. In 1925, with support of the circle, a young black female became the first Afro-American to attend the Pennsylvania School of Social and Health Work. The school, affiliated with the University of Pennsylvania, had admitted the young woman for a full year's work.[54]

The National Urban League

When the women of Norfolk founded a home to shelter black women migrating north to work, they soon discovered that their efforts would be meaningless if there were no support system for the migrants once they reached the northern cities. White women helped to establish the northern reception system. To aid those women who were trying to escape from the harsh realities of the South, the National League for the Protection of Colored Women was organized in 1905 by Frances Kellor, lawyer and female activist, and Ruth Standish Baldwin, founder of the New York Association for the Protection of Colored Women. Their main goal was to help penniless and homeless Afro-Americans from southern rural areas, particularly women, to find employment and living quarters in New York. Branches were established in Norfolk, Virginia; Philadelphia, Pennsylvania; and Baltimore, Maryland.[55] To assist the league, the Committee for Improving the Industrial Conditions of Negroes in New York was established.

For four years the Committee for Improving the Industrial Conditions of Negroes in New York and the National League for the Protection of Colored Women worked in tandem. In 1910, Baldwin called together representatives from the various organizations working in the interest of Afro-Americans in New York City. At this meeting, George Edmund Haynes, fellow of the Bureau of Social Research at the New York School of Philanthropy, and professor of social science at Fisk University in Nashville, presented a paper entitled "Negro Life in New York." Afterwards, a third group was formed, the Committee on Urban Conditions Among Negroes. To become more efficient and cost-effective, the three groups merged in 1911 to become the National League on Urban Conditions Among Negroes. With an interracial executive board and an annual budget of $8,500, the National League began to restructure its programs.[56] The program to aid black migrating women remained an integral unit. A Committee for the Protection of Women was formed, with seven or more members elected by the executive board.[57] In order to assist the committee, it was recommended that the National Association of Colored Women appoint correspondents in various cities, to assist the females who traveled through their communities.

The National League on Urban Conditions was incorporated in New York in 1913. Baldwin resigned as chair, and L. Hollingsworth Wood, a Quaker lawyer who was league treasurer, succeeded her. The league's purpose was broadened to address the needs of all Afro-Americans in urban settings, particularly those outside the Deep South. Beginning in 1916, the league sponsored a series of conferences to discuss problems associated with the large influx of black southerners into northern industrial centers. Since they had come from the South, they were to be assisted through direct contact with black staff workers, some of them educated in southern institutions.

One of the league's main purposes was "to secure and train Negro social workers." The organization carried out this goal by establishing full and partial fellowships for the training of young men and women for social service work. During the 1913–14 academic year, Nellie Quander of the New York School of Social Work and Uxenia B. Scott of Fisk University were appointed the first female fellows.[58] By 1919, the league was maintaining constant contact with college women and men, in an attempt to stimulate them to study and prepare for social work. This contact established what other interracial organizations had not been able to develop: a trained cadre of workers committed to a national organization.

By 1924, the league employed 175 people at its New York headquarters and in forty-one branches throughout the country. In addition, twenty-eight fellows were receiving training with league assistance. The 1924 operating budget was $300,000.[59] The league hired women as assistants and investigators, while men were usually hired as executives. Salaries for social workers ranged from $600 to $2,500 a year; black women working in a specialized field for the league earned between $900 and $1,200 a year, while comparable men earned between $1,200 and $1,500 a year. The league's male executives were paid between $1,500 and $2,000 a year.[60] Despite these salary differences, black women still sought positions with the league.

Purposes of the league cited in 1916 were "(1) to emphasize cooperation among social welfare agencies; (2) to secure and train Negro social workers; (3) to protect women and children from unscrupulous persons; (4) to fit workers for/to work; (5) to help secure playgrounds and other clean places of amusement; (6) to organize boys' and girls' clubs and neighborhood unions; (7) to help with probation oversight of delinquents; (8) to maintain a country home for convalescent women; and (9) to investigate conditions of city life as a basis for practical work."[61]

Black women in rural and urban areas throughout the South had been implementing most of these objectives since 1895. The major difference between the efforts of the league and those of black club women was in the ideal of the league expressed by Baldwin: "Let us work not as colored people nor as white people for the narrow benefit of any group alone, but TOGETHER, as American citizens for the common good of our common city, our common county."[62] Because of racial conditions and attitudes, most black women had been unable to elicit white support for their programs. In the League, the key officers, the finance committee, and the executive secretaries were black men, white men, or white women. Yet, as always in similar efforts in the past, the league's principal workers among the people were to be black women.

Even though the national headquarters set policy and established guidelines for the league's work, it was through the local branches that the objectives of the league were realized. In spite of the fact that in all branches the chief full-time administrative position of executive secretary was held by men, women were generally the implementors of league activities. The role of black women as community organizers and activists for the league became particularly significant during the great migration of 1916 and 1917.

The efforts of workers in Huntsville, Alabama, suggest the types of services performed by women. In that city, under the auspices of the Urban League branch, a Welfare Committee was organized. As a result, black women were appointed by the mayor to the juvenile probation board, which had eleven black members. The women also secured a rest place for women, promoted home nurse visitations, established a milk station and baby clinic, and developed plans for recreation activities for area girls. As a rule, similar programs and services were sponsored by Urban League branches in the South and North; direct contact with the masses remained the aim of the organization. As we have seen in the case of Atlanta, where local organizations already were performing similar functions, the league attempted to affiliate with such groups so as to become the official umbrella organization speaking for all Afro-Americans.

The National Association
for the Advancement of Colored People

Incorporated on 19 June 1911, the National Association for the Advancement of Colored People (NAACP) focused upon legal action to end racial discrimination. Lynchings, the denial of civil rights, and segregation were the three focal concerns during the organization's early years. On the opening day of the 1909 founding meeting in New York, Ida Wells Barnett, a member of the first executive committee of the NAACP, delivered a speech on lynching. Mary Church Terrell also attended the founding meeting and was appointed a member of the executive committee. Terrell organized the Washington, D.C., branch and became its vice president. From the inception of the NAACP, black women strove to raise operating funds for the organization, acquaint others with its goals, and establish branches in southern communities.

W.E.B. Du Bois, editor of the official organ of the NAACP, *The Crisis: A Record of the Darker Races* believed that it was imperative that Afro-Americans across the nation remain fully aware of the excellent self-help and social service work being done by black women. The second issue of the journal carried a column, "Talks About Women," by Mrs. J.E. Milholland. Beginning in May 1911, "News of Women's Clubs," by Addie W. Hunton, was a regular feature. Special articles about women and their roles in society were also included. *The Crisis*, with its vast circulation, enabled many other women to adapt noteworthy programs to their own needs.

Black women participated in many of the projects sponsored by the NAACP, but the one that rallied more women than any other was the campaign against lynching. Each month *The Crisis* listed the number of black persons in America lynched without a trial. Between 1900 and 1914, more than 1,100 persons were lynched. The majority were men, but by 1922, 83 women had been lynched.[63] The NAACP lobbied for antilynching bills, and on 31 May 1911, a delegation met with President Taft and presented a petition asking him to intervene to stop the lynchings. None of these efforts produced the desired results.

At the 1922 spring conference of the NAACP, sixteen black women formed the Committee of Anti-Lynching Crusades. The committee was fully and officially organized on 8 July 1922, with headquarters in Buffalo, New York, and Mary B. Talbert as national director. In each of forty states, one woman became state director. To reach as many citizens as possible, fifteen hundred women volunteered to disseminate information about the campaign and to raise one million dollars.[64] White women were among those who joined the effort. The committee women and the NAACP influenced the passage of antilynching laws in thirteen states, including Alabama and Tennessee, by July 1925.

Because of her leadership of the antilynching committee, her general support of the NAACP, and her contribution to the advancement of the race, on June 20, 1922, Mary B. Talbert became the first woman to receive the highest award given by the NAACP, the Spingarn Medal.[65]

The Commission on Inter-racial Cooperation

Unfortunately, the involvement of black women in the Commission on Inter-racial Cooperation (CIC) was not as harmonious as in the NAACP and the National Urban League. The CIC was created in December 1918, partly in response to problems facing Afro-Americans at the end of World War I. The movement of Afro-Americans to urban areas, and the visible progress of some, intensified the hostility of many whites toward black people. The educational director of the Phelps-Stokes Fund helped to arrange a conference in Atlanta in 1919. The white male delegates listed the following purposes:

(a) To study the Negro problem and discover what the *Negro Wanted*
(b) To agree upon a minimum program behind which *intelligent* white people might be rallied
(c) To line up white people in support of this program
(d) To enlist in its support at the same time the leaders of the Negro race
(e) To take the necessary steps to make the program effective
(f) To secure cooperation on the part of all agencies working in this field and to render assistance to them in the matter of better team work, and to avoid duplication."[66]

The ICC represented thirteen southern states, because the majority of Afro-Americans lived there. All of the CIC members were white professional men who had worked in some area of race relations. At the 17 February 1920 meeting in Atlanta, the members voted to include "representative leaders of Negroes."[67]

W.E.B. Du Bois openly criticized the type of Afro-American selected by whites to serve on the CIC. The whites recognized that greater cooperation among the races was necessary if programs which met the approval of Afro-Americans were to be established. However, because the commission stood for compromise, it could not have radicals and extremists as members. The compromise was evident: there must be progress, but progress at a slow pace within guidelines acceptable to whites. No specific black leadership group participated in the early organizing conferences. Referring to Charlotte Hawkins Brown and all the black men except John Hope, Du Bois called them "white folks niggers."[68] Most of the black women could not be so labeled, however.

After a study of the conditions of Afro-Americans, the CIC classified Afro-Americans and whites in three categories each. Afro-Americans were said to belong to one of three groups: the impatient masses who wanted equality immediately; thoughtful, educated Negro leaders, as earnest in their desire for equality but willing to be patient and work with whites; or radical, educated Negroes who did not wish to wait for progress. Whites also belonged to one of three groups: the masses who saw Afro-Americans as servants and could see no merit in racial cooperation; professional dema-gogues who advocated racial prejudice; or thoughtful white men and women, mostly college-trained, who sought justice for Afro-Americans.[69]

The list of categories suggests why many black women were reluctant to join the CIC and why they found it difficult to work with whites. As a rule, black women were interested not in labeling segments of their race, but rather in dealing with the effects of racial discrimination, poverty, and lack of formal education. They understood quite well why various black groups responded in different ways to the obstacles they encountered.

Women were not added to the commission until 17 November 1920, when a central committee was formed. During summer 1920, thirty-one black men and fifty-six white men had been hired to organize and develop county committees,[70] and by November 1920, eight hundred interracial committees existed in 1,300 counties in thirteen states.

In order to involve black women in the CIC initiatives, Estelle Haskin and Mary de Bardelehen established a framework through which women could organize. Mrs. Luke G. Johnson chaired the planning committee. All three of the women were white. To elicit support from black women, John-son and Haskin attended the 1920 annual meeting of the NACW at Tuske-gee. Lugenia Hope obtained permission for Johnson to speak on the last day of the conference. At a later conference, Johnson described her impres-sion of the women: "I saw these colored women, graduates of great institu-tions of learning. I saw lawyers, doctors, poets, sculptors and painters. I saw women of education, culture and refinement. I had lived in the South all my life, but didn't know such as these lived in the land."[71] Johnson's words constituted a clear and terrible indictment of the southern social system, which not only did not utilize the talents of many of its citizens, but even was unaware of their existence.

The day after the NACW meeting, ten premier leaders among black club-women met with Johnson and Haskin: Janie Porter Barrett, president, Virginia Federation of Colored Women's Clubs, Peak's Turnout, Virginia; Mary McLeod Bethune, president, Southeastern Federation of Colored Women's Clubs, and principal, Daytona Normal and Industrial School for Negro Girls, Daytona, Florida; Charlotte Hawkins Brown, president, North Carolina Federation of Colored Women, and principal, Palmer Memorial Institute, Sedalia, North Carolina; Mrs. M.L. Crosthwait, registrar, Fisk University; Lugenia Hope, Department of Neighborhood Work, NACW, and Morehouse College, Atlanta, Georgia; Lucy Laney, president, City Federation of Colored Women's Clubs, and principal, Haines Institute,

Fig. 26. In the South, only a few black women participated in interracial organizations. The leading clubwomen, in addition to their local and regional activities, represented the interests of the masses in the Women's Commission of the Commission on Inter-racial Cooperation. *Courtesy of the Atlanta University Center Woodruff Library.*

Augusta, Georgia; Mary J. McCrorey, chairman, Committee of Management, Charlotte Branch of YWCA, and Biddle University, Charlotte, North Carolina; Jennie Dee Moton, Tuskegee Institute, Tuskegee, Alabama; Margaret Murray Washington, honorary president, NACW, and Tuskegee Institute, Tuskegee, Alabama; and Marion B. Wilkerson, president, South Carolina Federation of Colored Women's Clubs, and State College, Orangeburg, South Carolina.

The women met at the home of Mrs. Washington. As Johnson told it:

> They did [come] — but oh how hard it was to get in touch with them — there was a gulf of distance, of mistrust and suspicion.
>
> I wanted to speak to them but didn't know how. I wanted to invite their frankness and their confidence but didn't know how. Only after an hour spent in the reading of God's word and in prayer, face to face on the platform of Christ Jesus did these white women and black women come to a liberty and frankness that made possible a discussion of those things which make for better civilization, for justice and righteousness and for Christian relations.

The day wore on — that prophetic day spent around the beautiful teak-wood table in Booker Washington's library. Those upon whom the responsibility rested felt the keenest pain as the Negro women made known the lack of protection for their daughters, their children and their homes, and the handicaps resting upon their lives and the lives of their little ones. When they told of the aching hearts and unspeakable fear for their young when they pillowed their heads for sleep, my heart broke and I have been trying to pass the story on to the women of my race.[72]

At the conclusion of the meeting, the women had agreed to explore what joint activities could further child welfare, transportation, education, suffrage, protection of black girls, press treatment of blacks, and elimination of lynching.

The black women were asked to draft a statement of their problems and submit them in correspondence. Only three of the ten responded. A consensus on lynching and suffrage was difficult to obtain: Lugenia Hope approved the first draft, but Margaret Washington and Jennie Moton submitted a second, more conservative draft to Johnson. Finally, points from the first and second drafts were combined with what was called the "Hope Amendment on Lynching."[73] The statement was presented at the CIC's Memphis conference. There it was decided that the best way to reach the women of the South was to share the results of the Tuskegee meeting with the leaders of church groups, YWCA, antituberculosis associations, federated clubs, and WCTU; practically every southern woman belonged to one or more of the organizations. Dr. Will Alexander, the CIC's paid director, persuaded the commission to allocate $7,500 needed by the women to hold a meeting of representatives of all these organizations.[74]

The CIC was not "popular with the rank and file of [white] club women in the South in 1920. Many women were indifferent while others were openly antagonistic."[75] Nevertheless, Haskin and Johnson continued to promote the CIC's causes. In October 1920, one hundred white women and four black women assembled in Memphis to commit themselves to interracial cooperation. Margaret Murray Washington addressed the assembly. The women agreed to aid Afro-Americans through establishment of day nurseries, kindergartens, clinics, and playgrounds; improvement of housing and sanitary conditions; provision of educational opportunities; improvement of traveling conditions; seeking justice in the courts; and suppression of lynching.[76] The list was drawn from the Tuskegee meeting. Suppression of lynching was to receive special emphasis. After the meeting in Memphis, Johnson was appointed chair of the CIC's Department of Woman's Work. The women were now officially under the umbrella of the larger group.

Because interracial coopertion was a concept alien to many southern white women, the Memphis conference did not bring about immediate significant changes. Therefore, in 1921 the Southeastern Federation of Colored Women's Clubs published a pamphlet, "Southern Negro Women and Race Cooperation."[77] The pamphlet was designed to accomplish what meetings with white women, the last of which was held in Georgia on 28–30 June 1921, had not been able to achieve. The pamphlet encouraged white women to assist black women in those matters affecting both groups. The publication contained clear statements of the Southeastern Federation's positions on race issues. The women who contributed to the text were Hope, Wilkerson, Laney, Brown, McCrorey, Barrett, Crosthwait, Washington, and Bethune.

Beginning with the statement that all black women, regardless of status, suffered from racial bias at some time or another, the pamphlet listed areas where black women came into contact with whites and troubling aspects of such contacts. In domestic service, the area of most frequent contact, a major concern was the long, irregular working hours of black women. Recommendations for alleviating the unfavorable conditions were regular hours of work; better conditions under which to work; clean, attractive, and "wholesome" rooming facilities; more attention to personal appearance and deportment; and more recreational opportunities. If these recommendations were to be implemented, white women would have to lead the way.

In the second area, child welfare, black women had already begun to address the problems of children who did not have adult supervision while their parents worked. The recommendations requested the support of white women in establishing additional day nurseries, playgrounds, and recreational centers; in providing for home and school visitation; and in securing more juvenile probation officers and reform schools.

The third section suggested ways to improve education. While all of the recommendations had received the attention of Afro-Americans since 1895, the authors of the pamphlet know that more needed to be done and could be done if white women agitated for improved facilities, extended terms, vocational training, adequate salaries, and additional training schools for teachers. The task was to convince the whites that improvements for Afro-Americans would bring about benefits for them as well.

Conditions of travel, the public press, suffrage, and lynching were other areas of concern. Lynchings, which polarized blacks and whites when they occurred, were considered an abomination, a flagrant abuse of personal liberties, and an affront to the American system of justice. Even though the women understood the need for a man who assaulted a woman to be punished, they were opposed to mob violence. To suppress lynching, white women were asked to protest lynchings when they occurred, to call for the punishment of leaders and participants in mobs and riots, and to request the cooperation of white churches and the press. Because of the southern myth that black men posed a threat to the sanctity of white women, and because of the fears generated by ignorance and hatred, the recommendations to end lynchings were expected to be the ones least likely to be implemented. Nevertheless, the black club women of the South staunchly supported the recommended seven-point plan of action. Through 1925, members from the Southeastern Federation of Colored Women's Clubs continued to work with the CIC Women's Department.

In each state where there was an CIC branch, much had been accomplished in many communities by 1925. The greatest influence was in the area of education; the southern states, as a direct result of commission involvement, provided additional educational services and facilities for Afro-Americans. These improvements were documented in a survey of public school systems and colleges conducted by the CIC in 1925. For example, Dr. Horace Bond, a prominent black educator, and the Louisville, Kentucky, CIC had assisted in raising $40,000 for Simmons University there. The board of trustees of the University of Louisville had pledged to establish a "colored" department for higher education. Until such time as the pledge could be fulfilled, the university would conduct extension courses at Simmons University. A pledge of one million dollars for "colored state institutions" was included in a proposed bond issue but was defeated at the polls. Kentucky, however, did supply additional teachers at increased salaries for black institutions.[78]

In South Carolina, the state paid particular attention to the Rosenwald schools, built for Afro-Americans through the Rosenwald Fund. The schools were supported in Florence County and on St. Helena's Island. The legislature continued to appropriate funds for the maintenance of Fairwald Industrial Schools. In Charleston, South Carolina, supervising visiting teachers were provided for the black schools. Tennessee also aided the Rosenwald schools. The state agricultural and industrial colleges received a state appropriation of $100,000. Of great significance in Tennessee was the law which provided for all schools meeting defined criteria to hold sessions for eight months; black schools had problems in meeting the criteria, however.

Virginia also benefitted from the CIC's positive force. A total of $50,000 was raised for Virginia Union University, and Manassas Industrial School's

$28,000 debt was paid. In Richmond the public library opened a branch for Afro-Americans. In Georgia, four teacher training schools in Savannah received $18,000, while the Athens CIC helped to raise bonds for the Teacher Training and Industrial Institute. A high school for Afro-Americans was erected in Waycross, Georgia.[79] Mrs. Jessie Daniel, state secretary for the Texas CIC supervised the restoration of $100,000 cut by the state legislature from the appropriation for maintenance of Prairie View Normal School. Other successes attributed to the state commissions and the CIC Women's Department included playgrounds, day nurseries, street repairs, fire protection, observation of Negro Health Week, and the investigation of housing for Afro-Americans.

A pattern was clear. The state CICs mediated between local officials and black institutions. Through the influence of persons on the various commissions, black educational institutions received increased support. Afro-Americans who had stated that white cooperation was needed in order to effect positive change had been proven partially correct. Whites, however, would still direct their attention to the institutions which they considered valuable; most of the schools which were given support had accepted the industrial education concept.

By 25 March 1925, the number of state commissions had increased so that a national interracial conference was held on the theme, "Problems Affecting the Racial Situation in the United States." The topics of health, housing, industry, and publicity were considered as they related to race relations. The three-day conference, cosponsored by the Commission on Race Relations of the Federated Council of Churches and the Commission on Interracial Cooperation, drew delegates, including black women, from many communities. Heralded as a "first," the conference permitted delegates to share success stories and encouraged the interaction of Afro-Americans and whites with similar attitudes about race.

At the end of 1925, the Commission on Inter-racial Cooperation was still active in many southern cities. Because it had existed as a functioning body only since 1919, the true measure of its impact in the South would not be realized until later years.

Conclusion

Even though black women living in different communities realized that some needs were unique to their areas, they also understood that certain needs were common to all communities where Afro-Americans lived. Because Tuskegee, Atlanta, Nashville, Hampton, and Baltimore were in the South, they presented similar economic, social, and political problems. As a result, black women in all five regions developed programs and organizations to respond to local, state, and regional concerns; the final goal was the advancement of Afro-Americans as a group. Generally, the programs were designed to serve self and others directly and to teach new ways to modify unfavorable conditions. Although the women were unable to provide solutions for all problems, they were able to change some people's behavior, provide services for many, and strengthen ties among separate southern communities.

The social service and self-help programs described in this book demonstrate the many achievements of black women:

1. These women were able to identify clearly the problems affecting them and other Afro-Americans.
2. In spite of limited resources, they were able to create programs which were meaningful and enduring.
3. Their efforts to provide social service programs often served to unify the black communities.
4. The women were willing to work within the existing social order to effect changes; yet, if necessary, they would challenge the attitudes of the larger white society and the conditions favored by whites.
5. The programs developed by these black women won for them the approval and support of traditionally white organizations and individuals, and so furthered interracial understanding and cooperation.

The small group of national leaders of black women spoke for the masses at national and international conferences. Generally, these leading educated black women were also regional leaders who served as presidents of state federations of black women's clubs. In many cases the same women concurrently held key local, regional, and national offices and so made public policy decisions for black women. Because the decisions generally flowed from a genuine desire to "lift the race," and in many cases after 1897 emerged from the general and executive sessions of NACW national conventions, they reflected the needs of black people. As this study proves, as a direct result of the implementation of national, regional, and local objectives, racial uplift did occur. Dedicated cadres of workers, usually volunteer, always existed at the level of greatest importance for racial advancement—the local community. Capable leadership, adequate funds, community support, and the potential to fulfill a defined need were essential if programs were to succeed. In the regions studied in this book, the programs which survived after 1925 were those which possessed all of the necessary components.

Because of the urgent need to improve the conditions under which the majority of Afro-Americans lived in the United States, black women did not permit personal differences and group conflicts to impede the implementation of programs for any length of time. However, they were not able to work as well with white women or with organizations created by whites as they were with all-black organizations. Token inclusion in national movements led by white women did not mean that black women were treated as equal partners in these groups. Often, when the white women gained victory, they again raised racial barriers.

The Commission on Inter-racial Cooperation, the NAACP, and the Urban League were all recognized as interracial organizations which were striving to create new Afro-American social institutions, to change negative attitudes held by whites, and when possible to influence the passage of racially positive legislation. If black women had not been active in all three, the gains would not have been so great. Through their involvement in the interracial organizations, black women proved that they were willing to affiliate with any group which sought the advancement of all Afro-Americans. Even when confronted with inequities in treatment and white reluctance to move at an acceptable pace, the black women remained members. At times, interracial cooperation did require black women to develop new strategies. In order to gain the support of whites, they modified their public declarations against social evils to some extent, relinquished the possibility of holding visible leadership positions within the groups, and at times acquiesced in allowing priorities to be determined by whites or by black males. In return, they saw increased attention and financial support given to programs and goals that they had championed since 1895. In many cases, the interracial thrust won program sanction from governmental officials, greater exposure for the programs, and greater financial assistance from whites. Except for some of the NAACP legal projects, the programs of the Urban League, the CIC, and the NAACP were all similar in purpose and scope to those that long had been proposed and implemented.

The YWCA and the Commission on Inter-racial Cooperation attempted to work with black women to solve the racial problems of the South. Until after 1925, neither organization was willing to allow black women equal participation on all levels in the organizations. Even so, through their black female members, the YWCA, the CIC, the NAACP, and the Urban League initiated programs which improved the quality of life for many Afro-Americans.

Whether in groups of black women only, or in biracial groups, the black female demonstrated her competence, industry, and intelligence. There is no greater evidence of her value to Afro-Americans as a group than the lives she influenced, the lasting institutions and programs she founded, and the positive course for racial betterment that she set for future generations.

Notes

Abbreviations

ADAU	Archives Department, Trevor Arnett Library, Atlanta University, Atlanta, Georgia. Now titled the Atlanta University Center Woodruff Library, Atlanta, Georgia
AMCHU	Archival and Museum Collection, Hampton University, Hampton, Virginia
BCA	Baltimore City Archives, Baltimore, Maryland
GPO	United States Government Printing Office, Washington, D.C.
LC	Library of Congress, Washington, D.C.
MSRC	Moorland-Spingarn Research Center, Howard University, Washington, D.C.
SCFU	Special Collections, Fisk University Library, Fisk University, Nashville, Tennessee
TUAC	Archival Collection, Hollis Burke Frissell Library, Tuskegee University, Tuskegee, Alabama

Chapter 1

1. E.C. Hobson and C.E. Hopkins, *A Report Concerning the Colored Women of the South,* Trustees of the John F. Slater Fund Occasional Paper No. 9 (Baltimore, 1896), pp. 6–14.
2. Mrs. Warren Logan, "Colored Women of the Country Districts," *Tuskegee Messenger* 29 (Apr. 1913): 7.
3. Mary Church Terrell, "Being a Colored Woman in the United States," Mary Church Terrell Papers, Collection 102, Box 3, Folder 53, p. 1, Manuscript Division, MSRC.
4. John Hope and Kelly Miller to Robert R. Moton, 5 June 1916 and 5 July 1916, R.R. Moton Collection, TUAC.

5. Serena Sloan Butler, "Heredity," *Spelman Messenger,* June 1897.
6. "Along the Color Line," *The Crisis: A Record of the Darker Races* [hereafter cited as *Crisis*], Feb. 1911, p. 8. Mary Church Terrell, "Club Work of Colored Women," *Southern Workman,* Aug. 1901, p. 435.
7. "The Awakening of Woman," *National Association Notes,* Neighborhood Union Collection, Box 148–1917, ADAU. Reproduced by permission.
8. Butler, "Heredity," pp. 2–3.
9. Amelia Perry Pride to Mrs. [Orra] Langhorne, 23 June 1899, Student Files, AMCHU.
10. Margaret Murray Washington, "Are We Making Good?", *Spelman Messenger,* Nov. 1915, p. 8.
11. I.C. Norcum, "Negro Women's Club Work," *Hampton Bulletin*, Sept. 1911, pp. 50–51.
12. Logan, "Colored Women of the Country Districts," p. 7.
13. Lucy C. Laney, "The Burden of the Educated Colored Woman," *Hampton Negro Conference No. 3,* ed. Hugh Browne, Edwina Kruse, et al. (Hampton, Va.: Hampton Institute Press, July 1899), pp. 39–41. Available in AMCHU.
14. Ibid., p. 42

Chapter 2

1. James Weldon Johnson, "Should the Negro be Given an Education Different From that Given to Whites?", in *Twentieth Century Negro Literature or a Cyclopedia of Thought on the Vital Topics Relating to the American Negro*, ed. D.W. Culp (Toronto: J.L. Nichols, 1902), p. 73.
2. Ibid., p. 74.
3. Charles Henry Turner, "Will the Education of the Negro Solve the Race Problem?", in *Twentieth Century Negro Literature*, ed. Culp, pp. 164–65.
4. Roscoe Conkling Bruce, "Freedom Through Education," in *Negro Orators and Their Orations*, ed. Carter G. Woodson (Washington, D.C.: Associated Publishers, 1925), p. 594. This was an address delivered on Memorial Day, 1905, to the Memorial Society of Harvard University, Sanders Theater, Memorial Hall, Cambridge, Mass.
5. Henry Lee Moon, ed., *The Emerging Thought of W.E.B. DuBois: Essays and Editorials from The Crisis* (New York: Simon and Schuster, 1972), pp. 125–127.
6. Archibald Grimke, William A. Hazel, and I.D. Barnett, "Address to the Country," p. 2, Archibald Grimke Papers, Box 8, MSRC.
7. E. Franklin Frazier, "A Note on Negro Education," *Opportunity: A Journal of Negro Life* [hereafter cited as *Opportunity*] 3 (Mar. 1924): 77.
8. D.O.W. Holmes, *The Evolution of the Negro College* (New York: Teachers College of Columbia University, 1934), p. 159.

9. D.J. Jordan, "Is it Time for the Negro Colleges in the South to be Put into the Hands of the Negro Teachers?", in *Twentieth Century Negro Literature,* ed. Culp, pp. 129–30.

10. Nathan B. Young, "Is it Time for the Negro Colleges in the South to be Put into the Hands of the Negro Teachers?", in *Twentieth Century Negro Literature,* ed. Culp, p. 127.

11. Jordan, "Is it Time for the Negro Colleges in the South to be Put into the Hands of Negro Teachers?", pp. 130–31.

12. W.T.B. Williams, *Report on Negro Universities in the South* (New York: Slater Trustees, 1913), p. 16.

13. Ibid.

14. "Social Progress," *Opportunity* 3 (July 1925): 222.

15. Buell B. Gallagher, *American Caste and the Negro College* (New York: Gordon Press, 1966), p. 64.

16. Address of H.B. Frissell at the Sphinx Club Dinner, 8 Jan. 1912, p. 4. Summer School File, AMCHU.

17. Booker T. Washington, "Some Results of the Armstrong Idea: An Address Delivered at Hampton Institute by Booker T. Washington, LL.D., on January 31, 1909, in Celebration of Founder's Day," *Southern Workman,* Mar. 1909, p. 171.

18. Ibid., p. 6.

19. Frontispiece, Hampton Institute Catalog, Jan. 1900, AMCHU.

20. C. John Walton, *Hampton Normal and Agricultural Institute* (Washington, D.C.: GPO, 1923), p. 4.

21. John Hope to Paul H. Hamus, 30 June 1916, R.R. Moton File, Box 9, TUAC.

22. *Southern Workman and Hampton School Record,* Jan. 1900, p. 50.

23. Letter from David Owl to Sidney David Frissell, 1 Aug. 1960, Student File, Indian Records, AMCHU.

24. *Forty-first Annual Report of the Principal of the Hampton Normal and Agricultural Institute, 1909* (Hampton, Va.: Press of the Hampton Normal and Agricultural Institute [1909]), p. 53.

25. Ibid.

26. "The Dixie Hospital," *Southern Workman,* July 1902, pp. 374–5.

27. Ibid., p. 95.

28. Hampton Training School for Nurses and Dixie Hospital, *Annual Report of the Hampton Training School for Nurses and Dixie Hospital, 1896–1897* (Hampton, Va.: Hampton Institute, 1897), pp. 12–16.

29. Hampton Training School for Nurses and Dixie Hospital, *Twelfth Annual Report of the Hampton Training School for Nurses and Dixie Hospital, 1902–1903* (Hampton, Va.: Hampton Institute, 1803), p. 1.

30. Hampton Training School for Nurses and Dixie Hospital, *Sixth Annual Report of the Hampton Training School for Nurses and Dixie Hospital, 1897–1898* (Hampton, Va.: Hampton Institute, 1898), p. 14.

31. Ibid., pp. 15–16.

32. Ibid., p. 10.
33. Ibid., pp. 14–15.
34. Hampton Training School for Nurses and Dixie Hospital, *Tenth Annual Report of the Hampton Training School for Nurses and Dixie Hospital, 1901* (Hampton, Va.: Hampton Institute, 1901), p. 11.
35. Hampton Training School for Nurses and Dixie Hospital, *Twelfth Annual Report of the Hampton Training School*, insert.
36. *Opportunity* 1 (July 1923): 224.
37. *The Hampton Normal and Agricultural Institute Principal's Report for the Year Ending June 30th, 1895* (Hampton, Va.: Hampton, Virginia, Normal School Steam Press Print [1895]), p. 23.
38. *Forty-first Annual Catalog—The Hampton Normal and Agriculture Institue* (Hampton, Va.: The Institute Press, 1909), p. 63.
39. "Extracts from Letters of Jane Stuart Woolsey, 1868–72," in *Memories of Old Hampton* (Hampton, Va.: The Institute Press, 1909), p. 39. Published for the Armstrong League of Hampton Workers.
40. Booker T. Washington, *Twenty-five Years of Tuskegee* (New York: Doubleday, Page, 1906); rptd. from *World's Work*, Apr. 1906, p. 1.
41. Booker T. Washington, "Industrial Education," in *The Negro Problem: A Series of Articles by Representative American Negroes for Today* (New York: J. Pott, 1903), pp. 16, 19.
42. Ibid., p. 24.
43. Booker T. Washington, "Will the Education of the Negro Solve the Race Problem?", in *Twentieth Century Negro Literature*, ed. Culp, p. 149.
44. Booker T. Washington, *Twenty-five Years*, p. 2.
45. Booker T. Washington, "Industrial Education," pp. 11, 13.
46. Booker T. Washington, *Some Results*, p. 5.
47. "Along the Color Line," *The Crisis* (Nov. 1912), p. 10.
48. J.L. Nichols and William H. Crogman, *Progress of a Race of the Remarkable Achievement of the American Negro: From the Bondage of Slavery, Ignorance, and Poverty to the Freedom of Citizenship, Intelligence, Affluence, Honor, and Trust* (Naperville, Ill.: J.L. Nichols, 1920), p. 414.
49. "Social Progress," *Opportunity* 3 (Aug. 1925): p. 253.
50. *Tuskegee Normal Catalogue, 1896–1897* (Tuskegee, Ala.: Tuskegee Institute Press, 1897), p. 95.
51. "Tuskegee's Work in the Southland," *Afro-American Ledger,* 13 Aug. 1912.
52. Asa H. Gordon, *The Georgia Negro: A History* (Ann Arbor, Mich.: Edwards Brothers, 1937), p. 154.
53. *Atlanta University Bulletin, November 1898–May 1899* (Atlanta, Ga.: Atlanta Univ., 1898), p. 1.
54. George A. Towns, "Is the Idea of the Tuskegee and Calhoun Schools the Solution of the Negro Problem?", May 1899, p. 7; George A. Towns Collection, ADAU. Reproduced by permission.

55. Ibid.
56. Clarence Bacote, *The Story of Atlanta University: A Century of Service* (Atlanta, Ga.: Atlanta Univ., 1969), pp. 128–29.
57. "Student Teachers," *Atlanta University Bulletin* (Atlanta, Ga.: Atlanta Univ., Dec. 1895), p. 3.
58. "Letters from Graduates," *Atlanta University Bulletin* (Atlanta, Ga.: Atlanta Univ., Dec. 1895), p. 2.
59. *Spelman Seminary Catalog, 1893* (Atlanta, Ga.: Spelman Seminary, 1893), p. 22.
60. Ibid.
61. "Annual Report," *Spelman Messenger,* May 1896, p. 2.
62. "Annual Report," *Spelman Messenger* (Supplement), Mar. 1898, p. 9.
63. "Annual Report," *Spelman Messenger,* June 1900, pp. 5–6.
64. "Twenty-third Annual Report of Spelman Seminary," *Spelman Messenger,* Mar. 1904, p. 3.
65. W.N. Hartshorn, ed., *An Era of Progress and Promise, 1863–1910* (Boston: Priscilla Publishing, 1910), p. 76.
66. Ibid., p. 81.
67. Ibid., p. 85.
68. Lucy Hale Tapley to W.E.B. Du Bois, Various Lectures, NAACP Administrative File, Box C 334, Manuscript Division, LC.
69. Minnie Lee Thomas, "The Work of the Industrial Department of Spelman Seminary," *Spelman Messenger,* Apr. 1896, p. 6.
70. *Spelman Seminary Catalog, 1893*, p. 18.
71. Nora A. Gordon, "Some Characteristics of the Heathen," *Spelman Messenger,* May 1895, p. 1.
72. Lena F. Clark, "An Autobiography," *Spelman Messenger,* May 1895, p. 2; "The Value of a Missionary Training to any Young Woman," *Spelman Messenger,* Jan. 1896, p. 4.
73. Lucy Hale Tapley, "Spelman College," *Opportunity* 1 (Apr. 1923): 16; "Celebration," *Opportunity* 1 (Apr. 1923): 99.
74. "Spelman Graduates," *Spelman Messenger,* Mar. 1904, p. 7.
75. George Haynes to Trustees of Fisk University, 12 Apr. 1915, George E. Haynes Papers, SCFU.
76. *Fisk University News* 11 (Oct. 1920): 2.
77. Fisk University, *Catalog of Fisk University, 1923–1924* (Nashville, Tenn.: Fisk Univ., 1916), p. 16.
78. *Fisk University News* 10 (Nov. 1919): 9.
79. *Fisk University News* 6 (Apr. 1916): 20–22.
80. "Social Progress," *Opportunity* 4 (Aug. 1925): pp. 247–50; Joe A. Richardson, *A History of Fisk University, 1865–1946* (University, Ala.: Univ. of Alabama Press, 1980), pp. 94–95.
81. "Fisk University Faculty, 1915–1916," George E. Haynes Papers, 1909–1922, Box 4 – Folder 22, SCFU.

82. "Education for Service," *Fisk University News* 11 (June 1919).
83. "From a Letter from Mrs. Althea Brown Edmiston, W.C. Africa," *Fisk University News* 6 (Dec. 1915): 27.
84. Fisk University, *Catalog of Fisk University, 1923–1924* (Nashville, Tenn.: Fisk Univ., 1923), pp. 93–95.
85. Meharry Medical College, *Meharry Medical College–Walden University Bulletin, 1906* (Nashville, Tenn.: Meharry Medical College, 1906), p. 3.
86. Meharry Medical College, *Meharry Medical College Bulletin* (Nashville, Tenn.: Medical College, 1915), pp. 84–85.
87. Ibid., p. 95.
88. "To Celebrate Fortieth Anniversary," *Afro-American Ledger*, 10 Sept. 1912.
89. "To the Officers and Members of the federated Charities, March 6, 1917," Baltimore Federated Charities Association, Annual Reports — RG 29–51, Box 10, BCA.
90. Advertisement, *Afro-American Ledger*, printed throughout Aug. 1924.

Chapter 3

1. R.R. Wright, Jr., "Negro in Unskilled Labor," in *The Negro's Progress in Fifty Years: The Annals of the American Academy*, ed. Emory R. Johnson (Philadelphia: American Academy and Political and Social Science, 1913), pp. 25–26.
2. Ibid.
3. Addie W. Hunton, "The Colored Woman as an Economic Factor," *New York Column*, Feb. 1916, Women's Work File, Monroe Work Collection, TUAC.
4. Ibid.
5. *Proceedings of the Hampton Negro Conference, No. 6* (Hampton, Va.: Hampton Institute Press, July 1902), and *Report of the Committee on Business and Labor Conditions in Richmond, Va.* (Hampton, Va.: Hampton Institute Press, July 1900), pp. 12–26; both in AMCHU.
6. "Conference on Negro Migration — Pittsburgh, June 12, 1917," George E. Haynes Papers, 1909–1922, Box 4, SCFU.
7. Ibid.
8. Paul Williams, "The Shadow of Equality: The Negro in Baltimore, 1864–1911" (Ph.D. diss., Univ. of Wisconsin, 1972), p. 365.
9. "A Trip Through Wise Bros.' Establishment," *Afro-American Ledger*, 23 Nov. 1912.
10. Quoted in George E. Haynes, *The Negro at Work During the World War and During Reconstruction* (New York: Negro Universities Press, 1921), p. 437.
11. *Proceedings of the First International Congress of Working Women, Oct. 28 to Nov. 5, 1919; Nov. 4th Session,* pp. 32–34. National Women's Trade Union League Papers, Manuscript Division, LC.
12. "Women Set for Labor Union Meeting," *Chicago Defender*, 12 Nov. 1921, Women's Work File, Monroe Work Collection, TUAC.

13. "Report of Conditions Found in Investigation of 'Work or Fight' Laws in Southern States," NAACP Administrative Files, Box 417, 19 Aug. and 26 Oct. 1918, 1918–1919, Manuscript Division, LC.
14. E. Ross Haynes, "Two Million Negro Women at Work," *Southern Workman,* Feb. 1922, p. 64.
15. "Opportunities for the Educated Colored Woman," *Opportunity* 1 (Mar. 1923): 8.
16. Monroe N. Work, "Research With Respect to Cooperation Between Urban and Rural Communities," *Opportunity* 1 (Feb. 1923): 9.
17. "Women Workers," *Opportunity* 3 (Aug. 1925): 1.

Chapter 4

1. Maryland State School Survey Commission, *The 1941 Survey of the Maryland Public Schools and Teachers Colleges;* and W.E.B. Du Bois and Augustus Granville Dill, eds., *The College-Bred Negro American: Report of a Social Study Made Under the Direction of Atlanta University, Together with the Proceedings of the Sixth Conference for the Study of the Negro Problem, Held at Atlanta University on May 24th, 1910* (Atlanta, Ga.: Atlanta Univ. Press, 1910), p. 17.
2. J. Walter Huffinton, *Supervision of Colored Schools in Maryland* (Baltimore: McCoy Hall — State Board of Education, 1918), pp. 21–23.
3. "Along the Color Line," *Crisis,* 1912, p. 10.
4. K. Elizabeth Trammel, "The Relation of the Rural Teacher to Her Community," *Negro Farmer,* 26 Aug. 1916, Tuskegee Institute Extension Collection, Box 1, TUAC.
5. *Atlanta University Bulletin* (Atlanta, Ga.: Atlanta Univ., Nov. 1895), p. 3.
6. "Along the Color Line," *Crisis,* May 1912, p. 10.
7. Monroe Work, "Education in the South," *Fisk University News* (Oct. 1919): 36.
8. "A Memorial to the Legislature of Georgia on the Proposed Amendment Touching the Distribution of the School Fund," 1919, p. 1, Neighborhood Union File, ADAU. By permission.
9. Ibid.
10. "White Leaders Back Better Negro Schools," *Fisk University News* 10 (Feb. 1920): 11; *Atlanta University Bulletin* (Atlanta, Ga.: Atlanta Univ., Nov. 1914), p. 7.
11. *Opportunity* 3 (Sept. 1925): 26; "Education in Georgia," *Opportunity* 3 (Aug. 1925): 1.
12. W.E.B. Du Bois and Augustus Dill, eds., *The Common School and the Negro American: Report of a Social Study made by Atlanta University under the Patronage of the Trustees of the John F. Slater Fund, with the Proceedings of the 16th Annual Conference for the Study of the Negro Problem, held at Atlanta University on Tuesday, May 30, 1911* (Atlanta, Ga.: Atlanta Univ. Press, 1911), p. 106.

13. *Southern Workman,* Sept. 1899, p. 299.
14. "Summer School," Sept. 1912, Extension File, AMCHU.
15. Ibid.
16. George P. Phenix — Vice Principal, to Haynes, 12 Jan. 1917, George E. Haynes Papers, Box 3, SCFU.
17. "The Hampton Summer School," *Southern Workman,* Sept. 1910, p. 396.
18. "The Colored Training School," *Afro-American Ledger,* 3 Sept. 1910, p. 4.
19. Ibid.
20. *Sixty-seventh Annual Report of the Board of School Commissioners to the Mayor and City Council of Baltimore for the Year Ending December 31, 1895* (Baltimore: William J.C. Dulany Co., Public Printers, 1896), pp. ix–xviii.
21. "Our Public Schools," *Afro-American Ledger,* 19 Oct. 1895; "The Next Mayor, Mr. Hooper Is an Ideal Citizen," *Afro-American Ledger,* 2 Nov. 1895; "Colored Teachers for Colored Schools Was a Slogan of the Campaign," *Afro-American Ledger,* 22 Feb. 1896.
22. "Aiming to Secure Better School Facilities," *Afro-American Ledger,* 5 Oct. 1912; "School Board Urges New School Building," *Afro-American Ledger,* 16 Nov. 1912.
23. "Local Jots," *Afro-American Ledger,* 19 Jan. 1913; *Eighty-eighth Annual Report of the Board of School Commissioners to the Mayor and City Council of Baltimore for the Scholastic Year Ending June 30, 1917* (Baltimore: King Brothers, City Printer, 1918), p. 11.
24. "The Town," *Afro-American Ledger,* 25 May 1918, p. 6. "What Others Say," *Southern Workman*, July 1920, p. 338.
25. "Three Delegations Clash at School Board Meeting," *Afro-American Ledger,* 23 May 1925.
26. "School Federation Outlines Program," *Afro-American Ledger,* 16 May 1925, p. 18; "School Funds Held up by Injunction," *Afro-American Ledger,* 27 June 1925, p. 1.
27. Arthur Wright and Edward Redcay, *The Negro Rural School, Inc.: Anna T. Jeans Foundation, 1907–1933* (Washington, D.C.: The Negro Rural School Fund, 1933), p. 8. Wright was president of the Jeanes Foundation's Board of Trustees. See also Certificate of Incorporation, p. 8, James C. Napier Papers, Box 2, SCFU.
28. "Report of the Manual Training of Colored Public Schools of Henrico County, Virginia for Session 1908 and 1909" [pamphlet], p. 1, James C. Napier Papers, Box 2, SCFU.
29. Ibid., pp. 2–3.
30. Ibid., p. 5.
31. B.C. Caldwell, "The Work of the Jeanes and Slater Funds," in *The Negro's Progress in Fifty Years,* ed. E.R. Johnson, pp. 173–75; James H. Dillard, "Negro Rural School Fund Statement VIII, March 9, 1910," James C. Napier Papers, Box 2, SCFU.
32. "Supervising Teachers," James C. Napier Papers, Box 2, SCFU.

33. Camilla Weems, "Supervising Rural Schools," *Spelman Messenger,* Nov. 1915, p. 6.
34. *What Hampton Graduates Are Doing, 1868–1904* (Hampton, Va.: Hampton Institute Press, n.d.), p. 60, AMCHU.
35. Lorenzo Hall, "Back to the Farm," 1910, pp. 2–3, Georgia Washington File, AMCHU; "Seventeenth Annual Report of the People's Village School, 1909–1910" [pamphlet], p. 11, Georgia Washington File, AMCHU.
36. "Outline of Course of Study, etc., People's Village School — Mt. Meigs, Alabama," Education Unit, AMCHU.
37. Georgia Washington to Dr. Frissell, 6 June 1906, Education Unit, AMCHU.
38. Hartshorn, ed., *An Era of Progress,* p. 366.
39. Hall, "Back to the Farm," pp. 3–4.
40. Georgia Washington, "Twenty-second Annual Report of the Principal of the People's Village School with Treasurer's Report, 1914–1915," p. 11, Mt. Meigs, Montgomery County, Alabama, AMCHU.
41. "The Peoples' [sic] Village School, Mount Meigs, Montgomery County, Alabama," n.d., AMCHU.
42. Ibid.
43. "Tuskegee Graduates," p. 51, Monroe Work Collection, Box 3, TUAC; *Tuskegee Almuni Bulletin,* v. 6, nos. 8–9 (Aug.–Sept. 1924), TUAC; *Spelman Messenger,* Aug. 1934, p. 7.
44. *What Hampton Graduates Are Doing,* p. 8.
45. Hartshorn, ed., *An Era of Progress,* p. 334.
46. "School for the Colored Blind and Deaf," *Afro-American Ledger,* 27 Aug. 1898; *Fisk Women After Graduation* (Nashville, Tenn.: Fisk Univ., 1908), SCFU.
47. "National Association of Teachers in Colored Schools," *Southern Workman,* Sept. 1915, pp. 471–73.
48. "The Horizon," *The Crisis,* Oct. 1917, p. 314.
49. "Vitalizing Negro Education," *Opportunity* 1 (Aug. 1923): 298.

Chapter 5

1. Helen W. Ludlow, "The Negro in Business in Hampton and Vicinity," *Southern Workman,* Sept. 1904, p. 491; *What Hampton Graduates Are Doing,* p. 1.
2. "The Race in Hampton, Va.," *Afro-American Ledger,* 25 Feb. 1899, p. 1.
3. Quoted in Florence Lattimore, *A Place of Delight: The Locust Street Social Settlement for Negroes at Hampton, Virginia* (Hampton, Va.: The Press of the Hampton Normal and Agricultural Institute, 1915), p. 6.
4. Ibid.
5. Addie W. Hunton, "A Social Center at Hampton, Va.," *Southern Workman,* June 1912, pp. 145–46.
6. "Work of Uplift Shown Results," *Afro-American Ledger,* 31 Aug. 1912.

7. "The Old Folks House," *Afro-American Ledger,* Oct. 1898.
8. *What Hampton Graduates Are Doing,* p. 26.
9. Amelia Perry Pride to Charlotte Davis, 5 Mar. 1904, Amelia Perry Pride File, Faculty Collection, AMCHU.
10. Helen W. Ludlow, "Industrial Classes for Colored Women and Children," *Southern Workman,* Jan. 1902, pp. 27–32; Ludlow, "The Huntington Industrial Classes for Women and Children," *Southern Workman,* Febr. 1902, p. 78.
11. "Extension Work — 1909," pp. 1–2, Extension Work Collection, AMCHU.
12. Ibid., p 34.
13. Ibid., p. 4.
14. Ibid., p. 5.
15. *Hampton Negro Conference, No. 1* (Hampton, Va.: Hampton Institute Press, 1897), p. 8, AMCHU.
16. Hugh Browne, Edwina Kruse, et al., eds., *Hampton Negro Conference, No. 3* (Hampton, Va. : Hampton Institute Press, July 1899), pp. 37–46.
17. *Afro-American Ledger,* Aug. 1899, p. 1.
18. Fannie Barrier Williams, "The Problem of Employment for Negro Women," *Southern Workman,* Sept. 1903, p. 432.
19. "Extension Work — 1909," pp. 5, 8, Extension Work Collection, AMCHU.
20. Janie Barrett, "Virginia Federation of Colored Women," *Hampton Bulletin,* Sept. 1911; *Fifteenth Annual Report of the Hampton Negro Conference, The Hampton Normal and Agricultural Institute* (Hampton, Va.: Press of the Hampton Normal and Agricultural Institute, 1911), pp. 45–50.
21. "The Woman's Conference," in *Hampton Negro Conference, No. 3,* ed. Browne, Kruse, et al., p. 43.
22. Ludlow, "Virginia's Negro Reform School," *Southern Workman,* Nov. 1904, p. 606.
23. Hunton, "Women's Clubs: State Conventions," *Crisis,* Sept. 1911, p. 211; Barrett, "Virginia Federation of Colored Women," p. 48; Mrs. John E. Milholland, "Talks About Women," *Crisis* Feb. 1911, p. 28.
24. William A. Aery, "Helping Wayward Girls," *Southern Workman,* Nov. 1915, pp. 598–604; J.E. Davis, "A Virginia Asset — The Virginia Industrial School for Colored girls," *Southern Workman,* Aug. 1920, p. 357.
25. Barrett, "The Virginia Industrial School," p. 357; Aery, "Industrial Home School for Colored Girls at Peak in Hanover County, Virginia," *Southern Workman,* Oct. 1919, pp. 473–4.
26. Janie Porter Barrett, Caroline D. Pratt, and Ida A. Tourbellot, "Community Clubs for Women and Girls," in *Hampton Leaflet* (Hampton, Va.: Press of Hampton Normal and Agricultural Institute, 1912), p. 1, AMCHU.
27. Ibid., p. 10.
28. L.A. Jenkins, "Annual Report of L.A. Jenkins, Assistant District Agent for 1915 to Mr. J.B. Pierce, District Agent," 1915, pp. 1–3, Extension File, AMCHU.

29. Ibid., p. 4.
30. "Homemakers' Clubs of Virginia," *Southern Workman*, Apr. 1917, p. 201.
31. "Negro Organization Society," *Southern Workman*, Dec. 1915, pp. 46–47.
32. "Negro Organization Society of Virginia—Minutes of Executive Committee, December 29, 1914," pp. 2–3, and "Second Session of Executive Committee Negro Organization Society, December 29, 1914," both in Negro Organization Society File, AMCHU.
33. Allen Washington, Associate Commandant, to Mrs. Maggie Burley, Supervisor of Teachers, 30 Jan. 1915, in Letters and Documents from Allen Washington to Dr. Martin, Jan. 1916 to Feb. 1917, Letters 1 Folder, Charities and Corrections, Negro Organization Society File, AMCHU.
34. Elizabeth Cobb Jordan, "The Impact of the Negro Organization Society on Public Support for Education in Virginia, 1912–1950" (D.Ed. diss., Univ. of Virginia, 1978), p. 54.

Chapter 6

1. Booker T. Washington to W.T. Harris, 2 May 1982, Press Copies of Letters Sent to Federal Officials, 1892–1907, Record Group 12, National Archives, Washington, D.C.; John Johnson, *Report of the Fifth Tuskegee Conference, 1896* (Baltimore: Slater Trustees, 1896), p. 6.
2. John Johnson, *Fifth Tuskegee Conference*, p. 5.
3. Ibid., p. 6.
4. Ibid., p. 11; August Meier, *Negro Thought in America: Racial Ideologies in the Age of Booker T. Washington* (Ann Arbor: Univ. of Michigan Press, 1963), p. 99.
5. *Thirtieth Annual Catalogue, 1910–1911, The Tuskegee Normal and Industrial Institute* (Tuskegee, Ala.: Tuskegee Institute Press, 1911), p. 3, TUAC; "Annual Negro Conference, 1910–1911," p. 3, Booker T. Washington Papers, Tuskegee Records, Extension Work 1911, A–F, Box 983, Manuscript Division, LC.
6. U.S. Department of Agriculture Extension Service, Tuskegee Institute, Alabama, "The Structure and Functions of Negro Extension Work," Office of Cooperative Extension Work in Agriculture and Home Economics, State Land Grant College, and U.S. Department of Agriculture Cooperating Circular 401-E, Tuskegee Institute, Extension File, Box 4, TUAC.
7. James L. Sibley, "Homemakers Clubs for Negro Girls," *Southern Workman*, Feb. 1915, pp. 81–86.
8. N. Juanita Coleman, "Home Demonstration Work in Alabama," *Southern Workman*, Sept. 1920, pp. 412–14.
9. "Cooperative Extension Work in Agriculture and Home Economics, State of Alabama: Outline for Rural Negro Women's and Girls' Clubs," 1 Sept. 1920, Extension File, Box 4, TUAC.
10. Mrs. Washington to Mrs. Hope, 6 Nov. 1914, Neighborhood Union Box 14–B, 1914, 1915, 1916, ADAU. By permission.

11. "The Summary: A Monthly Statement Issued by the Agricultural Extension Staff, Tuskegee Institute, Alabama, July and August 1921: Statistical Report Showing the Nature and Scope of Work in Process of Completion Among Negro Women and Girls in Alabama at the Close of the First Half of the Year, Beginning January 1, 1921, Ending June 30, 1921, Compiled by Miss R.B. Jones, State Agent Negro Woman," p. 5, Extension File, Box 4, TUAC.
12. Ibid., p. 9.
13. Margaret Murray Washington, "Women of Alabama," *Afro-American Ledger,* 16 Sept. 1899.
14. "Seventeenth Anniversary of Tuskegee Woman's Club," *Tuskegee Student,* 14 June 1913, in Women's Work File, Monroe Work Collection, TUAC.
15. "Tuskegee Institute Extension Work," undated, Monroe Work Collection, Box 3, TUAC.
16. "Synopsis of the Lecture by Mrs. Booker T. Washington on the Organization of Women's Clubs," 22 June 1910, Booker T. Washington Papers, Margaret Murray Washington File, TUAC.
17. Ibid.
18. *Twenty-ninth Annual Catalogue, 1909–1910, The Tuskegee Normal School and Industrial Institute* (Tuskegee, Ala.: Tuskegee Institute Press, 1910), p. 99, TUAC.
19. "Seventeenth Anniversary of Tuskegee Woman's Club."
20. *National Association Notes*, Mar. 1913, available in Margaret Murray Washington File, TUAC.
21. Anne M. Evans to Mrs. Washington, 1 Mar. 1916; Mrs. Washington to Evans, 8 Mar. 1916; Evans to Mrs. Washington, 13 Mar. 1916; all in Margaret Murray Washington File, TUAC.
22. "Seventeenth Anniversary of Tuskegee Woman's Club."
23. Mrs. M.M. Washington, "The Tuskegee Woman's Club," *Southern Workman,* Aug. 1920, p. 365.
24. *National Association Notes,* Mar. 1913, p. 6; "Woman's Work," *Tuskegee Student,* 18 July 1916; "Seventeenth Anniversary of Tuskegee Woman's Club," p. 368.
25. "Negro Women Federation of Clubs Meeting," *Montgomery Times,* 9 July 1912, in Women's Work File, Monroe Work Collection, TUAC.
26. "Negro Women and Successful Meet," *Montgomery Advertiser,* 10 June 1925, in Women's Work File, Monroe Work Collection, TUAC.

Chapter 7

1. Rev. E.R. Carter, "The Colored Poor of Atlanta," *Spelman Messenger,* Apr. 1900, p. 1.
2. Mills Lane, *The People of Georgia: An Illustrated Social History* (Savannah, Ga.: Beehive Press, 1975), p. 288.
3. *The Guardian,* 29 Sept. 1906, p. 1, William H. Hunt Papers, Box 55–5, Manuscript Division, MSRC.

4. "Along the Color Line," *Crisis,* Dec. 1910, p. 9.

5. "Along the Color Line," *Crisis,* June 1916, p. 63.

6. "The Horizon," *Crisis,* Dec. 1916, p. 89; "The Horizon," *Crisis,* Jan. 1917, p. 143.

7. Thomas Chase, ed., *Mortality Among Negroes in Cities: Proceedings of the Conference for Investigation of City Problems Held at Atlanta University, May 26–27, 1896* (Atlanta, Ga.: Atlanta Univ. Press, 1903), introduction and pp. 6, 18.

8. *Social and Physical Conditions of Negroes in Cities: Report of an Investigation under the Director of Atlanta University and Proceedings of the Second Conference for the Study of Problems Concerning Negro City Life, Held at Atlanta University, May 25–26, 1897* (Atlanta, Ga.: Atlanta Univ. Press, 1897), introduction.

9. Ibid., p. 33.

10. "The Gate City Free Kindergarten—1917," p. 3, Gate City Kindergarten File 1905–1935, Neighborhood Union Box 5, ADAU. By permission.

11. Ibid.

12. "The Story of the Gate City Free Kindergarten Association," Gate City Kindergarten File 1905–1935, Neighborhood Union Box 5, ADAU. By permission.

13. Ibid.

14. "Gate City Day Nursery Association" [pamphlet], p. 1, Frankie Adams Collection Box 1, ADAU. By permission.

15. "The Carrie Steel Logan Home," Carrie Steel Logan Home File, Neighborhood Union Box 5, ADAU. By permission.

16. "An Investment in Child Life Today," Leonard Street Orphanage, Atlanta (1890–1935) File, Neighborhood Union Box 5, ADAU. By permission.

17. Neighborhood Union Minutes, 8 July 1908, Minutes Book, p. 1, Neighborhood Union Box 5, ADAU. By permission.

18. Ibid.

19. Neighborhood Union Minutes, 16 July 1908, Minutes Book, p. 9, Neighborhood Union Box 5, ADAU. By permission.

20. Neighborhood Union Minutes, 23 July 1908, Minutes Book, pp. 10–11, Neighborhood Union Box 5, ADAU. By permission.

21. Neighborhood Union Minutes, 9 Sept. 1908, Minutes Book, p. 37, Neighborhood Union Box 5, ADAU. By permission.

22. Neighborhood Union Minutes, 14 Oct. 1908, Minutes Book, p. 39, Neighborhood Union Box 5, ADAU. By permission.

23. Neighborhood Union Minutes, 11 Nov. 1908, Minutes Book, p. 40, Neighborhood Union Box 5, ADAU. By permission.

24. Annual Inter-Collegiate Track Meet Program, Neighborhood Union Box 5, ADAU. By Permission.

25. Neighborhood Union Minutes, 9 Sept. 1910, Minutes Book, p. 56, Neighborhood Union Box 5, ADAU. By permission.

26. Neighborhood Union Charter, 30 Jan. 1911, Neighborhood Union, Box 14-B, 1911, 1912, 1913, ADAU. By permission.

27. "Treating Negro Problem at Basis," *Atlanta Constitution*, 2 Feb. 1911.

28. William M. Slaton, Superintendent, to Mrs. Hope, 12 June 1912, Neighborhood Union Box 14–B, 1911, 1912, 1913, ADAU. By permission.

29. Mrs. Hope's Notebook, Neighborhood Union Box 5, ADAU. By permission.

30. "Annual Report of the Neighborhood Union, 1913–1914," *Spelman Messenger,* Dec. 1914, p. 7.

31. Ibid.

32. Hattie Rutherford Watson, "Work on the Neighborhood Union," *Spelman Messenger*, Nov. 1916, pp. 5–6. Letter from Neighborhood Union to Mr. Z. Nespor, Field Secretary, National War Department Commission, 31 July 1917, ADAU. By permission.

33. Mills Lane, *People of Georgia*, p. 292.

34. Mrs. Hope, on behalf of Women's Civic and Social Improvement Committee, to School Board, 19 Aug. 1913, in Neighborhood Union Box 14–B, 1914, 1915, 1916, ADAU. By permission. *Spelman Messenger*, Dec. 1914, p. 7.

35. Ibid.

36. Ibid.

37. Women's Social Improvement Committee to Atlanta Mayor Walter A. Sims, the City Council, the Board of Education, and W.A. Swinton, Superintendent of City Public Schools, 29 Sept. 1923, in Neighborhood Union Box 2, 1923, 1924, 1925, ADAU. By permission.

38. "The Conservation of Negro Health — National Negro Health Week, March 21–27, 1915," p. 4, George Haynes Collection, Box 5, Folder 12, SCFU.

39. Ibid.

40. L.D. Shivery, "Atlanta Health Campaign — June 12, 1914," Neighborhood Union Box 14–B, 1914, 1915, 1916, ADAU. By permission.

41. "See What's Going to Happen," June [1916], Neighborhood Union Box 14–B, 1914, 1915, 1916, and "Atlanta Clean Up and Paint Up Campaign," Neighborhood Union Box 2, ADAU. Both by permission.

42. "Report of Colored Department," 1919, pp. 21–22, Neighborhood Union Box 2, ADAU. By permission.

43. "Annual Report of Atlanta Anti-Tuberculosis Association for the Year 1919," Neighborhood Union Box 2, ADAU. By permission.

44. "Report of Negro National Health Week — April 3–9, 1921," pp. 1–2, Neighborhood Union Box 14–B, 1914, 1915, 1916, ADAU. By permission.

45. Ibid., p. 2.

46. T. Arnold Hill, Secretary to Mr. Eugene K. Jones, Associate Director of the National League on Urban Conditions Among Negroes, to Mrs. Hope, 8 May 1914, in Neighborhood Union Box 14–B, 1914, 1915, 1916, ADAU. By permission.

47. "Neighborhood Union," 1925, Neighborhood Union Box 2, ADAU. By permission.

48. Mrs. Hope's Memorable Speeches (1919–1924), Notebook, Neighborhood Union Box 5, ADAU. By permission.

Chapter 8

1. Lester C. Lamon, *Black Tennesseans, 1900–1930* (Knoxville: Univ. of Tennessee Press, 1977), p. vi.
2. Ibid., p. 2.
3. Ibid., p. 15.
4. "Will It Sleep Always—Local Negro Business League Taking Rip Van Winkle Snooze," *Globe*, 8 Nov. 1907; "Double Resurrection Needed," *Globe,* 26 Feb. 1909; Lamon, *Black Tennesseans,* p. 176.
5. R.C. Grant, comp., *The Nashville Colored Directory* (Nashville, Tenn., 1925), p. 8; "Statement to the Honorable Committee of Negro Board of Trade," George E. Haynes Papers, 1909–1922, Box 5–Folder 1, SCFU.
6. Lamon, *Black Tennesseans,* p. 24.
7. "George Haynes to Friends," 20 May 1911, George E. Haynes Papers, 1909–1922, Box 4, SCFU.
8. George E. Haynes to Interested Persons: "Suggested Steps that May Be Taken in Improving Conditions among Colored People of Nashville, 27 May 1911," George E. Haynes Papers, 1909–1922, Box 4, SCFU.
9. Lamon, *Black Tennesseans,* p. 217.
10. George E. Haynes to Methodist Training School, Jan. 1905, George E. Haynes Papers, 1909–1922, Box 4–Folder 4, SCFU.
11. "Work in Nashville, Tennessee," George E. Haynes Papers, 1909–1922, Box 4, SCFU.
12. "Supervisors Report of Bethlehem House Work for September and October, 1915," George E. Haynes Papers, 1909–1922, Box 5–Folder 8, SCFU.
13. "Report of the Director, June 1 to Sept. 15, 1915, to the Executive Board of the National League on Urban Conditions Among Negroes," p. 4, R.R. Moton Collection, Box 10–File 10, National Urban League, TUAC.
14. *Catalogue of Fisk University, 1915–1916* (Nashville, Tenn.: Fisk Univ., 1916), p. 55.
15. Fayette Avery McKenzie, "Race Cooperation," *Fisk University News* 6 (May 1916): 6.
16. "Colored Residents to Hold Meeting," [Nashville] *Tennessean*, 9 Feb. 1918, in George E. Haynes Papers, 1909–1922, Box 4, SCFU.
17. "Phyllis Wheatley Club's Record," *Globe*, 3 Jan. 1908, pp. 172, 174; Grant, *Nashville Colored Directory,* p. 47.
18. Grant, *Nashville Colored Directory*, p. 47.
19. "Emancipation Anniversary," *Globe,* 11 Jan. 1907; *Globe*, 18 Jan. 1907.
20. "Women's Meeting Held in the Interest of 'Day Home' Project," *Globe*, 22 Feb. 1907.
21. "Meeting of the Day Home Club," *Globe,* 30 Oct. 1908.
22. Grant, *Nashville Colored Directory*, p. 25.
23. Ibid.

24. "Like Forest Fire — Negroes Purchase Land in New University Place," *Globe*, 1 Mar. 1907.
25. Grant, *Nashville Colored Directory*, p. 27.

Chapter 9

1. "Women in Fight Against Amendment," *Afro-American Ledger*, 21 Oct. and 6 Nov. 1909.
2. "Along the Color Line," *Crisis*, Nov. 1912, p. 7.
3. Flyer, NAACP Administrative File, 25 Jan.–Mar. 1917; telegram to Hallie Brown from James W. Johnson, NAACP Administrative File, 23 Jan. 1917; and telegram from Brown to Johnson, NAACP Administrative File, 8 Feb. 1923; all in Intermarriage C309, Manuscript Division, LC.
4. Fannie Barrier Williams, "Do We Need Another Name?", *Southern Workman*, Jan. 1904, p. 35.
5. "Along the Color Line," *Crisis*, July 1914, p. 116.
6. *Directory of the Charitable and Beneficient Organizations of Baltimore and Maryland Together with a Summary of Laws, etc., and an Introduction by Amos G. Warner, Ph.D.* (Baltimore: Charity Organization Society, 1892), p. 3. "One Woman Banker Among Fifteen Million People," Mary Church Terrell Collection, Box 102–3, Manuscript Division, MSRC. Arnold H. Taylor, *Travail and Triumph: Black Life and Culture in the South Since the Civil War* (Westport, Conn.: Greenwood, 1976), p. 108.
7. *Directory of the Charitable and Beneficent Organizations*, p. 25.
8. Ibid.
9. "The Oblate Sisters of Providence," Mary Church Terrell Collection, Box 102–3, Manuscript Division, MSRC.
10. *Directory of the Charitable and Beneficent Organizations,* p. 53; *Twenty-ninth Annual Report of St. Elizabeth's Home of Baltimore City for Colored Children under the Charge of the Franciscan Sisters, St. Paul Street, Baltimore, for the Year Ending December 31, 1910* (Baltimore: St. Mary's Industrial School, 1911), pp. 7–8.
11. Ibid., pp. 9, 16.
12. "Day Nursery Association for Colored Children," *Afro-American Ledger*, 27 Aug. 1910; "Day Nursery Will Reopen in October," *Afro-American Ledger*, 16 Aug. 1912; "Day Nursery Association Opens New Building," *Afro-American Ledger*, 19 Oct. 1912.
13. Ida R. Cummings, "Report of Colored Empty Stocking and Fresh Air Circle, July 1912," *National Association Notes*, June 1913, p. 15.
14. Ibid., p. 16.

15. Ibid.; "The Colored Fresh Air Farm Closed," *Afro-American Ledger*, 14 Sept. 1912.
16. *Report of the Charities Endorsement Committee Conducted under the Auspices of the Merchants and Manufacturers Association, Chamber of Commerce and City Club*, 31 Dec. 1914, Charities Collection 29–1, BCA.
17. *History of the Women's Civic League* (Baltimore: Lord Baltimore Press, 1936), p. 7.
18. Ibid., p. 92.
19. S.C. Fernandis, "Report of the Women's Cooperative Civic League," in *Civic Courier, 1912–1914* (Baltimore: Lord Baltimore Press, Apr. 1914), p. 4.
20. "The Looking Glass," *Crisis,* June 1916, pp. 70–71.
21. Margaret G. Hawkins, "Report of the Women's Cooperative Civic League" [1920], p. 5, Archives, Women's Civic League, Baltimore, Md.
22. *The Family Welfare Association — Member of the Baltimore Alliance, Annual Report 1922* (Baltimore: Family Welfare Association, 1922), p. 5. Ira A. Reid, *The Negro Community of Baltimore* (New York: Department of Research, National Urban League, 1935), p. 31.
23. "Negroes at Work in Baltimore, Maryland," *Opportunity* 1 (May 1923): 12.
24. Ibid.

Chapter 10

1. Mary Church Terrell, "Colored Woman's League," p. 2, Mary Church Terrell Collection, Box 102–3, Manuscript Division, MSRC.
2. Ibid.
3. Ibid.
4. Margaret Murray Washington, "National Association of Colored Women's Clubs," *National Association Notes*, June 1913, p. 5.
5. "Colored Women's League," pp. 7–8.
6. "Woman's Era Club," *National Association Notes*, Apr. 1900. Available in Mary Church Terrell Collection, Box 102–12, Manuscript Division, MSRC.
7. "What the National Association Has Meant to Colored Women," Mary Church Terrell Collection, Box 102–3, Manuscript Division, MSRC. "National Association of Colored Women," and Addie W. Hunton, "NACW 1912–1914," *New York Call*, 1916, in Women's Work File, Monroe Work Collection, TUAC.
8. "National Association of Colored Women," *Southern Workman,* Sept. 1916, pp. 494–95. "Mrs. Mary B. Talbert, Women's President," *New York Age*, 17 Aug. 1916, in Women's Work File, Monroe Work Collection, TUAC.
9. Mary B. Talbert, "The Frederick Douglass Home," *Crisis,* Feb. 1917, pp. 174–76.
10. Ida B. Wells, "National Asociation Colored/Women's Clubs," *The Woman's Forum,* Sept.–Oct. 1922, in Mary Church Terrell Collection, Manuscript Division, LC.

11. Margaret Murray Washington to Nannie H. Burroughs, 5 July 1924, and Burroughs to Washington, 11 July 1914, both in Nannie H. Burroughs Papers, Box 31, Manuscript Division, LC.
12. "Mrs. Bethune to Enlarge Program of Women's Clubs," *New York Age*, 14 Nov. 1925, in Women Work File, Monroe Work Collection, TUAC.
13. "Mrs. Booker T. Washington, Honored Guest of Nashville's Women's Club," *Globe*, 11 May 1917.
14. Gordon, *The Georgia Negro*, pp. 206–207; "Along the Color Line," *Crisis,* Jan. 1914, p. 117.
15. Addie W. Hunton, "Women's Club," *Crisis,* May 1911, pp. 17–18. "National Association of Colored Women," *Milford (N.H.) Cabinet*, 22 Aug. 1912, in Women's Work File, Monroe Work Collection, TUAC. Passie Fenton Atley, "Kindergarten for Colored Children," *Southern Workman*, Jan. 1901, pp. 103–106.
16. Eleanor Flexner, *Century of Struggle: The Woman's Rights Movement in the United States* (Cambridge, Mass.: Harvard Univ. Press, 1975), pp. 224, 247.
17. Myra V. Merriman to [Mary White] Ovington; and W.E.B. Du Bois to Mrs. Paul Gaston Darrott, 27 Jan. 1921; both in NAACP Administrative Subject File, Box C–384, National Woman's Party, 27 Oct. 1920–9 May 1921, Manuscript Division, LC. Letter of Nomination from Sallie W. Stewart to Bishop John Hurst, NAACP Administrative Subject File, Spingarn Medal, Feb. to March 1921; and NAACP Release, 19 Jan. 1921, NAACP Administrative Subject File, Box C–384, National Woman's Party; both in Manuscript Division, LC.
18. International Council of Women of the Darker Races, Printed Sheet, 10 Nov. 1924, Mary Church Terrell Collection, Box 102–12, Manuscript Division, MSRC.
19. "A Tearful Retribution," *Afro-American Ledger,* 22 Feb. 1912, p. 1.
20. "Women Discussed Important Problems at Convention," *Washington Tribune,* 17 Aug. 1922. Available in Women's Work File, Monroe Work Collection, TUAC.
21. "Booker T.'s Wife Heads World Order," *Chicago Defender*, 26 Aug. 1922, in Women's Work File, Monroe Work Collection, TUAC.
22. "World International Council—Darker Races," *New York Age*, 18 Aug. 1923, in Women's Work File, Monroe Work Collection, TUAC.
23. M.M. Washington, International Council of Women of the Darker Races, Prepared Statement in Mary Church Terrell Collection, Box 102–12, Manuscript Division, MSRC.
24. Janie Porter Barrett to M.M. Washington, 12 Feb. 1925, M.M. Washington Collection, TUAC.
25. "Situation Grave in International Women's Council," *Montgomery Advertiser,* 8 May 1925, in Women's Work File, Monroe Work Collection, TUAC. "Women Achieve and Do While Men Wine and Dine," *Afro-American Ledger*, 16 May 1925, p. 2.

Chapter 11

1. "Suffering Suffragists," *Crisis*, June 1912, pp. 76–77; "Along the Color Line," *Crisis*, June 1911, p. 101.
2. "Suffering Suffragists."
3. "Chicago Women Join Suffragettes," *Afro-American Ledger*, 11 Jan. 1923, p. 1.
4. "Suffrage Paraders," *Crisis*, Apr. 1913, p. 296.
5. "Votes for Women," *Crisis*, Nov. 1917, p. 8.
6. "The Elections," Crisis, Dec. 1917, p. 62.
7. June Sochen, *Herstory: A Woman's View of American History* (New York: Alfred Publishing, 1974), p. 279.
8. National Women's Party, 30 Dec. 1920, NAACP File, 27 Oct. 1920–9 May 1921, Manuscript Division, LC.
9. National League of Republican Colored Women, Feb. 1925, Nannie H. Burroughs Papers, Box 31, Manuscript Division, LC.
10. "The Temperance Convention," news article published before 1808, Bumstead Papers, ADAU. By permission.
11. *What Hampton Graduates Are Doing*, p. 72.
12. "Editorial Comment," *Afro-American Ledger*, 22 Nov. 1913; "Across the Color Line," *Crisis*, Sept. 1913, p. 216.
13. Addie W. Hunton, "Woman's Clubs: Caring for Young Women," *Crisis*, June 1911, pp. 120–21.
14. "Colored YWCA," *Southern Workman*, Aug. 1916, p. 442.
15. "YWCA Student Conference," *Southern Workman,* Aug. 1918, p. 1.
16. National Student Council – YWCA, 5 Nov. 1924, Lucy Slowe Papers, Box 90-10, Manuscript Division, MSRC.
17. "YWCA," *Afro-American Ledger*, 22 Feb. 1896.
18. "YWCA," *Afro-American Ledger,* 16 May 1896.
19. "YWCA," *Afro-American Ledger*, 19 July 1922.
20. *Afro-American Ledger,* 27 Jan. 1912.
21. "Some of the Dangers Confronting Southern Girls in the North," in *Hampton Negro Conference, No. 2* (Hampton, Va.: Hampton Institute Press, July 1898), p. 64, AMCHU.
22. Ibid., p. 65.
23. Ibid., p. 67.
24. Browne, Kruse, et al., eds., *Hampton Negro Conference No. 3*, p. 46.
25. "Young Women's Christian Association Work Report by Mrs. Laura D. Titus – Norfolk, Va.," *Hampton Bulletin,* Sept. 1911, pp. 54–59.
26. Ibid.
27. Laura D. Titis, "A Negro Young Women's Christian Association," *Southern Workman,* Dec. 1914, p. 701.
28. Neighborhood Union Box 5, YWCA–Atlanta File, ADAU. By permission.
29. Ibid.

30. Ibid.
31. Ibid.
32. "A Statement of Policy—Colored Women and the YWCA, March 12, 1920," Neighborhood Union Box 5, YWCA-Atlanta File, ADAU. By permission.
33. "The Latest Farce From the YWCA," Neighborhood Union Box 5, YWCA-South File, ADAU. By permission.
34. "Too Much Paternalism—May 1, 1920," Neighborhood Union Box 5, YWCA-South File, ADAU. By permission.
35. "Minutes of the Meeting," Neighborhood Union Box 5, YWCA-South File, ADAU. By permission.
36. "Discuss Extension of 'Y' Work in South Among Negro Women," *New York Age*, 12 Mar. 1921, Women's Work File, Monroe Work Collection, TUAC.
37. Ibid.
38. "Secretaries Train," *Afro-American Ledger,* 30 Dec. 1921, Women's Work File, Monroe Work Collection, TUAC.
39. "Extract from an Open letter to the President," *Crisis*, Aug. 1917, p. 164.
40. "What Colored Women Are Doing in War," *Marietta (Ohio) Leader*, 11 July 1918, Women's Work File, Monroe Work Collection, TUAC.
41. Herbert Hoover, "An Appeal to the Negroes of the United States," *Spelman Messenger*, Nov. 1918, p. 5.
42. "Food Conservation Movement Being Pushed Among Negroes," *Spelman Messenger*, Nov. 1918, p. 6.
43. Jane Olcott, comp., *The Work of Colored Women* (New York: Colored Work Commission, War Work Council, National Board-YWCA, 1919), p. 69.
44. "Broadening Opportunities for Colored Girls," *War Work Bulletin*, 3 May 1918, p. 2, in Neighborhood Union 14–B, 1918 YWCA File, ADAU. By permission.
45. Olcott, *Work of Colored Women,* p. 73.
46. Olcott, *Work of Colored Women,* p. 5.
47. "Broadening Opportunities for Colored Girls"; E. Rose Batterham, "Negro Girls and the YWCA," *Crisis*, Sept. 1919, p. 437.
48. Olcott, *Work of Colored Women.*
49. Ibid., p. 10.
50. "$400,000 To Be Spent for Work Among Colored Girls," Women's Work File, Monroe Work Collection, TUAC.
51. "To Establish Many Recreation Centers for Colored Girls," *New York Age*, 2 Nov. 1918, in Women's Work File, Monroe Work Collection, TUAC.
52. Olcott, *Work of Colored Women*, p. 122.
53. Belle Davis "The Circle for Negro Relief," *Opportunity* 3 (Mar. 1925): 86–90.
54. Ibid.
55. John Hope Franklin and Isidore Star, *The Negro in Twentieth Century America: A Reader in the Struggle for Civil Rights* (New York: Vintage, 1967), p. 108; Guichard Parris and Lester Brooks, *Blacks in the City: A History of the National Urban League* (Boston: Little, Brown, 1971), pp. 5, 9; Hollingsworth

Wood, "The Urban League Movement," *Journal of Negro History* 9 (Apr. 1924): 117.

56. Eugene K. Jones, "The National Urban League," *Opportunity* 3 (Jan. 1925): 13.
57. Constitution of the National League on Urban Conditions Among Negroes, George E. Haynes Papers, 1909–1922, Box 4, SCFU.
58. "A Quarter Century of Progress in the Field of Race Relations," Neighborhood Union Box 5, Pamphlet–1935, ADAU. By permission.
59. Jones, "National Urban League."
60. "Securing, Training, and Placing Negro Social Workers," NAACP Administrative File, Labor General, 14 Jan. 1919–Apr. 1919, C319, Manuscript Division, LC.
61. "Bulletin—National League on Urban Conditions Among Negroes," NAACP Administrative File, National Urban League 9 Jan. 1914–13 Jan. 1919, C384, Manuscript Division, LC.
62. Ibid.
63. "A Million Women United to Suppress Lynching," *Negro Star,* 13 Oct. 1922, Monroe Work Collection, Women's Work File, TUAC.
64. Ibid.
65. NAACP Administrative Files, Subject File Awards, Spingarn Medal, 1922, Box 210, Manuscript Division, LC.
66. "Origin and Purpose," Commission on Inter-racial Cooperation Collection, File 17 A–Z, ADAU. By permission.
67. Ibid., p. 2.
68. W.E.B. Du Bois, *Crisis* Editor to Robert B. Elerezer, Commission on Inter-racial Cooperation, 12 Mar. 1926, Commission on Inter-racial Cooperation Collection, File 17, ADAU. By permission.
69. "Origin and Purpose," pp. 3–4, Commission on Inter-racial Cooperation Collection, File 17 A–Z, ADAU. By permission.
70. Ibid.
71. "Background of the Women's Department," p. 12, Commission on Inter-racial Cooperation Collection, File 17 B–1, ADAU. By permission.
72. Ibid., p. 14.
73. "Background of the Women's Department," p. 17, Commission on Inter-racial Cooperation Collection, File 17 B–1, ADAU. By permission.
74. Ibid., p. 21.
75. Ibid., p. 4.
76. "Conscience Answers the Call," p. 5, Commission on Inter-racial Cooperation Collection, File 17 A–Z, ADAU. By permission.
77. *Southern Negro Women and Race Cooperation* (Southeastern Federation of Negro Women's Club, 1921), pp. 2–6, R.R. Moton Collection, Interracial Conference, Box 52–File 344, TUAC.
78. "Survey of Activities, 1925," pp. 8–9, Commission on Inter-racial Cooperation Collection, File 17, ADAU. By permission.
79. Ibid., pp. 9, 10.

A Note on Sources

By necessity and choice, the documentation for this book is principally from primary sources. Because Afro-American women's history represents a relatively new field of historical inquiry and because nineteenth- and early twentieth-century records relating to women's history in general and black women's history specifically are still in the process of being collected and catalogued, there are still too few scholarly secondary sources. To understand and appreciate as fully as possible black women's beliefs, aspirations, and motivations, to glimpse the "underside" of their lives, it was necessary to read their exact words and peruse their letters, notebooks, and diaries.

The archives of Atlanta University, Fisk University, Hampton University, Spelman College, and Tuskegee University provided invaluable data on many of the lesser-known women, the accomplishments of black women generally, and the black experience in America. Other repositories of primary sources that proved helpful were the Moorland-Spingarn Research Center at Howard University, the Library of Congress, the National Archives, and the Baltimore City Archives. Of special historical significance and value in reconstructing black women's history are the Mary Church Terrell Collections at Howard University and the Library of Congress, the Neighborhood Union Collection at Atlanta University, and the Student Files at Hampton University. Also to be noted is the Monroe Work Women's Work File at Tuskegee University. Work collected and categorized from the leading black and white newspapers hundreds of relevant articles relating to black women. In many instances, because issues of the newspapers are no longer available in any form, Work's collection provides the only source.

Index